A PRACTICAL INTRODUCTION TO COMPUTER VISION WITH OPENCV

A PRACTICAL INTRODUCTION TO COMPUTER VISION WITH OPENCV

Kenneth Dawson-Howe
Trinity College Dublin, Ireland

WILEY

This edition first published 2014
© 2014 John Wiley & Sons Ltd

Registered office

John Wiley & Sons Ltd, The Atrium, Southern Gate, Chichester, West Sussex, PO19 8SQ, United Kingdom

For details of our global editorial offices, for customer services and for information about how to apply for permission to reuse the copyright material in this book please see our website at www.wiley.com.

Library of Congress Cataloging-in-Publication Data applied for.

ISBN: 9781118848456

Set in 10/12pt Times by Aptara Inc., New Delhi, India

1   2014

I am grateful to many people for their help and support during the writing of this book. The biggest thanks must go to my wife Jane, my children, William and Susie, and my parents, all of whose encouragement has been unstinting.

I must express my thanks to my students for their interest and enthusiasm in this subject. It is always refreshing to hear students discussing how to solve vision problems in tutorials and great to hear their solutions to problems which are often different (and sometimes better) than my own.

I thank my colleagues (in particular Arthur Hughes, Jeremy Jones and Hilary McDonald) for their encouragement and support.

Contents

Preface

Perception is essential in order for any entity to interact in a meaningful way with its environment. Humans draw on many senses (such as sight, sound, touch and smell) to perceive the world. Most machines can only receive input through simple input devices, such as keyboards and mice, or through wired and wireless communication channels. However, in recent years, cameras and microphones have been added as standard parts of computers and mobile devices (such as phones and tablets). At the same time, the speed of these devices has increased significantly, making it possible to start to process this data in a meaningful manner. Computer Vision is about how we can automate image or video understanding on machines. It covers the techniques used to automate tasks ranging from industrial inspection (where the image understanding problem is constrained to one which we could easily address 20 years ago) to video understanding in order to guide autonomous robots so that they can interact in a meaningful and safe manner in a world designed for humans.

This book provides a brief introduction to this exciting field, covering the basics of image processing and providing the reader with enough information to solve many practical problems. Computer vision systems are becoming ubiquitous. They are in our homes (in the interfaces of the games consoles which our children use), in our cameras and phones (providing automatic face detection and red eye removal), on our streets (determining the licence plates of vehicles passing through toll gates), in our offices (providing biometric verification of identity), and even more so in our factories, helping to guide robots to manufacture goods (such as cars) and automatically inspecting goods to ensure they look right. Yet it seems that we are only at the beginning of how computer vision can be employed, and we can expect significantly more vision systems to emerge.

For those interested in this field as developers (and that hopefully includes you as you are reading this book) there is very good news as there are a number of high quality systems in which computer vision solutions can be developed, of which two stand out in particular: MATLAB® and OpenCV. MATLAB® provides an environment that allows relatively rapid prototyping of vision solutions. OpenCV is a high quality library for C and C++, with wrappers for Python and Java (on Windows, Linux, MacOS, FreeBSD, OpenBSD, Android, Maemo and iOS), which provides implementations of many state-of-the-art vision techniques. OpenCV is the platform of choice for many vision developers, is developed collaboratively by the vision community and is available free of charge for educational and commercial use. OpenCV code snippets are provided throughout this book so that readers can easily take the theory and easily create working solutions to vision problems.

This text is intended to:

1. Provide a solid academic background to basic computer vision.
2. Provide enough material for a one-semester course in computer vision. Larger, all encompassing, textbooks are very off-putting to new students in this (or any) field.
3. Facilitate practical use of computer vision. The goal is to bridge the gap between the theory and the practical implementation of computer vision and so explanations of how to use the relevant OpenCV library routines are included, accompanied by a full working program including the code snippets from the text in the website mentioned below.
4. Allow students to solve real practical problems by providing images and videos for the 20 application problems in Chapter 10.

Electronic Resources

The electronic resources which accompany this text inlcude:

• the code examples from the text along with images generated from the code to give an idea of the processing done by each section of the code.
• Powerpoint slides for each of the chapters.
• the media (images and videos) for each of the application problems in Chapter 10 of the book.
• links to information on OpenCV.

The resources are available at https://www.scss.tcd.ie/publications/book-supplements/A-Practical-Introduction-to-Computer-Vision-with-OpenCV and at (a shorter alternative which redirects to the above page) https://www.scss.tcd.ie/Kenneth.Dawson-Howe/PracticalVisionBook

Teaching Computer Vision Using This Text

A computer vision course based on this text would consist of around 22–28 one-hour lectures together with tutorials and labs. Anticipated lecture hours by topic are as follows:

• Introduction: 1–2 hours
• Images (2.1 Cameras – 2.3 Colour images): 2 hours
• Images (2.4 Noise – 2.5 Smoothing): 2 hours
• Histograms (Chapter 3): 2 hours
• Binary Vision (Chapter 4): 2–3 hours
• Geometric Transformations (Chapter 5): 1–2 hours
• Edges (6.1 Edge detection): 2 hours
• Edges (6.2 Contour segmentation): 1–2 hours
• Edges (6.3 Hough transform): 1–2 hours
• Features (7.1 Moravec corner detection – 7.3 FAST corner detection): 1 hour
• Features (7.4 SIFT): 1 hour
• Recognition (8.1 Template matching and 8.2 Chamfer matching): 1 hour

- Recognition (8.3 Statistical pattern recognition): 1 hour
- Recognition (8.4 Cascade of Haar classifiers): 1 hour
- Recognition (8.6 Performance): 1 hour
- Video (Chapter 9): 2–3 hours

For tutorials, it is suggested that the class be broken into groups of three or four students (all in a single large venue) and that the groups should be asked to come up with solutions to some of the vision problems in Chapter 10 (using the vision techniques they have learnt). The intention is that the students discuss how to solve the problems, coming up with ways of combining the techniques that they have learnt in order to solve them. There is more than one solution to all of the problems, so some of the groups should present their solutions to the class, and the class and lecturer should discuss how appropriate the solutions are. For labs and assignments, the same problems can be used, as OpenCV provides the functionality to allow students to prototype solutions to these problems.

1

Introduction

Computer vision is the automatic analysis of images and videos by computers in order to gain some understanding of the world. Computer vision is inspired by the capabilities of the human vision system and, when initially addressed in the 1960s and 1970s, it was thought to be a relatively straightforward problem to solve. However, the reason we think/thought that vision is easy is that we have our own visual system which makes the task seem intuitive to our conscious minds. In fact, the human visual system is very complex and even the estimates of how much of the brain is involved with visual processing vary from 25% up to more than 50%.

1.1 A Difficult Problem

The first challenge facing anyone studying this subject is to convince themself that the problem is difficult. To try to illustrate the difficulty, we first show three different versions of the same image in Figure 1.1. For a computer, an image is just an array of values, such as the array shown in the left-hand image in Figure 1.1. For us, using our complex vision system, we can perceive this as a face image but only if we are shown it as a grey scale image (top right).

Computer vision is quite like understanding the array of values shown in Figure 1.1, but is more complicated as the array is really much bigger (e.g. to be equivalent to the human eye a camera would need around 127 million elements), and more complex (i.e. with each point represented by three values in order to encode colour information). To make the task even more convoluted, the images are constantly changing, providing a stream of 50–60 images per second and, of course, there are two streams of data as we have two eyes/cameras.

Another illustration of the difficulty of vision was provided by psychologist John Wilding considering his own visual system:

> As I look out of my window, I see grass and trees, gently swaying in the wind, with a lake beyond ... An asphalt path leads down through the trees to the lake and two squirrels are chasing each other to and fro across it, ignoring the woman coming up the path ...

A Practical Introduction to Computer Vision with OpenCV, First Edition. Kenneth Dawson-Howe.
© 2014 John Wiley & Sons, Ltd. Published 2014 by John Wiley & Sons, Ltd.

67	67	66	68	66	67	64	65	65	63	63	69	61	64	63	66	61	60
69	68	63	68	65	62	65	61	50	26	32	65	61	67	64	65	66	63
72	71	70	87	67	60	28	21	17	18	13	15	20	59	61	65	66	64
75	73	76	78	67	26	20	19	16	18	16	13	18	21	50	61	69	70
74	75	78	74	39	31	31	30	46	37	69	66	64	43	18	63	69	60
73	75	77	64	41	20	18	22	63	92	99	88	78	73	39	40	59	65
74	75	71	42	19	12	14	28	79	102	107	96	87	79	57	29	68	66
75	75	66	43	12	11	16	62	87	84	84	108	83	84	59	39	70	66
76	74	49	42	37	10	34	78	90	99	68	94	97	51	40	69	72	65
76	63	40	57	123	88	60	83	95	88	80	71	67	69	32	67	73	73
78	50	32	33	90	121	66	86	100	116	87	85	80	74	71	56	58	48
80	40	33	16	63	107	57	86	103	113	113	104	94	86	77	48	47	45
88	41	35	10	15	94	67	96	98	91	86	105	81	77	71	35	45	47
87	51	35	15	15	17	51	92	104	101	72	74	87	100	27	31	44	46
86	42	47	11	13	16	71	76	89	95	116	91	67	87	12	25	43	51
96	67	20	12	17	17	86	89	90	101	96	89	62	13	11	19	40	51
99	88	19	15	15	18	32	107	99	86	95	92	26	13	13	16	49	52
99	77	16	14	14	16	35	115	111	109	91	79	17	16	13	46	48	51

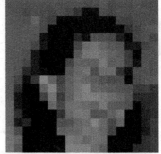

Figure 1.1 Different versions of an image. An array of numbers (left) which are the values of the grey scales in the low resolution image of a face (top right). The task of computer vision is most like understanding the array of numbers

> *This is the scene I experience, a world of objects with background, acted upon and sometimes acting and interacting in events. I have no problem seeing and hearing and smelling and feeling all these things because they affect my senses directly and they make up the real world.*
>
> *Or do they? I can look again and notice things I missed before, or see the scene in new ways. There is a white wall framing the window I am looking through and the window in fact fills less of my field of view that the wall, but I did not even notice the wall at first, and my impression was that the scene through the window was a panorama right across in front of me. There are metal bars dividing the window into squares and the glass is obscured with dust and spots but for me the view seems complete and un-obscured. The 'grass' is patches of colour ranging from nearly white in the bright sun to nearly black in the shade but I 'saw' green grass in light and shade. Other changing greenish shapes were for me permanent leafy branches moved by a wind I neither saw nor felt, and two constantly varying grey shapes were squirrels moving with a purpose. Another shape increasing in size and changing in position was an approaching woman. (Wilding, 1983)*

1.2 The Human Vision System

If we could duplicate the human visual system then the problem of developing a computer vision system would be solved. So why can't we? The main difficulty is that we do not understand what the human vision system is doing most of the time.

If you consider your eyes, it is probably not clear to you that your colour vision (provided by the 6–7 million cones in the eye) is concentrated in the centre of the visual field of the eye (known as the macula). The rest of your retina is made up of around 120 million rods (cells that are sensitive to visible light of any wavelength/colour). In addition, each eye has a rather large blind spot where the optic nerve attaches to the retina. Somehow, we think we see a continuous image (i.e. no blind spot) with colour everywhere, but even at this lowest level of processing it is unclear as to how this impression occurs within the brain.

The visual cortex (at the back of the brain) has been studied and found to contain cells that perform a type of edge detection (see Chapter 6), but mostly we know what sections of the brain do based on localised brain damage to individuals. For example, a number of people with damage to a particular section of the brain can no longer recognise faces (a condition known as prosopagnosia). Other people have lost the ability to sense moving objects (a condition known as akinetopsia). These conditions inspire us to develop separate modules to recognise faces (e.g. see Section 8.4) and to detect object motion (e.g. see Chapter 9).

We can also look at the brain using functional MRI, which allows us to see the concentration of electrical activity in different parts of the brain as subjects perform various activities. Again, this may tell us what large parts of the brain are doing, but it cannot provide us with algorithms to solve the problem of interpreting the massive arrays of numbers that video cameras provide.

1.3   Practical Applications of Computer Vision

Computer vision has many applications in industry, particularly allowing the automatic inspection of manufactured goods at any stage in the production line. For example, it has been used to:

- Inspect printed circuits boards to ensure that tracks and components are placed correctly. See Figure 1.2.
- Inspect print quality of labels. See Figure 1.3.
- Inspect bottles to ensure they are properly filled. See Figure 1.3.

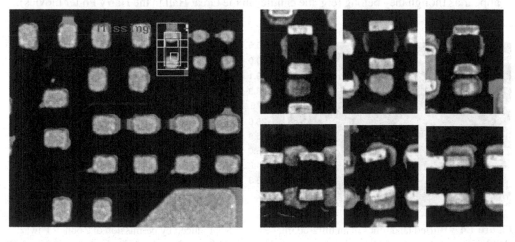

Figure 1.2   PCB inspection of pads (left) and images of some detected flaws in the surface mounting of components (right). Reproduced by permission of James Mahon

Figure 1.3 Checking print quality of best-before dates (right), and monitoring level to which bottles are filled (right). Reproduced by permission of Omron Electronics LLC

- Inspect apples to determine if there is any bruising.
- Locate chocolates on a production line so that a robot arm can pick them up and place them in the correct locations in the box.
- Guide robots when manufacturing complex products such as cars.

On the factory floor, the problem is a little simpler than in the real world as the lighting can be constrained and the possible variations of what we can see are quite limited. Computer vision is now solving problems outside the factory. Computer vision applications outside the factory include:

- The automatic reading of license plates as they pass through tollgates on major roads.
- Augmenting sports broadcasts by determining distances for penalties, along with a range of other statistics (such as how far each player has travelled during the game).
- Biometric security checks in airports using images of faces and images of fingerprints. See Figure 1.4.
- Augmenting movies by the insertion of virtual objects into video sequences, so that they appear as though they belong (e.g. the candles in the Great Hall in the Harry Potter movies).

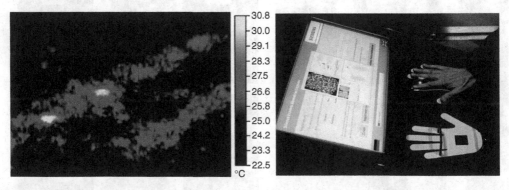

Figure 1.4 Buried landmines in an infrared image (left). Reproduced by permission of Zouheir Fawaz, Handprint recognition system (right). Reproduced by permission of Siemens AG

- Assisting drivers by warning them when they are drifting out of lane.
- Creating 3D models of a destroyed building from multiple old photographs.
- Advanced interfaces for computer games allowing the real time detection of players or their hand-held controllers.
- Classification of plant types and anticipated yields based on multispectral satellite images.
- Detecting buried landmines in infrared images. See Figure 1.4.

Some examples of existing computer vision systems in the outside world are shown in Figure 1.4.

1.4   The Future of Computer Vision

The community of vision developers is constantly pushing the boundaries of what we can achieve. While we can produce autonomous vehicles, which drive themselves on a highway, we would have difficulties producing a reliable vehicle to work on minor roads, particularly if the road marking were poor. Even in the highway environment, though, we have a legal issue, as who is to blame if the vehicle crashes? Clearly, those developing the technology do not think it should be them and would rather that the driver should still be responsible should anything go wrong. This issue of liability is a difficult one and arises with many vision applications in the real world. Taking another example, if we develop a medical imaging system to diagnose cancer, what will happen when it mistakenly does not diagnose a condition? Even though the system might be more reliable than any individual radiologist, we enter a legal minefield. Therefore, for now, the simplest solution is either to address only non-critical problems or to develop systems, which are assistants to, rather than replacements for, the current human experts.

Another problem exists with the deployment of computer vision systems. In some countries the installation and use of video cameras is considered an infringement of our basic right to privacy. This varies hugely from country to country, from company to company, and even from individual to individual. While most people involved with technology see the potential benefits of camera systems, many people are inherently distrustful of video cameras and what the videos *could* be used for. Among other things, they fear (perhaps justifiably) a Big Brother scenario, where our movements and actions are constantly monitored. Despite this, the number of cameras is growing very rapidly, as there are cameras on virtually every new computer, every new phone, every new games console, and so on.

Moving forwards, we expect to see computer vision addressing progressively harder problems; that is problems in more complex environments with fewer constraints. We expect computer vision to start to be able to recognise more objects of different types and to begin to extract more reliable and robust descriptions of the world in which they operate. For example, we expect computer vision to

- become an integral part of general computer interfaces;
- provide increased levels of security through biometric analysis;
- provide reliable diagnoses of medical conditions from medical images and medical records;
- allow vehicles to be driven autonomously;
- automatically determine the identity of criminals through the forensic analysis of video.

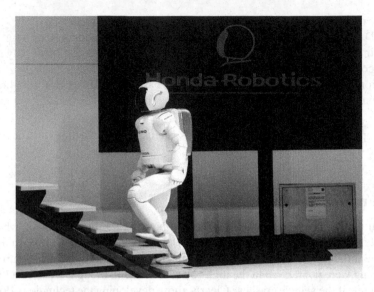

Figure 1.5 The ASIMO humanoid robot which has two cameras in its 'head' which allow ASIMO to determine how far away things are, recognise familiar faces, etc. Reproduced by permission of Honda Motor Co. Inc

Ultimately, computer vision is aiming to emulate the capabilities of human vision, and to provide these abilities to humanoid (and other) robotic devices, such as ASIMO (see Figure 1.5). This is part of what makes this field exciting, and surprising, as we all have our own (human) vision systems which work remarkably well, yet when we try to automate any computer vision task it proves very difficult to do reliably.

1.5   Material in this Textbook

This textbook is intended to provide an illustrated introduction to the area of computer vision. It provides roughly the amount of material which can be covered in a one-semester, year four or five university course. While this text covers the theory behind basic computer vision, it also provides a bridge from the theory to practical implementation using the industry standard OpenCV libraries (by explaining how the operations can be invoked in OpenCV).

In Chapter 2, we consider the basics of cameras and images, along with consideration of the noise that is exhibited by many images and the techniques through which this noise can be removed or attenuated.

In Chapter 3, we consider how image information can be summarised in the form of a histogram and how those histograms can be used in order to enhance images or to extract information from the images.

Chapter 4 looks at the most commonly used technique for industrial vision – that of binary vision, where we simplify images so that every point is either black or white. This approach makes the processing much easier (assuming that the binary image can be obtained correctly).

Chapter 5 looks at how we model and remove distortion from images and cameras (which is often introduced by the camera/lens system).

Chapter 6 describes the extraction and use of edges (locations at which the brightness or colour changes significantly) in images. These cartoon-like features allow us to abstract information from images. Edge detection does not perform well at corners, and in Chapter 7 we look at corner/feature points that can act as a complement to edges or can be used on their own to provide less ambiguous features with which to match different images or objects.

In Chapter 8, we look at a number of common approaches to recognition in images, as in many applications we need to determine the location and identity of objects (e.g. license plates, faces, etc.).

Chapter 9 looks at the basics of processing videos, concentrating particularly on how we detect moving objects in video feeds from static cameras (a problem that occurs frequently in video surveillance), how we track objects from frame to frame and how we can assess performance in video processing.

Finally, in Chapter 10, we present a large number of vision application problems to provide students with the opportunity to solve real problems (which is the only way to really appreciate how difficult computer vision is). Images or videos for these problems are provided in the resources associated with this book.

We end this introduction with a quote from the 19th century: '... apprehension by the senses supplies after all, directly or indirectly, the material of all human knowledge, or at least the stimulus necessary to develop every inborn faculty of the mind. It supplies the basis for the whole action of man upon the outer world ... For there is little hope that he who does not begin at the beginning of knowledge will ever arrive at its end' (von Helmholtz, 1868).

1.6   Going Further with Computer Vision

This text contains roughly the amount of material that could be covered in a one semester introductory course on computer vision. There are many very large comprehensive vision texts, which allow students to delve more deeply and broadly into computer vision. A few that come highly recommended are (Sonka, et al., 2007), (González & Woods, 2007), and (Marques, 2011).

For those wishing to go further with computer vision and OpenCV, I would recommend the practical textbook by Baggio (Daniel Lélis Baggio, 2012). This leads the reader through a series of relatively advanced vision application problems on a variety of platforms.

2

Images

Images are central to computer vision, as they are the representation that we obtain from imaging devices (such as cameras; see Section 2.1). They provide us with a representation of the visual appearance of a scene (see Sections 2.2 and 2.3), which we can process to enhance certain features of interest, before we attempt to abstract information. Images generally exhibit some degree of noise (see Section 2.4) which can be attenuated by various simple image processing techniques (see Section 2.5).

2.1 Cameras

A camera consists of a photosensitive image plane (which senses the amount of light that falls upon it), a housing which prevents stray light from falling onto the image plane and a lens in the housing which allows some light to fall onto the image plane in a controlled fashion (i.e. the light rays are focused onto the image plane by the lenses).

2.1.1 The Simple Pinhole Camera Model

One of the simplest, but reasonably realistic, models of a camera is the pinhole camera model in which the lens is instead treated as a simple pinhole (see Figure 2.1). All rays of light that hit the image plane must come through the pinhole of the camera in front of the photosensitive image plane. This is a simplification of most real imaging systems, as typically various parts of imaging systems (such as the lenses) introduce distortions into the resultant images. This basic model is extended to cope with these distortions in Section 5.6.

The mapping from a point in the 3D world (x, y, z) to a point on the image plane (i, j), for the simple pinhole camera, can be modelled as

$$\begin{bmatrix} i.w \\ j.w \\ w \end{bmatrix} = \begin{bmatrix} f_i & 0 & c_i \\ 0 & f_j & c_j \\ 0 & 0 & 1 \end{bmatrix} \begin{bmatrix} x \\ y \\ z \end{bmatrix} \qquad (2.1)$$

A Practical Introduction to Computer Vision with OpenCV, First Edition. Kenneth Dawson-Howe.
© 2014 John Wiley & Sons, Ltd. Published 2014 by John Wiley & Sons, Ltd.

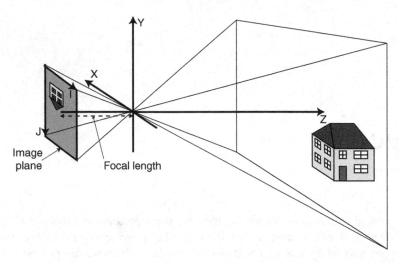

Figure 2.1   The simple pinhole camera model showing the relationship the real 3D world (on the right-hand side) and the images captured on the image plane (on the left-hand side). The pinhole in this case is the origin in the XYZ coordinate system and, in reality, the image plane would need to be enclosed in a housing, which prevented any stray light from hitting the image plane

where w can be treated as a scaling factor in the homogeneous coordinates being used to describe the image points, f_i and f_j describe a combination of the camera focal length and the size of the pixels in the I and J directions respectively, and (c_i, c_j) are the coordinates of the point at which the optical axis intersects the image plane (sometimes referred to as the optical centre). Note that the optical axis is the perpendicular line from the image plane, which extends through the pinhole of the camera.

2.2   Images

An image is a picture (generally a 2D projection of a 3D scene) captured by a sensor. It is a continuous function of two coordinates in the image plane; usually expressed as (i,j) or (column, row) or somewhat confusingly (x,y). To process such an image on a digital computer it must be both

- Sampled into a matrix (M rows and N columns), and
- Quantised so that each element in the matrix is given an integer value. In other words, the continuous range is split into some number of intervals (k) where most commonly $k = 256$.

In OpenCV, images are represented using the `Mat` *data structure, and individual pixel values may be accessed and assigned using the* `at` *function. For example, the following code sets some of the bits to zero in each pixel in a grey-scale image. Note that type*

`CV_8UC1` *means a 1 channel (C1) image with where each pixel value is stored in 8 bits, unsigned (8U):*

```
void ChangeQuantisationGrey( Mat &image, int num_bits )
{
   CV_Assert( (image.type() == CV_8UC1) &&
      (num_bits >= 1) && (num_bits <= 8) );
   uchar mask = 0xFF << (8-num_bits);
   for (int row=0; row < image.rows; row++)
     for (int col=0; col < image.cols; col++)
       image.at<uchar>(row,col) =
                  image.at<uchar>(row,col) & mask;
}
```

2.2.1 Sampling

Digital images are created by sampling a continuous image into discrete elements. Digital image sensors consist of a 2D array of photosensitive elements, and each element (pixel/image point/sampling point) in the array has some fixed area over which is it photosensitive. Typically, between elements there is some small (border) area which is not photosensitive, so it is possible (but not likely) that objects in the real world (such as a distant telephone line) could be completely missed by the sensor if the light from those objects fell only in the border regions. The bigger issue, however, with sampling is that pixels represent the average value (luminance/chrominance) over a discrete area which in the real world could be projected from a single object, but equally (particularly at the boundaries of objects) could be a summation of light reflected from multiple objects.

The number of samples in an image limits the objects that can be distinguished/recognised in the image (e.g. see Figure 2.2, in which the people can only be distinguished in the upper pictures). Hence, it is essential that the resolution (the number of pixels) is sufficient for our purpose (whatever that may be). At the same time, too high a resolution will have more detail than we need which may make processing harder and will definitely make it slower.

In OpenCV, image sampling (the number of pixels in the image) can be changed using the `resize` *function. Note that image size can be specified by the number of rows and columns or by a single Size data type:*

```
resize( image, smaller_image,
               Size( image1.cols/2, image.rows/2 ));
resize( image, smaller_image, Size( image1.cols/2, image.rows/2 ));
```

2.2.2 Quantisation

Each pixel in a digital image $f(i, j)$ is a function of scene brightness. The brightness values are continuous, but we need to represent them discretely using digital values. Typically, the number of brightness levels per channel is $k = 2^b$ where b is the number of bits (often 8).

Figure 2.2   Four different samplings of the same image; top left 256x192, top right 128x96, bottom left 64x48 and bottom right 32x24

The question which must be asked is: how many bits are really necessary to represent the pixels? The more bits that are used the more memory the image will require; but as progressively fewer bits are used it is clear that information is being lost. Considering Figure 2.3, you should perceive little different between the 8-bit and the 6-bit images although the latter requires 25% fewer bits. There are clearly issues with the 4-bit and 2-bit images, although it is still possible for us to recognise many objects in these images. So it appears that the number of bits required actually depends on the purpose to which the image is to be put. If a machine is to automatically interpret a scene, though, we typically require more quantisation levels than might be expected, as otherwise false contours (e.g. in the sky in the 2-bit and 4-bit images in Figure 2.3) and incorrect segmentation occurs.

> *In OpenCV, image quantisation may be changed simply by masking some of the bits (as shown previously) or may also be done by changing the representation (e.g. converting from 32-bit to 16- or 8-bit images).*

Figure 2.3 Four different quantizations of the same grey-scale image; top left 8 bits, top right 6 bits, bottom left 4 bits and bottom right 2 bits

2.3 Colour Images

Colour (multispectral) images (Plataniotis & Venetsanopoulos, 2000) (Gevers, Gijsenij, van de Weijer, & Geusebroek, 2012) have multiple channels, whereas grey-scale (monochromatic) images (sometimes, incorrectly, referred to as black and white images) have only one channel. A grey-scale image represents the luminance (Y) at every point a scene. A colour image represents both luminance and chrominance (colour information) within the scene. This information can be represented in a number of ways but in all cases requires multiple channels of image data. Hence, colour images (with the same sampling and quantisation) are bigger and more complex than grey-scale images, as we must somehow decide how to process each of the channels of information. Note that much of image processing was developed specifically for grey-scale images and its application to colour images is often not very well defined.

Computer vision was for many years based on grey-level images, mainly based on two premises:

- Humans can understand grey-level images, so why bother with colour?
- Grey-scale images are smaller and less complex (a number for each point).

However, colour does provide more useful information that can assist with many tasks, such as segmentation of the image into physically separate entities (objects, surfaces, etc.). For example, looking at Figure 2.4 you should find it much easier to separate/segment the different trees in the colour image.

Figure 2.4   RGB colour image (left) and the same image in grey-scale (right)

Humans are sensitive to light at wavelengths between 400 nm and 700 nm and hence most camera image sensors are designed to be sensitive at those wavelengths.

Colour images are more complex than grey-scale images and are typically represented using a three-channel colour space (Koschan & Abidi, 2007), a number of which are described in the following sections.

2.3.1   Red–Green–Blue (RGB) Images

The most common representation for colour images is to use three channels correspond-ing, roughly, to the red (700 nm), green (546.1 nm) and blue (435.8nm) wavelengths (see Figure 2.5). What this means in effect is that the photosensitive elements in the camera are spectrally sensitive to wavelengths which are centred on those colours (see Figure 2.6).

Figure 2.5   RGB Image (top left) shown with red channel (top right), green channel (bottom left) and blue channel (bottom right)

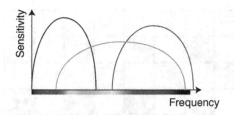

Figure 2.6 Spectral sensitively curves for blue (left), green (middle) and red (right) photosensitive elements

---

In OpenCV, colour images are also represented using the Mat *data structure but use multiple channels for each pixel. Individual values for each channel can be accessed using the* at *function. For example, to invert a colour image (type* CV_8UC3 *meaning a three-channel image where each value is 8 bits, unsigned):*

```
void InvertColour( Mat& input_image, Mat& output_image )
{
  CV_Assert( input_image.type() == CV_8UC3);
  output_image = input_image.clone();
  for (int row=0; row < input_image.rows; row++)
    for (int col=0; col < input_image.cols; col++)
      for (int channel=0; channel < input_image.channels(); channel++)
        output_image.at<Vec3b>(row,col)[channel] = 255 -
                    input_image.at<Vec3b>(row,col)[channel];
}
```

When displaying the image, a combination of these three channels is presented to the user.

It is worth noting that even though there are around 16.8 million (256*256*256) possible colours using this representation, there are some colours that cannot be represented using this model.

RGB colour information can easily be converted to grey-scale using a formula such as:

$$Y = 0.299R + 0.587G + 0.114B \qquad (2.2)$$

It is also worth pointing out that in most cameras the elements that are photosensitive to different wavelengths are not co-located. Instead, they are set out in a regular pattern, such as that shown in Figure 2.7, and RGB values are interpolated in some way from these sensed values. This means that the image received is not even a proper sampling of the continuous image, but rather is interpolated from the data received by the sensor elements.

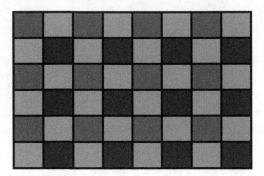

Figure 2.7 Sample arrangement of photosensitive cells in an RGB camera where the red, green and blue boxes represent individual photosensitive cells which are sensitive to wavelengths around red, green, and blue respectively. This pattern is referred as the Bayer pattern and is used in modern CCD and older CMOS cameras

In OpenCV, we can convert between colour representations and grey-scale using the cvtColor *function, and can split colour images into their component channel images using the* split *function:*

```
Mat bgr_image, grey_image;
cvtColor(bgr_image, grey_image, CV_BGR2GRAY);
vector<Mat> bgr_images(3);
split(bgr_image, bgr_images);
Mat& blue_image = bgr_images[0];
```

RGB values are normally stored in BGR format in OpenCV (i.e. the opposite order to what you might expect).

In OpenCV, to efficiently process images we must avoid use of the at *function (as this adds significant computational costs). Instead, we must use pointers to the image data within the* Mat *structures. Unfortunately, this produces code that is hard to understand. For example, consider the following code for inverting a three-channel image (type* cv_8uc3 *meaning a three-channel image with where each value is 8 bits, unsigned):*

```
int image_rows = image.rows;
int image_columns = image.cols;
for (int row=0; row < image_rows; row++) {
  uchar* value = image.ptr<uchar>(row);
  uchar* result_value = result_image.ptr<uchar>(row);
  for (int column=0; column < image_columns; column++)
  {
    *result_value++ = *value++ ^ 0xFF;
    *result_value++ = *value++ ^ 0xFF;
    *result_value++ = *value++ ^ 0xFF;
  }
}
```

More complex examples are provided in the sample image processing code provided in the resources accompanying this text.

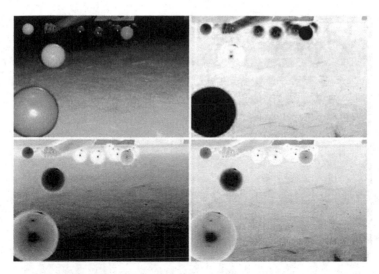

Figure 2.8 CMY Image (top left) shown with yellow channel (top right), magenta channel (bottom left) and cyan channel (bottom right)

2.3.2   Cyan–Magenta–Yellow (CMY) Images

The CMY model is based on the secondary colours (RGB are the primary colours), and is a subtractive colour scheme; that is the values of the C, M and Y are subtracted from pure white in order to get the required colour (see Figure 2.8). For this reason, it is often employed as a colour model within printers where white is the starting point.

> *In OpenCV, CMY is not directly supported but we could convert to CMY values by using the InvertColour routine shown previously.*

Conversion from an RGB image is straightforward: $C = 255 - R$, $M = 255 - G$, $Y = 255 - B$

2.3.3   YUV Images

The YUV colour model is used for analogue television signals (PAL, NTSC . . .) and is comprised of luminance (Y) together with two colour components: blue minus luminance (U) and red minus luminance (V) (see Figure 2.9). The transformation from RGB is again quite straightforward

- $Y = 0.299R + 0.587G + 0.114B$
- $U = 0.492^*(B - Y)$
- $V = 0.877^*(R - Y)$ (2.3)

The human vision system is much more sensitive to luminance than it is to chrominance, and this fact is exploited when images are encoded in television signals in order to reduce

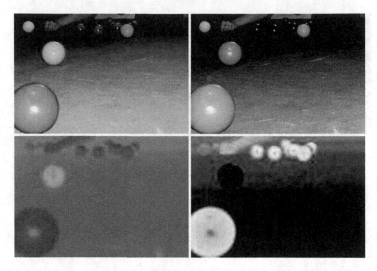

Figure 2.9 YUV image (top left) shown with luminance (Y) channel (top right), U channel (bottom left) and V channel (bottom right)

the amount of data that needs to be transmitted. For example, in YUV420p format 4 bytes of luminance (Y) are transmitted for every 2 bytes of chrominance (1 U and 1 V).

In OpenCV, to convert to YUV:

```
cvtColor(image, yuv_image, CV_BGR2YUV);
```

2.3.4   Hue Luminance Saturation (HLS) Images

The HLS model is frequently used in computer vision because, as well as separating the luminance and the chrominance, it separates the chrominance into hue and saturation, giving us quantities which we can talk about easily (e.g. dark blue, light red, etc.). The luminance typically ranges from 0 to 1. The hue describes the colour and ranges from 0 to 360°. The saturation S is the degree of strength or purity of the colour and ranges from 0 to 1. In practical implementations, all of these quantities are typically scaled to the 0 to 255 range (although in OpenCV hue values range between 0 and 179). See Figure 2.10 for a visual representation of these axes.

The most important fact to take from Figure 2.10, though, is the circular nature of the hue axis. This means that the minimum (0) and maximum (179) hue values are only 1 apart. These values correspond to red pixels, and if the hue channel in Figure 2.11 is examined it can be observed that the red snooker balls are represented by both black and white pixels (i.e. hue values near 0 and near 179 respectively). This means that if processing the hue channel one must be extremely careful, and typically special processing needs to be developed. For

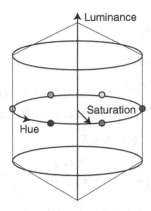

Figure 2.10 HLS space. The different colours are around the circular hue axis, the depth of the colours is indicated by how far along the saturation axis the colour is (from the centre), and the luminance indicates the brightness. The space is shown as wide in the middle and smaller at high and low values of luminance as there is no effective/reliable colour information when something is very dark or very bright

example, if averaging hue values 0, 178, 1, 177 and 179, the result should be 179, rather than 107!

In OpenCV, we can convert to HLS using:

```
cvtColor(bgr_image, hls_image, CV_BGR2HLS);
```

Note that the saturation and luminance values range from 0 to 255, but the hue value ranges from 0 to 179.

Figure 2.11 HLS Image (top left) shown with luminance channel (top right), hue channel (bottom left) and saturation channel (bottom right)

To convert RGB to HLS we use the following formulas (assuming R, G and B have been normalised to between 0.0 and 1.0):

$$L = \frac{Max(R,G,B) + Min(R,G,B)}{2}$$

$$S = \begin{cases} \frac{Max(R,G,B) - Min(R,G,B)}{Max(R,G,B) + Min(R,G,B)} & \text{if } L < 0.5 \\ \frac{Max(R,G,B) - Min(R,G,B)}{2 - (Max(R,G,B) + Min(R,G,B))} & \text{if } L \geq 0.5 \end{cases}$$

$$H = \begin{cases} \frac{60.(G-B)}{S} & \text{if } R = Max(R,G,B) \\ 120 + \frac{60.(B-R)}{S} & \text{if } G = Max(R,G,B) \\ 240 + \frac{60.(R-G)}{S} & \text{if } B = Max(R,G,B) \end{cases} \tag{2.4}$$

From the above formulas, the L and S values will be between 0.0 and 1.0, and the H value should range between 0.0 and 360.0, although we will need to add 360.0 to any H value which is less than 0 and subtract 360.0 from any value greater than or equal to 360.0.

2.3.5   Other Colour Spaces

There are a large number of other colour spaces available to use. Bear in mind that most of these are just alternative representations of the image. In theory, they contain no more or less information that an RGB image or a CMY image or HSV image. However, they do contain more information than a grey-scale image as in this case information has been discarded (in comparison to an original colour image). OpenCV provides support (in terms of conversion functions) for six other colour spaces:

1. HSV. Hue Saturation Value, is similar to HLS but the definitions of channels differ somewhat.
2. YCrCb is a scaled version of YUV, which is often used in image and video compression.
3. CIE XYZ is a standard reference colour space, where the channel responses are similar to the different cone responses in the human eye.
4. CIE $L^*u^*v^*$ is another standard colour space defined by CIE which is intended to be provide a perceptually uniform colour space where the differences between colours are proportional to our perceived differences. L^* is a measure of luminance and u^* and v^* are chromaticity values.
5. CIE $L^*a^*b^*$ is a device independent colour space that includes all colours that can be perceived by humans.
6. Bayer is the pattern widely used in CCD sensors, and is used if we have raw sensor data (i.e. that have not been interpolated). See Figure 2.7.

2.3.6   Some Colour Applications

In some applications we need to identify which pixels represent a particular colour. For example, to locate road signs we will be particularly interested in red, yellow, blue, black and white. We can identify specific colours by creating simple formulas that identify them (as will be shown in the two examples which follow) but it should be noted that this should really be addressed in a more rigorous fashion, such as described in Section 3.5. Equations of the type

Figure 2.12   Colour image (left), selection of skin pixels by selecting all points with (Saturation $>=$ 0.2) AND (0.5 < Luminance/Saturation <3.0) AND (Hue $<= 28°$ OR Hue $>= 330°$) (right)

shown here are likely to fail as the criteria are not based on a sufficient quantity of images (with varying objects and lighting, etc.). Also the criteria themselves are really too crude, effectively identifying large subspaces in colour space (which will result in unnecessary false positives – e.g. points identified as skin pixels when they do not represent skin).

2.3.6.1   Skin Detection

Skin detection can be performed by simply analysing pixels values. Through simple experimentation it was found that

$$\text{(Saturation} >= 0.2) \text{ AND } (0.5 < \text{Luminance/Saturation} < 3.0) \text{ AND}$$
$$\text{(Hue} <= 28° \text{ OR Hue} >= 330°) \tag{2.5}$$

will identify many skin pixels. However, as can be seen the right image in Figure 2.12, this also identifies other pixels (such as parts of the flag). For more information on skin detection see (Kakumanu, Makrogiannis, & Bourbakis, 2007).

In OpenCV, we can determine if a pixel might represent skin as follows:

```
uchar H = hls_image.at<Vec3b>(row,col)[0];
uchar L = hls_image.at<Vec3b>(row,col)[1];
uchar S = hls_image.at<Vec3b>(row,col)[2];
double LS_ratio = ((double) L) / ((double) S);
bool skin_pixel = (S >= 50) && (LS_ratio > 0.5) &&
      (LS_ratio < 3.0) && ((H <= 14) || (H >= 165));
```

Figure 2.13 Selection of red-eye pixels by selecting all points with (Luminance >= 0.25) AND (Saturation >= 0.4) AND (0.5 < Luminance/Saturation <1.5) AND (Hue <= 14° OR Hue >= 324°)

2.3.6.2 Red Eye Detection

A similar evaluation can be performed to identify red eye pixels:

$$(Luminance >= 0.25) \text{ AND } (Saturation >= 0.4) \text{ AND}$$
$$(0.5 < Luminance/Saturation < 1.5) \text{ AND } (Hue <= 14° \text{ OR } Hue >= 324°) \quad (2.6)$$

This was determined experimentally and could be improved upon, but it was found to be a good starting point for the identification of red eye, as shown in Figure 2.13. For more information about red eye detection see (Gasparini & Schettini, 2009).

In OpenCV, we can determine if a pixel might represent a red eye point as follows:

```
uchar H = hls_image.at<Vec3b>(row,col)[0];
uchar L = hls_image.at<Vec3b>(row,col)[1];
uchar S = hls_image.at<Vec3b>(row,col)[2];
double LS_ratio = ((double) L) / ((double) S);
bool red_eye_pixel = (L >= 64) && (S >= 100) &&
                     (LS_ratio > 0.5) && (LS_ratio < 1.5) &&
                     ((H <= 7) || (H >= 162));
```

2.4 Noise

Images are normally affected by noise (anything that degrades the ideal image) to some degree, and this noise can have a serious impact on processing. Noise is caused by the environment, the imaging device, electrical interference, the digitisation process, and so on. We need to be able to both measure noise and somehow correct it.

The most common measure of noise is the signal to noise ratio. For an image $f(i, j)$ the signal to noise ratio is defined as follow:

$$S/N ratio = \sum_{(i,j)} f^2(i,j) \Big/ \sum_{(i,j)} v^2(i,j) \qquad (2.7)$$

where $v(i, j)$ is the noise. In this section we will consider two types of noise, how noise affects images and how we can simulate noise (so that we can evaluate how well our techniques remove it).

2.4.1   Types of Noise

The two most commonly encountered types of noise are Gaussian noise (see Section 2.4.1.1) and salt and pepper noise (see Section 2.4.1.2).

2.4.1.1   Gaussian Noise

Gaussian noise is a good approximation to much real noise. Noise $v(i, j)$ is modelled as having a Gaussian distribution around some mean (μ), which is usually 0, with some standard deviation (σ). For an example, see Figure 2.14.

Figure 2.14   Colour and grey-scale images (left) with Gaussian noise added with a mean of 0 and a standard deviation of 20 (right). The signal to noise ratios of the noisy images are 43.3 (colour image) and 40.3 (grey-scale image), with respect to the original images

In OpenCV, we can add Gaussian noise to an image as follows:

```
void addGaussianNoise(Mat &image, double average=0.0,
                      double standard_deviation=10.0)
{
  // We need to work with signed images (as noise can be
  // negative as well as positive).  We use 16 bit signed
  // images as otherwise we would lose precision.
  Mat noise_image(image.size(), CV_16SC3);
  randn(noise_image, Scalar::all(average),
                     Scalar::all(standard_deviation));
  Mat temp_image;
  image.convertTo(temp_image,CV_16SC3);
  addWeighted(temp_image, 1.0, noise_image, 1.0, 0.0, temp_image);
  temp_image.convertTo(image,image.type());
}
```

2.4.1.2 Salt and Pepper Noise

Impulse noise is corruption with individual noisy pixels whose brightness differs significantly from that of the neighbourhood. Salt and pepper noise is a type of impulse noise where saturated impulse noise affects the image (i.e. it is corrupted with pure white and black pixels). For an example see Figure 2.15.

Figure 2.15 Colour and grey-scale images (left) with 10% Salt and pepper noise (right). The signal to noise ratio of the noisy images are 7.5 (colour image) and 6.7 (grey-scale image)

In OpenCV, we can add salt and pepper noise to an image as follows:

```
void addSaltAndPepperNoise(Mat &image, double noise_percentage)
{
  int image_rows = image.rows;
  int image_columns = image.cols;
  int image_channels = image.channels();
  int noise_points = (int) (((double) image_rows*
            image_columns*image_channels)*noise_percentage/100.0);
  for (int count = 0; count < noise_points; count++)
  {
    int row = rand() % image_rows;
    int column = rand() % image_columns;
    int channel = rand() % image_channels;
    uchar* pixel = image.ptr<uchar>(row) +
                            (column*image_channels) + channel;
    *pixel = (rand()%2 == 1) ? 255 : 0;
  }
}
```

2.4.2   Noise Models

Noise must be joined with the image data in some way. The way in which we model this depends upon whether the noise is data independent or data dependent.

2.4.2.1   Additive Noise

In the case of data independent noise (i.e. noise where the amount of noise is not related to the image data itself), an additive noise model is appropriate:

$$f(i,j) = g(i,j) + v(i,j) \tag{2.8}$$

where $g(i,j)$ is the ideal image, $v(i,j)$ is the noise and $f(i,j)$ is the actual image. Examples of additive noise are shown in Figure 2.14 and Figure 2.16.

2.4.2.2   Multiplicative Noise

In the case of data dependent noise (i.e. noise where the amount of noise is related to the image data itself), a multiplicative noise model is appropriate:

$$f(i,j) = g(i,j) + g(i,j).v(i,j) \tag{2.9}$$

where $g(i,j)$ is the ideal image, $v(i,j)$ is the noise and $f(i,j)$ is the actual image.

2.4.3 Noise Generation

In order to evaluate noise, we often need to simulate noise so that it can then be removed/reduced and the extent to which we are successful assessed. Assume that we are generating noise with a Gaussian distribution with a 0 mean and a standard deviation of σ.

We first determine the probability distribution $p(k)$ and the cumulative probability distribution $p_{cum}(k)$ of all possible values of the noise from the greatest possible negative change to the greatest possible positive change (typically k = -255..255).

$$p(k) = e^{-k^2/2\sigma^2}/\sigma\sqrt{2\pi} \quad k = -(G-1), \dots, -1, 0, 1, \dots, G-1 \quad (2.10)$$

$$p_{cum}(k) = p_{cum}(k-1) + p(k)$$

$$p_{cum}(-(G-1)) = p(-(G-1))$$

Once the cumulative distribution has been determined, we can then compute a noise value for each pixel in the image as follows.

For every pixel (x,y)

$$f^*(i,j) = g(i,j) + \text{argmin}_k(\text{rand}() - p_{cum}[k])$$

Set

$$f'(x,y) = 0 \qquad \text{if } f^*(x,y) < 0$$

$$f'(x,y) = G-1 \qquad \text{if } f^*(x,y) > G-1$$

$$f'(x,y) = f^*(x,y) \quad \text{otherwise} \qquad (2.11)$$

Note the argmin function gives the index of the smallest value, in this case choosing the k within the cumulative distribution whose value is closest to the random number. Also note that the truncation (to ensure that the values remain within $0 \dots 255$) alters the Gaussian nature of noise somewhat.

2.4.4 Noise Evaluation

The evaluation of noise can be done either subjectively or objectively. In a subjective evaluation images are shown to observers who appraise them according to a list of criteria and give marks.

In an objective evaluation, given an image $f(i, j)$ and a known reference image $g(i, j)$ we compute a measure of difference between them. For example

$$\text{Mean Quadratic Difference} = \sum\sum (g(i,j) - f(i,j))^2$$

$$\text{Mean Absolute Difference} = \sum\sum |g(i,j) - f(i,j)|$$

Or we can compute the signal to noise ratio assuming $v(i,j) = f(i,j) - g(i,j)$ \quad (2.12)

Obviously, this objective evaluation does have a slight problem in that we must either know the ideal image or the noise in advance. Hence, as in the examples in this section, we often artificially add noise to see how good our techniques are at removing it.

2.5   Smoothing

Removing or, more likely, reducing noise can be achieved by a variety of methods, a number of which are presented here. Note that different techniques are appropriate in different circumstances, often due to assumptions underlying the techniques or the nature of the image data.

The most commonly used approaches to noise reduction are linear smoothing transformations, where the computation can be expressed as a linear sum (e.g. see Section 2.5.1 and Section 2.5.2).

Noise suppression using linear smoothing transformations typically results in the blurring of sharp edges. A number of nonlinear transformations (which cannot be expressed as a simple linear sum) have been proposed to deal with this (e.g. see Section 2.5.3 and Section 2.5.4). Generally, these transformations require that some logical operation/test is performed at every location in the image.

None of the techniques described here can eliminate the degradations if they are large blobs or thick stripes. In such cases, image restoration techniques (in the frequency domain) may provide a solution.

2.5.1   Image Averaging

If there are multiple images of exactly the same scene, then they can be averaged to reduce the noise. The average of n images is:

$$f'(i,j) = \frac{1}{n} \sum_{k=1..n} f_k(i,j) = \frac{1}{n} \sum_{k=1..n} g_k(i,j) + v_k(i,j) \qquad (2.13)$$

This assumes an additive noise model. Also assuming that

- all the $g_k(i,j)$ are the same (i.e. the scene and camera are static)
- there is statistical independence between the noise $v_k(i,j)$ in each image
- the noise $v_k(i,j)$ has a Gaussian distribution with a 0 mean and a σ standard deviation

then the averaging of the image will alter the distribution of the noise, maintaining the Gaussian nature but reducing the standard deviation by a factor of $\sqrt{n}$. An example is shown in Figure 2.16.

In OpenCV, we can average images as follows:

```
addWeighted(image1,0.5,image2,0.5,0.0,average_image);
```

Note that in the case of salt and pepper noise, the noise is averaged into the image and hence this type of smoothing is not particularly appropriate for such noise.

If the scene is not static (e.g. if there were moving objects in the scene) then the averaging would introduce some unwanted effects. See Figure 9.6.

Figure 2.16 Original image (left), with Gaussian noise added (middle, 0 mean and 30 standard deviation) and the average of 8 such noisy images (right). Note how closely the final image approximates the first one. The signal-to-noise ratio in the middle image is 17.5, whereas it has increased to 129.7 in the averaged image

2.5.2   Local Averaging and Gaussian Smoothing

If only one image is available, averaging can still be performed but must be done in a local neighbourhood around each point (rather than using the corresponding points from multiple frames). The simplest form of this averaging is, for each point in the image, to simply compute the local average of the current point and its 8 closest neighbours (i.e. to compute the local average of a 3x3 block of pixels centred on the current point).

Where each of the points is equally weighted, the technique is referred to as local averaging. It is possible to change the weights, for example so that points closer to the current point are given higher weights. One very common such weighting is defined by the Gaussian distribution and use of such weighted averages is referred to at Gaussian smoothing. For example, consider the following:

$$h_1 = \frac{1}{9}\begin{bmatrix} 1 & 1 & 1 \\ 1 & 1 & 1 \\ 1 & 1 & 1 \end{bmatrix} \qquad h_2 = \frac{1}{10}\begin{bmatrix} 1 & 1 & 1 \\ 1 & 2 & 1 \\ 1 & 1 & 1 \end{bmatrix} \qquad h_3 = \frac{1}{16}\begin{bmatrix} 1 & 2 & 1 \\ 2 & 4 & 2 \\ 1 & 2 & 1 \end{bmatrix} \quad (2.14)$$

h_1 is a 3x3 local averaging filter, h_2 is a 3x3 Gaussian smoothing filter with a small value of sigma (the standard deviation of the Gaussian function), and h_3 is a 3x3 Gaussian smoothing filter with a larger value of sigma. See Figure 2.17 (b) and (c) and Figure 2.18 (b) and (c).

As we are averaging neighbouring pixels, we introduce blurring into the image which reduces the visible (Gaussian) noise. Unfortunately, this blurring also has a major impact on boundaries/edges (places where the image changes grey-scale or colour very rapidly) within the image, making the image fuzzier and hence (in some cases) harder to process accurately.

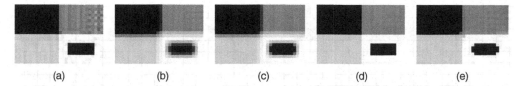

| (a) | (b) | (c) | (d) | (e) |

Figure 2.17   Test image (a) after 3x3 local averaging (b), Gaussian smoothing (c), rotating mask (d) and median filtering (e)

However, it may be necessary to accept this blurring in order to reduce the noise to an acceptable level.

In OpenCV, we can apply local averaging (using a 3x3 filter) as follows:

```
blur(image,smoothed_image,Size(3,3));
```

Gaussian smoothing (using a 5x5 filter and a sigma of 1.5) can be performed as follows:

```
GaussianBlur(image,smoothed_image,Size(5,5),1.5);
```

In the case of salt and pepper noise, again the noise will be smoothed into the image and hence this is not the most appropriate filter for such noise.

Filter masks can be larger than 3x3, in which case the effect (reduction in noise and increase in blurring) will become more significant.

Application of such filtering techniques is typically performed using convolution techniques, in which a convolution mask ($h(i,j)$ representing the weights of the smoothing filter) is convolved with the input image $f(i,j)$ in all possible locations, in order to create an output image $f'(i,j)$:

$$f'(i,j) = \sum_m \sum_n f(i,j).h(i - m, j - n) \tag{2.15}$$

Figure 2.18   Church image corrupted with Gaussian noise with a 0 mean and a standard deviation of 20 (left), after 3×3 local averaging (centre left), Gaussian smoothing (centre), rotating mask (centre right) and median filtering (right). The signal-to-noise ratios of these images are (a) 37.3, (b) 115.5, (c) 130.6, (d) 107.1 and (e) 112.1 respectively, when compared with the original image before noise was added

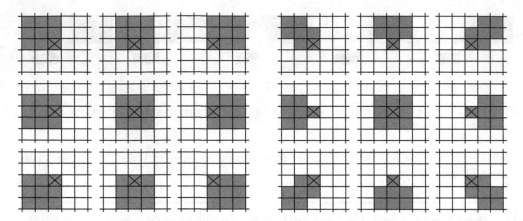

Figure 2.19 Two sets of masks used for the rotating mask smoothing filter. The current point is marked by an X and the same 5x5 region is shown nine times in each set of masks

$h(i,j)$ is generally is non-zero only for a small region (e.g. in a 3x3 filter, values are only non-zero between −1 and +1). The filter mask is usually square and an odd number of pixels high/wide to ensure symmetry around the current point (e.g. 3x3 or 5x5).

2.5.3   Rotating Mask

The rotating mask is a nonlinear operator that applies one of nine possible local averaging filters depending on which image region is most homogeneous (i.e. self-similar).

Relative to the current point, nine masks are defined all of which include the current point (see Figure 2.19). The shape and size of the masks can vary (e.g. in Figure 2.19 the first set is just all possible 3x3 regions including the current point and the second set is an alteration of this which is more shaped/targeted).

When averaging, we apply one of the masks to the image data to get an output value for the current point (i.e. we determine a local average of the points that correspond to those in the mask). The main question is which mask to choose for any given point. What we are trying to achieve is to reduce noise in the current point, and hence we want to average the current point with other similar points from the same physical stimulus (i.e. surface or object). We cannot tell the physical origin of pixels, but we can approximate it to some extent by looking for the local region which is most consistent (self-similar). We do this by calculating the dispersion (the degree to which the pixels are on average different from the average value) for each mask and choose the one with the minimum dispersion.

Algorithm 2.1

> For each $f(i,j)$
> > Calculate the dispersion for all masks.
> > Pick the mask with the minimum dispersion.
> > Assign output point $f'(i,j)$ the average of that mask.

This technique can be applied iteratively until there are no or very few changes. The larger the mask size, the faster the convergence will be (i.e. less iterations will be necessary).

Rotating mask smoothing is not supported in OpenCV, but is quite easy to implement.

Averaging with a rotating mask is quite effective at suppressing noise and sharpening the image (edges), although it will be significantly slower than simple local averaging. See Figure 2.17 (d) and Figure 2.18 (d) for examples.

Dispersion (D) is computed by determining the average of the squared difference of each point in the mask less the average of the mask:

$$D = \frac{1}{n} \sum_{(i,j) \in \text{Mask}} \left(f(i,j) - \frac{1}{n} \sum_{(i',j') \in \text{Mask}} f(i',j') \right)^2 \tag{2.16}$$

This can be reorganised somewhat in order to make a direct implementation of it more computationally efficient:

Expanding out the square:

$$D = \frac{1}{n} \sum_{(i,j) \in \text{Mask}} \left[f(i,j)^2 - \frac{2}{n} \cdot f(i,j) \cdot \sum_{(i',j') \in \text{Mask}} f(i',j') + \frac{1}{n^2} \left(\sum_{(i',j') \in \text{Mask}} f(i',j') \right)^2 \right] \tag{2.17}$$

Bringing the summation inside:

$$D = \frac{1}{n} \left(\sum_{(i,j) \in \text{Mask}} f(i,j)^2 - \frac{2}{n} \left(\sum_{(i',j') \in \text{Mask}} f(i',j') \right)^2 + \frac{n}{n^2} \left(\sum_{(i',j') \in \text{Mask}} f(i',j') \right)^2 \right) \tag{2.18}$$

Cancelling some n's and doing a little subtraction:

$$D = \frac{1}{n} \left(\sum_{(i,j) \in \text{Mask}} f(i,j)^2 - \frac{1}{n} \left(\sum_{(i',j') \in \text{Mask}} f(i',j') \right)^2 \right) \tag{2.19}$$

This formula is significantly less expensive (computationally) than the original.

Note that the rotating mask can be applied to images with salt and pepper noise, but can result in undesirable effects particularly if noise is present near object boundaries.

2.5.4 Median Filter

Another nonlinear smoothing operation is to replace each pixel with the median of the pixels in a small region (e.g. 3x3) centred around the pixel. The median value is the middle value

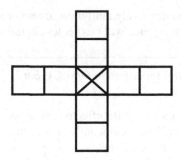

Figure 2.20   Non-square mask for use in median filtering

in an ordered list. So, for example, if a 3x3 region contained the grey levels (25 21 23 25 18 255 30 13 22), the ordered list would be (13 18 22 21 23 25 25 30 255) and the median would be 23. Note that the average value would have been 48 due to the single point of noise (i.e. the 255), so this technique is quite good at dealing with noise. In addition, this technique does not blur edges much and can be applied iteratively. In fact, the effect of median filtering is quite similar to that of averaging using a rotating mask. For examples, see Figure 2.17 (e) and Figure 2.18 (e).

In OpenCV, we can apply median filtering (with a 5×5 filter) to an image as follows:

```
medianBlur(image,smoothed_image,5);
```

Median filtering tends to damage thin lines and corners, although these effects can be reduced by using a non-rectangular region such as that shown in Figure 2.20. However, there will still be problems (e.g. consider the corners of square which is an angle of 45% to the horizontal). It has also been regarded as very computationally expensive as the basic algorithm is $O(k^2 \log k)$.

However, an algorithm developed by Perreault (Perreault, 2007) has reduced this to $O(1)$, although this technique does not appear to be in common use. In this approach, an intermediate representation of column histograms is used to summarise the columns that make up the region of points to be considered; for example, if considering the median of a nxn region then $nx1$ histograms are created for every column along one entire row. To move to a new row of points, we can simply remove the topmost points from the column histograms and add an extra point from the new row to be included (see the left-hand diagram in Figure 2.21). Also, when moving from column to column we can initially summarise the first n columns histogram in a single histogram (to compute the median) and then when moving to the next column we need only take the left-hand column histogram away and add a new column histogram on the right-hand side (see the right hand diagram in Figure 2.21). Note that each pixel is only accessed twice (to add and then remove it from a histogram).

The Perreault algorithm can be summarised as follows:

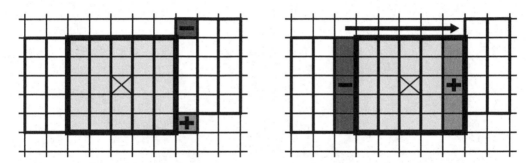

Figure 2.21 Using the Perreault approach the image is broken into column histograms. When considering a pixel a single column histogram to the right-hand side of the previous kernel is updated by removing the topmost pixel and adding a new pixel to the bottom (left). Then the kernel histogram is updated by removing the leftmost column (shown in red) and adding a new column to the right-hand side (shown in green) (right)

Algorithm 2.2

Given Input image X $(m * n)$, kernel radius k, Output image Y
for $row = 1$ to m
Initialise column histograms $h_{1..n}$ and histogram H
for $column = 1$ to n
$Y(column, row) =$ Median of H; Compute the median in an efficient manner (by keeping a count of the points less than or equal to the median when updating the histogram (H).
Remove $X(column+k+1, row-k-1)$ from $h_{column+k+1}$
Add $X(column+k+1, row+k)$ to $h_{column+k+1}$
Remove leftmost column from H: $h_{column-k}$
Add new column to right of H: $h_{column+k+1}$

There are a number of other things which must be done to make the implementation of this efficient. For example, use of processor SIMD instructions for manipulating histograms and ensuring that all the histograms remain in the cache (e.g. by processing the image in sections).

3

Histograms

An image histogram is an abstraction of an image where the frequency of each image (brightness/intensity) value is determined.

3.1 1D Histograms

In the case of a grey-scale image in which there are 256 grey scale intensities (0–255), 256 counts are computed indicating how many pixels each of the grey-scales in the image have. This can be visualised as in Figure 3.1.

The algorithm to derive such a histogram $h(g)$ from a grey-scale image $f(i,j)$ is:

Algorithm 3.1

```
// Initialise the histogram
for (g = 0; g <= 255; g++)
    h(g) = 0
// Compute the histogram
for (i = 0; i < MAX_column; i++)
    for (j = 0; j < MAX_row; j++)
        h(f(i,j))++
```

The histogram contains global information about the image and that information is completely independent of the position and orientation of objects in the scene. In some cases, the histogram or information derived from it (such as the average intensity and its standard deviation) can be used to perform classification (e.g. apples with bruises will result in dark spots, which will change the shape of the histogram when compared to histograms from good apples). However, care must be taken as image histograms are not unique and hence many very different images may have similar (or even the same) histogram.

A Practical Introduction to Computer Vision with OpenCV, First Edition. Kenneth Dawson-Howe.
© 2014 John Wiley & Sons, Ltd. Published 2014 by John Wiley & Sons, Ltd.

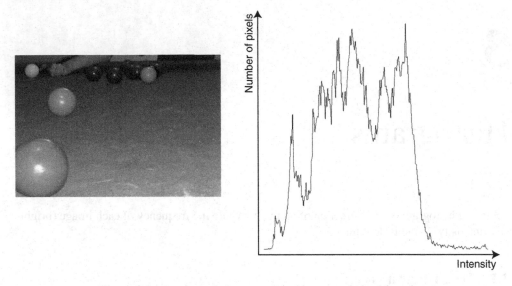

Figure 3.1 A grey-scale image and the histogram derived from it

In OpenCV, to compute a histogram for a grey-scale image (`grey_image`) with a particular quantisation (`number_bins`) we call `calcHist` as follows:

```
Mat display_image;
MatND histogram;
const int* channel_numbers = { 0 };
float channel_range[] = { 0.0, 255.0 };
const float* channel_ranges = channel_range;
int number_bins = 64;
calcHist( &gray_image, 1, channel_numbers, Mat(), histogram,
                         1, &number_bins, &channel_ranges );
OneDHistogram::Draw1DHistogram( &gray_histogram, 1,
                                         display_image );
```

3.1.1 Histogram Smoothing

Global and local maxima and minima in the histogram can also provide useful information although, as can be seen in Figure 3.1, there can be many local maxima and minima. To reduce this number, the histogram may be smoothed. This is done by creating a new array of values where each value is the average of a number of values centred on the corresponding value in the original histogram. This process is often referred to as filtering. See Figure 3.2 for an example.

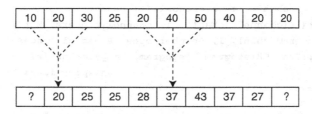

Figure 3.2   Smoothing of a 1D histogram using a local average with a filter width of 3

In OpenCV, to smooth a 1D histogram, replacing each element (except the first and last elements) by the average of its neighbours:

```
MatND smoothed_histogram = histogram[channel].clone();
for(int i = 1; i < histogram[channel].rows - 1; ++i)
  smoothed_histogram[channel].at<float>(i) =
     (histogram.at<float>(i-1) + histogram.at<float>(i) +
                        histogram.at<float>(i+1)) / 3;
```

One major question arises when doing this filtering (the same question arises with all filtering operations in image processing): what do we do at the ends of the histogram? Unfortunately there is no correct answer and typical solutions include:

- Altering the filter so that only supported values are included.
- Assuming that all unsupported locations have some constant value.
- Assuming that the representation wraps around in a circular fashion.
- Reflecting the values from inside the representation.

3.1.2   Colour Histograms

Another issue that arises is what to do with colour images. Often histograms are determined for each channel independently (see Figure 3.3 and Figure 3.4).

In OpenCV, to compute histograms for each channel on a colour image we simply split the image into separate channels/planes and histogram each one as normal:

```
MatND* histogram = new MatND[image.channels()];
vector<Mat> channels(image.channels() );
split( image, channels );
const int* channel_numbers = { 0 };
float channel_range[] = { 0.0, 255.0 };
const float* channel_ranges = channel_range;
int number_bins = 64;
```

```
for (int chan=0; chan < image.channels(); chan++)
    calcHist( &(channels[chan]), 1, channel_numbers, Mat(),
        histogram[chan], 1, &number_bins, &channel_ranges );
OneDHistogram::DrawlDHistogram(histogram, image.channels(),
                                        display_image );
```

The choice of colour model can have a huge effect on the usefulness of the colour histogram. For example, if you consider the hue histogram in Figure 3.4, it should be apparent that identifying the green cloth and the red balls in the image should be quite straightforward.

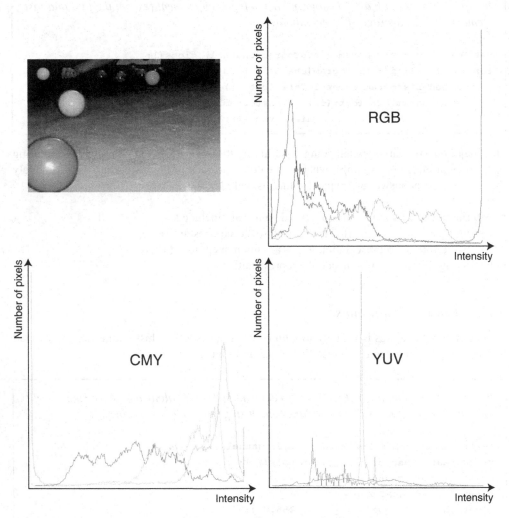

Figure 3.3 Histograms of the various channels from RGB, CMY and YUV representations of a colour image

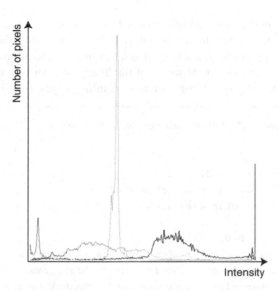

Figure 3.4 Histogram of the HLS channels from the colour image in Figure 3.3. Note that the hue histogram is represented by the coloured line and notice that the red balls and the green table are both clearly represented by peaks in the hue distribution. The luminance histogram is plotted in light grey and the saturation histogram is plotted in black

3.2 3D Histograms

In all of the histograms presented so far, the channels of colour data have been treated independently. This approach does not lend itself to the best possible segmentation of colours in the overall image. For example, most of the red points representing the ball in the snooker image have a high value of saturation as well as a limited range of hue value. If we want to achieve better segmentation, we would need to look at a 3D histogram of the colours (e.g. see Figure 3.5).

Figure 3.5 A 3D histogram (right) of the RGB channels from the colour image on the left. Note that the 0,0,0 point is shown on the front layer at the bottom left. The green axis goes from bottom left to bottom right of the front layer, the blue axis goes from bottom left to top left of the front layer and the red axis goes from bottom left of the front layer to bottom left of the bottommost layer. The average colour of each cell is shown as the border of the cell and the grey level intensity shown within in each cell indicates the relative number of pixels in each cell (black = 0, white = max). We can see several distinct peaks in the histogram for black points (front layer), grey points (2nd layer), red points (3rd layer) and white points (4th layer). The green image points are distributed across a few cells in the histogram

One practical problem of using 3D histogram is the number of cells within the histogram. If we assume 8 bits per channel then there are almost 16.8 million cells in the histogram. This is unacceptable as the histogram is typically used as a summary of the information in the image. To overcome this we reduce the quantisation of the histogram. For example, in Figure 3.5 a 3D histogram is shown with just 2 bits per channel resulting in just 64 cells in the histogram.

In OpenCV, to compute a 3-D colour histogram from an image:

```
MatND histogram;
int channel_numbers[] = { 0, 1, 2 };
int* number_bins = new int[image.channels()];
for (ch=0; ch < image.channels(); ch++)
        number_bins[ch] = 4;
float ch_range[] = { 0.0, 255.0 };
const float* channel_ranges[] = {ch_range,ch_range,ch_range};
calcHist( &image, 1, channel_numbers, Mat(), histogram,
            image.channels(), a_number_bins, channel_ranges );
```

3.3   Histogram/Image Equalisation

Often images may be difficult for a human observer to decipher due to the picture being, for example, too dark. It has been determined that humans can distinguish between 700 and 900 shades of grey under optimal viewing conditions (Kimpe & Tuytschaever, 2007), although in very dark or bright sections of a image the just noticeable difference (JND) reduces significantly. However, it is also clear that it is easier for humans to distinguish larger differences, so if the distribution of grey-scales in an image is improved, this facilitates understanding by human observers.

One technique for improving the distribution of grey-scales in an image is histogram equalisation. This technique attempts to distribute the grey-scales in an image evenly, so that the resulting histogram is flat (i.e. all grey-scales have exactly the same number of points). This is not really feasible (unless points of some common grey-scales in the input are mapped to multiple different grey-scales in the output), so instead the resulting histogram often has some grey-scales with no associated pixels, interspersed with high values. See Figure 3.6.

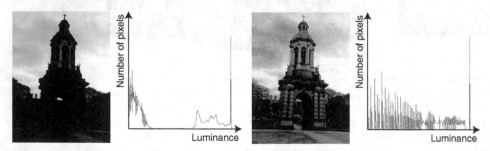

Figure 3.6   A colour image and its luminance histogram (left), together with a histogram-equalised version of the image and the resultant luminance histogram (right)

Note that when equalising a colour image (such as that in Figure 3.6) we generally only equalise the luminance channel as otherwise the colours can become distorted.

In OpenCV, when equalising an image, the computation of the histogram is hidden within OpenCV. Here we equalise the luminance channel of a HLS image:

```
split (hls_image, channels);
vector<Mat> channels( hls_image.channels() );
equalizeHist ( channels[1], channels[1] );
merge ( channels, hls_image );
```

The algorithm for histogram equalisation is as follows:

Algorithm 3.2

- Given a histogram *histogram(x)* of the luminance values from some input image $f(i,j)$.
- Create a look-up table *LUT(x)* to map the luminance values from the input image to the output image.

> *total_pixels_so_far = 0*
> *total_pixels = image.rows * image.cols*
> *output_grey_scale = 0*
> *for input_grey_scale = 0 to 255*
> *total_pixels_so_far = total_pixels_so_far +*
>   *histogram[input_grey_ scale]*
> *new_output_grey_scale = (total_pixels_so_far*256)/(total_pixels+1)*
> *LUT[input_grey_scale] = (output_grey_scale+1+*
>   *new_output_ grey_scale)/2*
> *output_grey_scale = new_output_grey_scale*

- Apply the lookup table *LUT(x)* to the input image to generate a new image $f'(i,j)$:

> *for every pixel f(i,j)*
> *f'(i,j) = LUT[f(i,j)]*

3.4   Histogram Comparison

Retrieving images that are similar to a given image or that contain particular content is a well-known imaging problem. Most image search engines provide this functionality, although most frequently it is addressed by using meta-data tags associated with each image (i.e. keywords associated with an image indicating roughly what their content is). It is possible to provide assistance to this process by analysing the colour distribution present in an image and this can be done by comparing histograms derived from the images. For example, see Figure 3.7.

Figure 3.7 Best matching images (based on histogram comparison using a 3D HLS histogram with 2 bits on each channel; that is a $4 \times 4 \times 4$ histogram). The reference image is the one on the top left (which gets a perfect matching score). The metrics shown in red are the correlation scores

There are a number of metrics that are commonly used to compare histograms:

- $D_{\text{Correlation}}\left(h_1, h_2\right) = \dfrac{\sum_i \left(h_1(i) - \overline{h_1}\right)\left(h_2(i) - \overline{h_2}\right)}{\sqrt{\sum_i \left(h_1(i) - \overline{h_1}\right)^2 \sum_i \left(h_2(i) - \overline{h_2}\right)^2}}$

- $D_{\text{Chi-Square}}\left(h_1, h_2\right) = \sum_i \dfrac{\left(h_1(i) - h_2(i)\right)^2}{\left(h_1(i) + h_2(i)\right)}$

- $D_{\text{Intersection}}\left(h_1, h_2\right) = \sum_i min\left(h_1(i), h_2(i)\right)$

- $D_{\text{Bhattacharyya}}\left(h_1, h_2\right) = \sqrt{1 - \dfrac{1}{\sqrt{\overline{h_1}.\overline{h_2}.N^2}} \sum_i \sqrt{h_1(i).h_2(i)}}$

where

- N is the number of bins in the histograms,
- $\overline{h_k} = {\sum_i \left(h_k(i)\right)}\big/{N}$

Alternatively, it is possible to use the **Earth Mover's Distance**, which determines the minimum cost for turning one distribution (in this case histograms) into another. In the discrete 1D domain this can be solved by iterating through the elements of the histograms follows:

$$EMD(-1) = 0$$

$$EMD(i) = h_1(i) + EMD(i-1) - h_2(i) \tag{3.1}$$

The final distance computed is

$$\sum_i |EMD(i)| \qquad (3.2)$$

It is possible to use the Earth Mover's Distance to compare colour histograms, which is generally formulated as a linear programming problem (See (Rubner, 1998) for further details).

In OpenCV, to compare histograms using correlation:

```
normalize ( histogram1, histogram1, 1.0);
normalize (histogram2, histogram2, 1.0);
double matching_score = compareHist ( histogram1,
                        histogram2, CV_COMP_CORREL );
```

We can also use Chi-Square (`CV_COMP_CHISQR`*), Intersection (*`CV_COMP_INTERSECT`*) or Bhattacharyya (*`CV_COMP_BHATTACHARYYA`*) metrics or alternatively can use the Earth Mover's Distance function (*`EMD ()`*)*

3.5 Back-projection

In Sections 2.3.6.1 and 2.3.6.2 we considered some very simple approaches to selecting particular colours within images. These approaches select rather crude subspaces within the colour spaces in which they are defined. A better approach to this problem is to:

1. Obtain a representative sample set of the colour(s) to be selected.
2. Create a histogram of the samples.
3. Normalise the histogram so that the maximum value is 1.0. This allows the histogram values to be treated as probabilities (i.e. the probability that a pixel with the corresponding colour is from the sample set).
4. Back-project the normalised histogram onto any image $f(i,j)$ where the similarity of the pixels in the image to those in the sample set is required, in effect providing a probability image $p()$ where $p(i,j)$ indicates the similarity between $f(i,j)$ and the sample set (i.e. $p(i,j) = h(f(i,j))$).

In OpenCV, given a colour histogram we can back-project it into a colour image of the same format (in this case HLS) to get the similarities of the pixels to those in the histogram as follows:

```
calcHist ( &hls_samples_image, 1, channel_numbers, Mat(),
    histogram,image.channels(),number_bins,channel_ranges);
normalize ( histogram, histogram, 1.0);
Mat probabilities = histogram.BackProject ( hls_image );
```

Figure 3.8   Back-projection (right image) of a (3D) HLS histogram of the skin pixels (centre image) of a colour image (left image). The 3D histogram was quantized to 3 bits per channel (i.e. the histogram was $8 \times 8 \times 8$) and this histogram was normalised so that the maximum value was 1.0

For example, see Figure 3.8, in which a sample set of skin pixels is histogrammed and back-projected into an image in order to identify skin regions in the image. Note that the size of the histogram bins is particularly important when doing this back-projection, particularly if the number of samples is limited. In this case it was found that $8 \times 8 \times 8$ bins in the histogram was appropriate. In addition, the choice of colour space can be quite important. In this example, use of RGB space gave a somewhat poorer answer.

3.6   k-means Clustering

One major problem with colour is the large range of possible colours that exist (e.g. the 16.8 million colours in 8 bit RGB space). We frequently want to reduce this number, for example to represent the colours of the clothing that someone is wearing or to allow images to be more faithfully compressed. To achieve this reduction of colours, one common technique which is used is clustering in 3D colour space (e.g. see Figure 3.9).

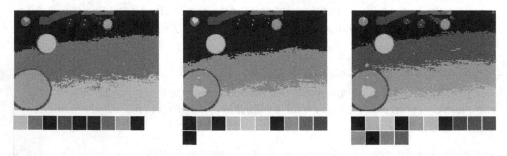

Figure 3.9   Three different k-means clustered images together with their colours derived from the image in Figure 3.3. Note that they were clustered using 10, 15 and 20 random starting exemplars respectively, although only those exemplars which eventually had any associated patterns (pixels) are shown below each image

The technique used in Figure 3.9 is the original k-means clustering algorithm. Note that there are many variations on this algorithm, but they all work in a similar fashion (e.g. see (Kanungo, Mount, Netanyahu, Piatko, Silverman, and Wu, 2002)).

We are searching for a number (k) of exemplars (i.e. specific colours) to best represent all of the colours in an image, and that number (k) is specified in advance. The colour of each pixel in the image is referred to as a pattern. A group of patterns associated with a particular exemplar is referred as a cluster.

- The starting exemplars are, for example,
  ○ picked randomly
  ○ chosen as the first k patterns
  ○ distributed evenly.
- First pass: For all patterns, allocate the pattern to the nearest exemplar. Re-compute the exemplar as the centre of gravity of all patterns associated with it after each new pattern is associated with it.
- Second pass: Use the final exemplars from the first pass and reallocate all patterns to the exemplars (these allocations may not be the same as last time . . . however the exemplars don't change).

A simple 1D illustration of k-means is shown in Figure 3.10.

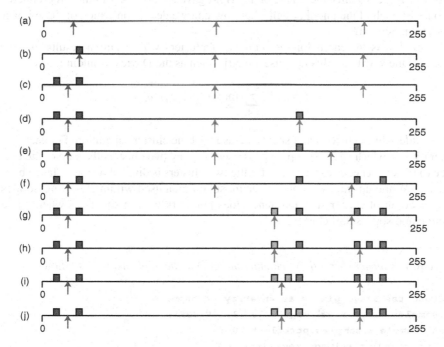

Figure 3.10 A 1D example of k-means. (a) Three starting exemplars, (b–i) new patterns are introduced and each is associated with the closest exemplar; that is red (b,c), green (d,e,f,h) or blue (g,i); with the relevant exemplar being recomputed after each new pattern is introduced, and finally (j) the patterns are associated with the closest exemplar in the second pass (with one green labelled pattern reclassified as part of the blue cluster)

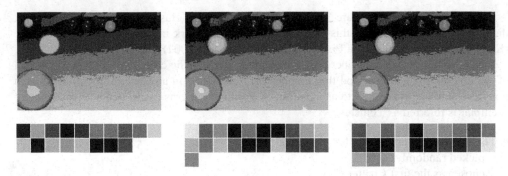

Figure 3.11 Three different k-means clustered images together with the colours derived from the image in Figure 3.3. Note that all three were clustered using 30 random starting clusters, although only those clusters/colours which eventually had any associated pixels are shown

Note that choosing the starting exemplars randomly means that the algorithm is non-deterministic. In Figure 3.11 the results of applying the k-means algorithm three times, each with 30 starting exemplars, are shown.

Deciding how many colours should be used to represent a region or an image is not straight-forward. In Figure 3.9 only the image on the right gave a reasonably faithful reproduction of the colours of each of the snooker balls, but how can we decide on which of these images is appropriate in general?

One approach is to search for the number of clusters whose output results the highest confidence. One way to do this is to use a metric such as the Davies–Bouldin index

$$DB = 1/k \sum_{1..k} \max_{i \neq j} ((\Delta_i + \Delta_j)/\delta_{i,j}) \tag{3.3}$$

which considers the k clusters and sums a measure of the cluster separation. For each cluster, the other cluster which is worst-separated is used: for any two clusters the sum of the average distance to the cluster centres ($\Delta_i + \Delta_j$) for the two clusters is divided by the distance between clusters $\delta_{i,j}$. While this metric is one of the most common used within clustering, it does not take any account of cluster size and hence does not work well in situations where there are some large and some small clusters.

In OpenCV, k-means (for a three-channel image) can be implemented as follows:

```
// Store the image pixels as an array of samples
Mat samples(image.rows*image.cols, 3, CV_32F);
float* sample = samples.ptr<float>(0);
for(int row=0; row<image.rows; row++)
  for(int col=0; col<image.cols; col++)
    for (int channel=0; channel < 3; channel++)
      samples.at<float>(row*image.cols+col,channel) =
               (uchar) image.at<Vec3b>(row,col)[channel];
```

```
// Apply k-means clustering, determining the cluster
// centres and a label for each pixel.
Mat labels, centres;
kmeans (samples, k, labels, TermCriteria)
        CV_TERMCRIT_ITER|CV_TERMCRIT_EPS, 100, 0.0001),
        iterations, KMEANS_PP_CENTERS, centres );
// Use centres and label to populate the result image
Mat& result_image = Mat( image.size(), image.type() );
for(int row=0; row<image.rows; row++)
   for(int col=0; col<image.cols; col++)
     for (int channel=0; channel < 3; channel++)
       result_image.at<Vec3b>(row,col)[channel] = (uchar)
           centres.at<float>( *(labels.ptr<int>(
                                row*image.cols+col )), channel);
```

k-means clustering is an example of unsupervised learning where the segmentation is learnt from the data presented. Unsupervised learning is learning that is done without feedback about whether the current classification is correct or not. Instead, the learning has to be based on some regularity within the input data that allows similar events/pixels/objects to be classified in the same way.

4

Binary Vision

Grey-scale images generally have 8 bits per pixel. While processing these images is easier in some ways than processing colour images, there is a simpler form of image, the binary image, in which processing is even more straightforward. In fact, a significant portion of practical applications of computer vision have been developed using binary vision (Marchand-Maillet and Sharaiha, 1999).

A binary image is one in which there is only a single bit per pixel (i.e. black or white). These images are created by thresholding (see Section 4.1) where the thresholds used are determined in a variety of ways (see Section 4.2 and Section 4.3). The resulting binary images are often post-processed using mathematical morphology (see Section 4.4) and the resulting segmented binary regions are extracted from the image using connected components analysis (see Section 4.5).

It is worth mentioning that binary images can be created from many types of image, such as intensity images, gradient images, difference images, and so on.

4.1 Thresholding

A binary image is created from a grey-scale image by thresholding. The binary thresholding algorithm is simply:

Algorithm 4.1

$$\text{For all pixels } (i,j)$$
$$f'(i,j) = 1 \text{ where } f(i,j) >= T$$
$$= 0 \text{ where } f(i,j) < T$$

Often grey-level 255 is used instead of binary 1 (so that the resulting image can be represented using a 8-bit format and displayed/processed in the same manner as the original grey-scale image).

The most efficient means of implementing this operation (which can often be done in hardware) is to use a lookup table. In other words, create a one-dimensional array (the lookup

A Practical Introduction to Computer Vision with OpenCV, First Edition. Kenneth Dawson-Howe.
© 2014 John Wiley & Sons, Ltd. Published 2014 by John Wiley & Sons, Ltd.

Figure 4.1   A binary version (right) of a grey-scale image (left) thresholded at grey-level 97

table) with the same number of elements as there are grey scales. Each cell in the array should then be initialised to 1 or 0 depending upon whether its index is above or below the threshold.

$$\text{For all grey levels } k = 0 \dots 255$$
$$\text{LUT}(k) = 1 \text{ where } k >= T$$
$$= 0 \text{ where } k < T$$
$$\text{For all pixels } (i,j)$$
$$g(i,j) = \text{LUT}(f(i,j))$$

The thresholding operation is generally used in order to separate some objects of interest from the background. Most typically the object(s) of interest are represented by 1 (or 255), but sometimes (such as in Figure 4.1) the binary image would have to be inverted for this to be the case.

In OpenCV, thresholding is performed as follows:

```
threshold(gray_image,binary_image,threshold,
                        255,THRESH_BINARY);
```

where `gray_image` *and* `binary_image` *are defined as* `Mat` *and* `gray_image` *contains a single channel image.*

4.1.1   Thresholding Problems

Arguably, the most important thing to note about binary imaging is that the foreground and the background that are being separated need to be distinct in the image being thresholded. If they are not distinct then it will be difficult (or even impossible) to accurately segment them using thresholding. However, there are a number of techniques (e.g. adaptive thresholding)

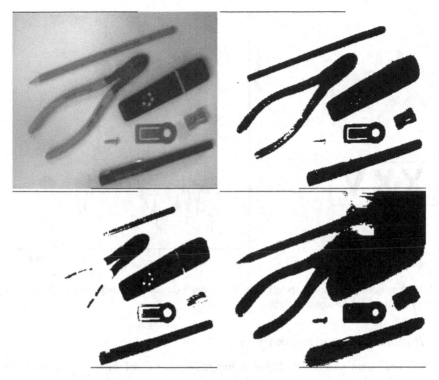

Figure 4.2 A grey-scale image (top left) together with a binary version where the threshold is 'correct' (top right), a version where the threshold is too low (bottom left) and a version where it is too high (bottom right)

which are used to try to deal with situations where the distinction between foreground and background is not clear, and there are a number of techniques (e.g. erosion, dilation, opening, closing) which aim to improve a binary image where the segmentation is imperfect.

Figure 4.2 shows examples of what happens when the threshold is not chosen correctly. However, even in the 'correctly' thresholded binary image there are some errors (e.g. much of the tip of the pencil is missing and the shadow above the highlighter pen has been erroneously included).

4.2 Threshold Detection Methods

While for some industrial applications thresholds are set manually, this can cause problems over time as lighting changes throughout the day. Even within industrial lighting enclosures, the lighting sources gradually become weaker over time. Hence, mechanisms are required to automatically determine thresholds (Sezgin and Sankur, 2004).

For the following sections we assume that we are given a grey-scale image $f(i,j)$ to threshold; its histogram has been computed $h(g) = \sum_{i,j} \begin{bmatrix} 1 & f(i,j) = g \\ 0 & otherwise \end{bmatrix}$, and turned into a probability distribution $p(g) = h(g) \Big/ \sum_g h(g)$.

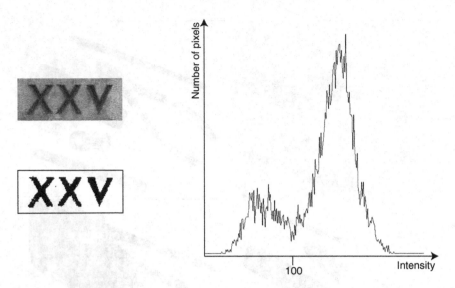

Figure 4.3   A grey-scale image (top left) which has been thresholded (bottom left) by selecting the anti-mode (100) from the histogram (right)

4.2.1   Bimodal Histogram Analysis

It is possible to determine a threshold for an image by analysis of the histogram of the image. If we assume that the background is predominantly centred around one grey-scale, and the foreground is predominantly centred around another grey-scale, then we can assume that the histogram will be bimodal (i.e. have two main peaks). Then, to find the threshold we can simply look for the anti-mode (the minimum value between the peaks).

Considering the histogram in Figure 4.3, though, we can see that while the overall shape of the histogram is bimodal, there are many local maxima and minima and hence finding the anti-mode is not straightforward. There are a few possibilities when addressing this, such as to smooth the histogram (to suppress the noisy peaks), or to use a variable step size (rather than considering each element of the histogram separately). We could also ignore all points that have a high gradient (as these represent boundaries) and this should provide better separation between the two modes of the histogram. Alternatively, we could histogram only the boundary points, and then take the mode of the resulting (hopefully unimodal) histogram.

However, these approaches tend to shift the anti-mode, resulting in poor threshold values. There are other approaches, described in the sections that follow, based on the analysis of the histogram (which represents the image), which are more reliable.

4.2.2   Optimal Thresholding

The preceding technique works reasonably well as long as the modes are reasonably well separated and as long as the noise is not too great. However, as the modes become closer together the anti-mode is no longer the optimal solution. Consider the two normal distributions in Figure 4.4 and their summation. The optimal threshold is where the two normal distributions intersect (the left-hand vertical line), whereas the anti-mode of the summed distributions is further to the right.

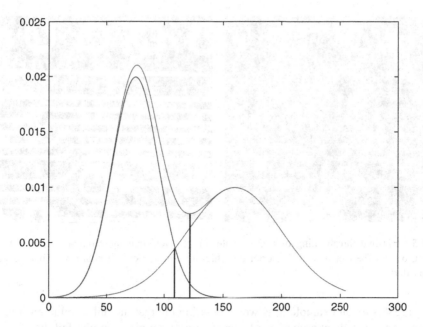

Figure 4.4 This chart shows in blue a normal distribution with an average grey-scale of 75 and a standard deviation of 20, in green a normal distribution with an average grey-scale of 160 and a standard deviation of 40 and in red the sum of the two distributions. The two vertical black lines show (on the left) the optimal distribution and (on the right) the anti-mode

If we can model the histogram as the sum of two normal, but possibly overlapping, distributions, we can use a technique called Optimal Thresholding. The algorithm for optimal thresholding iterates until it reaches a solution, although there is no intuitive way to explain why it returns the optimal answer.

The optimal thresholding algorithm:

Algorithm 4.2

1. Set $t = 0$, $T^t = $ <some initial threshold value>
2. Compute average values for the foreground and background based on the current threshold T^t

$$w_b(T^t) = \sum_{g=0}^{T^t-1} p(g) \qquad \mu_b(T^t) = \left.\sum_{g=0}^{T^t-1} p(g).g \middle/ w_b(T^t)\right.$$

$$w_f(T^t) = \sum_{g=T^t}^{255} p(g) = 1 - w_b(T^t) \qquad \mu_f(T^t) = \left.\sum_{g=T^t}^{255} p(g) \cdot g \middle/ w_f(T^t)\right.$$

3. Update the threshold (for the next iteration) by setting $T^{t+1} = \left(\mu_b\left(T^t\right) + \mu_f\left(T^t\right)\right) / 2$ and by incrementing $t = t + 1$.
4. Go back to 2 until $T^{t+1} = T^t$.

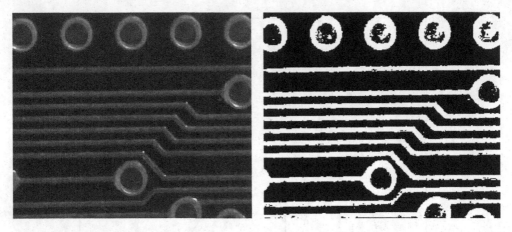

Figure 4.5 Optimal thresholding of a grey-scale image. Note that the circular holes are not well segmented, due to the fact that the material on which the printed circuit board was imaged was not sufficiently dark

See Figure 4.5 for an example. It is worth pointing out that the initial value must result in some object and some background pixels, or otherwise our program will fail due to a divide by zero error. Also bear in mind that the result will only be optimal if the histogram is the sum of two normal distributions.

4.2.3   Otsu Thresholding

Optimal thresholding makes the assumption that the histogram is the sum of two normal distributions. This is often not the case and so the result of optimal thresholding may not be acceptable. Another alternative was defined by Otsu (Otsu, 1979) where the spread of the pixel values on each side of the threshold is minimised:

Select the threshold T (by considering all possible thresholds) which minimises the within class variance $\sigma_W^2(T)$:

$$\sigma_W^2(T) = w_f(T)\,\sigma_f^2(T) + w_b(T)\,\sigma_b^2(T) \tag{4.1}$$

where $w_f(T)$ and $w_b(T)$ are the portions of the points which are foreground/background and $\sigma_f^2(T)$ and $\sigma_b^2(T)$ are the variances of the foreground and background grey-scale values:

$$w_f(T) = \sum_{g=T}^{255} p(g) \qquad \sigma_f^2(T) = \left. \sum_{g=T}^{255} p(g) \cdot \left(g - \mu_f(T)\right)^2 \middle/ w_f(T) \right.$$

$$w_b(T) = \sum_{g=0}^{T-1} p(g) \qquad \sigma_b^2(T) = \left. \sum_{g=0}^{T-1} p(g) \cdot \left(g - \mu_b(T)\right)^2 \middle/ w_b(T) \right. \tag{4.2}$$

where $\mu_f(T)$ and $\mu_b(T)$ are the means of the foreground and background grey-scale values:

$$\mu_f(T) = \sum_{g=T}^{255} p(g) \cdot g \Big/ w_{\mathrm{f}}(T) \qquad \mu_b(T) = \sum_{g=0}^{T-1} p(g) \cdot g \Big/ w_{\mathrm{b}}(T) \qquad (4.3)$$

The threshold with the smallest within class variance is also the threshold with the largest between class variance $\sigma_B^2(T)$ (which is easier to compute). This is because $\sigma_B^2(T) = \sigma^2 - \sigma_W^2(T)$ where μ and σ^2 are the mean and variance of the image data respectively.

Given two classes (f and b) the between class variance may be defined as

$$\sigma_B^2(T) = w_f(T)\left(\mu_f(T) - \mu\right)^2 + w_b(T)\left(\mu_b(T) - \mu\right)^2 \qquad (4.4)$$

which can be simplified as

$$\sigma_B^2(T) = w_f(T)\, w_b(T)\left(\mu_f(T) - \mu_b(T)\right)^2 \qquad (4.5)$$

given that $\mu = w_f(T)\,\mu_f(T) + w_b(T)\,\mu_b(T)$.

The reformulation allows us to determine the Otsu threshold from just the weights and the means. See Figure 4.6 for an example of Otsu thresholding.

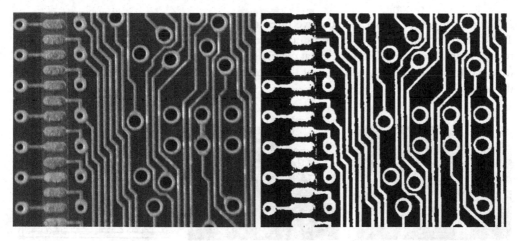

Figure 4.6   Otsu thresholding of a grey-scale image. Note that some points from the background of the pads (on the left-hand side) are being erroneously classified as foreground, and some of the points on the pads themselves are being erroneously classified as background. These issues can be dealt with by using very specific lighting configurations

In OpenCV, Otsu thresholding is performed by adding a flag to the call to the threshold function:

```
threshold( gray_image, binary_image, threshold,
                    255, THRESH_BINARY | THRESH_OTSU );
```

Note that in this case the passed `threshold` *value is ignored.*

4.3   Variations on Thresholding

4.3.1   Adaptive Thresholding

In all of the examples shown so far, global thresholding has been used (i.e. a single threshold has been applied to all points in the image). In some situations it is possible to significantly improve thresholding results by using multiple thresholds.

Consider the thresholding in Figure 4.7, where an optimal global threshold hides most of the written details of the diagram. Using adaptive thresholding (with 64 thresholds/image blocks) most of the details appear correctly.

The adaptive thresholding algorithm is:

Algorithm 4.3
1. Divide the image into sub-images (in Figure 4.7, 64 sub-images were used – an 8×8 grid).
2. For each of the sub-images compute a threshold.
3. For each point in the image determine a threshold by interpolating a threshold value from the four nearest thresholds using bilinear interpolation (see Section 5.5.2).

Note, in Figure 4.7, that the adaptive thresholding has not worked correctly everywhere. There are two black regions at the top (middle and right) which should be white, and one region near the centre of the image that clearly has the wrong threshold. It might be possible to avoid this problem by ensuring that the threshold values do not vary significantly across the image.

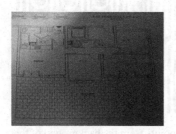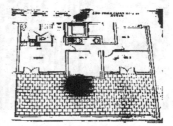

Figure 4.7   A grey-scale image (left) which has significant variation in lighting across the image, together with an optimally thresholded binary version (middle) and an adaptively thresholded binary version (right)

In OpenCV, adaptive thresholding is not performed in the manner described in this text (or in most textbooks):

```
adaptiveThreshold( gray_image, binary_image, output_value,
    ADAPTIVE_THRESH_MEAN_C, THRESH_BINARY, block_size, offset );
```

This function considers the difference between the current pixel and the local average of a `block_size` by `block_size` block of pixels centred around the current pixel, and sets the `binary_image` to `output_value` (usually 255) or 0 if the difference less the `offset` is greater than or less than 0 respectively. The `block_size` has a huge effect on the output. It is possible to compare the value to a Gaussian weighted average instead of the local average. In effect, a new threshold is being computed for every pixel based on the average of a local region around it. Sample output from the OpenCV adaptive thresholding routine is shown in Figure 4.8.

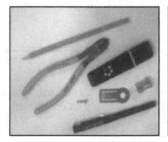

Figure 4.8 A 334×288 grey-scale image (left) which has significant variation in lighting across the image, together with two adaptively thresholded binary versions, computed using OpenCV's method, with a block size of 101×101 (middle) and 21×21 (right). An offset of 20 was used for both

4.3.2   Band Thresholding

In band thresholding two thresholds are used, one below and one above the object pixels:

$$\text{For all pixels } (i,j)$$
$$f'(i,j) = 1 \text{ for } f(i,j) \geq T_1 \text{ and } f(i,j) \leq T_2$$
$$= 0 \text{ otherwise}$$

In OpenCV, band thresholding can be implemented as follows:

```
threshold( image, binary_image1, low_threshold, 255, THRESH_BINARY );
threshold( image, binary_image2, high_threshold, 255,
                                        THRESH_BINARY_INV );
bitwise_and( binary_image1, binary_image2, band_thresholded_image );
```

Band thresholding is illustrated in Figure 4.9 and can be used to locate object boundaries, although the edge detectors described in Section 6.1 are more reliable and more appropriate.

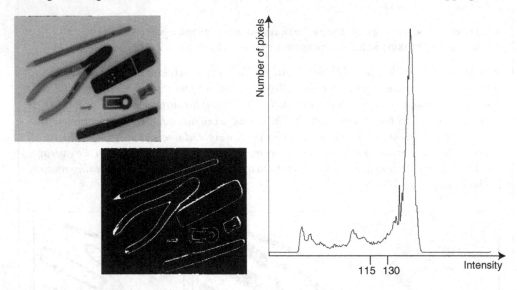

Figure 4.9 A grey-scale image (left) which has been band thresholded (bottom left) between grey-scales 115 and 130. A histogram of the original image is shown (right) with the relevant intensities highlighted

4.3.3   Semi-Thresholding

Semi thresholding is where object pixels retain their original grey-scale and background pixels are set to black.

$$
\text{For all pixels } (i,j)
$$
$$
f'(i,j) = f(i,j) \text{ for } f(i,j) \ge T
$$
$$
= 0 \text{ otherwise}
$$

See Figure 4.10 for an example.

In OpenCV, semi-thresholding can be implemented as follows:

```
threshold( gray_image, binary_image, threshold, 255, THRESH_BINARY );
bitwise_and( gray_image, binary_image, semi_thresholded_image );
```

4.3.4   Multispectral Thresholding

For colour images, it is not clear how thresholding should be applied. The most common thing to do is to convert the images to grey-scale and then threshold, although obviously thresholding

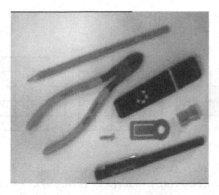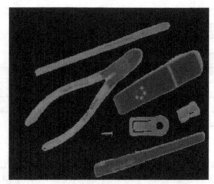

Figure 4.10 A grey-scale image (left) which has been semi-thresholded (right). In this case, pixels below the threshold have been considered as object pixels (as the background is brighter than the foreground)

can be applied to each channel independently (as in Figure 4.11). It is also possible to threshold within 3D colour space (effectively defining object pixels as those having a colour within a particular subspace of the 3D colour space).

4.4 Mathematical Morphology

Mathematical morphology (Najman and Talbot, 2013) is an approach to image processing based on set operations typically describing the algebra of nonlinear operators operating on object shape. It provides a unifying framework for describing many image processing and analysis operations and has allowed the development of techniques (such as those which follow) which otherwise are relatively hard to describe.

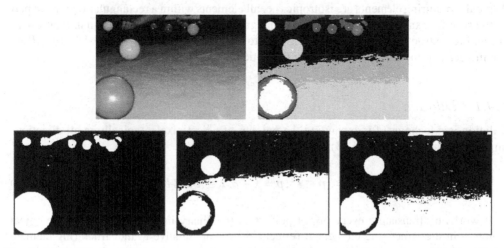

Figure 4.11 Otsu thresholding of the separate channels (bottom) of an RGB image (top left), and their combination (top right)

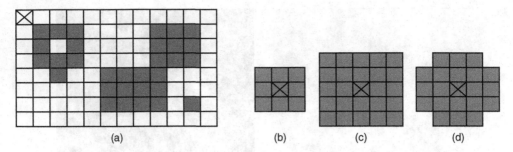

(a)   (b)   (c)   (d)

Figure 4.12 Sample binary image (a) = { (1,1), (1,2), (1,3), (1,8), (1,9), (1,10), (2,1), (2,3), (2,8), (2,9), (2,10), (3,1), (3,2), (3,3), (3,8), (3,9), (3,10), (4,2), (4,5), (4,6), (4,7), (4,8), (5,5), (5,6), (5,7), (5,8), (6,5), (6,6), (6,7), (6,8), (6,10) } which has a local origin in the top left corner, together with a 3×3 isotropic structuring element (b) = { (−1,−1), (−1,0), (−1,1), (−1,1), (0,0), (0,1), (1,−1), (1,0), (1,1) }, a 5×5 isotropic structuring element (c) and a 'circular' structuring element (d). Each of the structuring elements has its own local origin shown by an X

We consider a limited set of morphological operations (erosion, dilation, opening and closing) aimed primarily at enhancing the binary images in Sections 4.4.1, 4.4.2 and 4.4.3. We also look briefly at the application of morphological operators in grey-scale and colour images (see Section 4.4.4).

Morphological operations work by performing a logical test in every possible position in an image between a structuring element and the corresponding portion of the image. In other words, the structuring element is effectively translated to each possible position in the image, the logical operation is applied (comparing the structuring element to the image in some fashion) and the result is stored in a separate output image.

Binary images are treated as 2D sets, where the object points are the points in the sets. These sets use the same origin as the original image (see Figure 4.12 (a)). Structuring elements are typically small sets of object points defined (typically symmetrically) around their own origin. Typical structuring elements are isotropic (i.e. all elements within a rectangular region are part of the set); for example the 3×3 and 5×5 rectangular sets of object pixels shown in Figure 4.12 (b) and (c). Structuring elements do not have to be isotropic (e.g. see Figure 4.12 (d)). Both the images and the structuring elements theoretically have infinite support.

4.4.1 Dilation

Dilation is a technique for expanding the number of object pixels, typically in all directions simultaneously (see Figure 4.13):

$$X \oplus B = \{p \in \epsilon^2; p = x + b, x \in X \text{ and } b \in B\} \qquad (4.6)$$

It works by translating every object point x in the binary image X by each of the object points b in the structuring element B (effectively vectors relative to the structuring element origin). Hence each object point in the image X can result in a number of object points in the output set/image. Duplicates are not maintained.

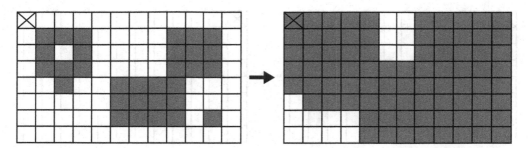

Figure 4.13 Dilation of a binary image (left) using a 3×3 isotropic structuring element (see Figure 4.12). The resultant dilated binary image is shown on the right. Note that the hole has been filled in and close objects have been joined together

---

In OpenCV, dilation using the default 3×3 isotropic structuring element is invoked as follows:

```
dilate( binary_image, dilated_image, Mat());
```

To change the structuring element (for example to a 5×5 isotropic structuring element):

```
Mat structuring_element( 5, 5, CV_8U, Scalar(1) );
dilate( binary_image, dilated_image, structuring_element );
```

This operation results in small holes being filled and fills in narrow gaps between larger groups of set points. It also increases the size of objects (i.e. the number of points in the set). Note that normal dilation in an imaging context uses an isotropic structuring element. Erosion using a 3×3 isotropic structuring element is shown in Figure 4.14.

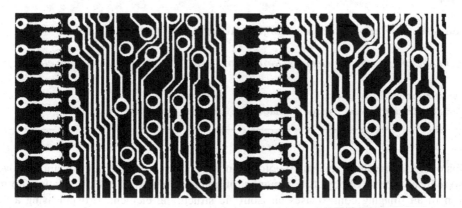

Figure 4.14 Binary image before (left) and after dilation (right) with a 3×3 isotropic structuring element

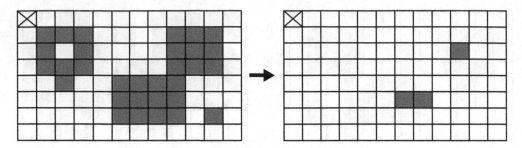

Figure 4.15 Erosion of a binary image (left) using a 3×3 isotropic structuring element (see Figure 4.12). The resultant eroded binary image is shown on the right. Note that the small point of noise has been removed, although at the same time the shape on the top left has been removed because of the missing pixel in the middle. The two connected larger blocks have been separated

4.4.2 Erosion

Erosion is a technique for shrinking object shapes by removing pixels from the boundary (see Figure 4.15):

$$X \ominus B = \{p \in \epsilon^2; p + b \in X \text{ for every } b \in B\} \qquad (4.7)$$

A point p is an element of the eroded output set if, and only if, that point is a member of the input image set X when translated by each (and all) of the structuring element points/vectors b. It can also be thought of as a matching problem where the structuring element is compared with the input image set at every possible location, and the output is marked only where the structuring element and the image match perfectly.

In OpenCV, erosion using the default 3×3 isotropic structuring element is invoked as follows:

```
erode( binary_image, eroded_image, Mat());
```

To change the structuring element (for example to a 5×5 isotropic structuring element):

```
Mat structuring_element( 5, 5, CV_8U, Scalar(1) );
erode( binary_image, eroded_image, structuring_element);
```

This operation results in any small points of noise and any narrow features being removed. It also reduces the size of objects (i.e. number of points in the set). Similar to dilation, normal erosion in an imaging context uses an isotropic structuring element. Erosion using a 3×3 isotopic structuring element is shown in Figure 4.16.

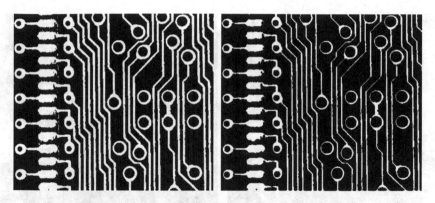

Figure 4.16 Binary image before (left) and after erosion (right) with a 3×3 isotropic structuring element

4.4.3 Opening and Closing

Erosion is the dual (i.e. mirror concept) of dilation and vice versa. While one expands the object pixels, the other shrinks them, and if we combine these operations together we get some interesting and useful effects.

An opening is an erosion operation followed by a dilation operation with the same structuring element (B):

$$X \bigcirc B = (X \ominus B) \oplus B \tag{4.8}$$

An opening removes noise (i.e. eliminates image details smaller than the structuring element), narrow features (such as bridges between larger groups of points), and smoothes the object boundaries. Unlike erosion and dilation though, it maintains the approximate size of the objects.

A closing is a dilation operation followed by an erosion operation, again with the same structuring element (B):

$$X \bullet B = (X \oplus B) \ominus B \tag{4.9}$$

A closing joins objects which are close together and fills in holes within objects. It tends to distort the shape of objects somewhat. Like opening, closing roughly maintains the size of objects.

In OpenCV, opening and closing are invoked as follows:

```
Mat five_by_five_element( 5, 5, CV_8U, Scalar(1) );
morphologyEx( binary_image, opened_image, MORPH_OPEN,
                              five_by_five_element );
morphologyEx( binary_image, closed_image, MORPH_CLOSE,
                              five_by_five_element );
```

Note that in many applications it is common to see a closing followed by an opening to clean up binary image data (e.g. see Figure 4.17 and Figure 4.18).

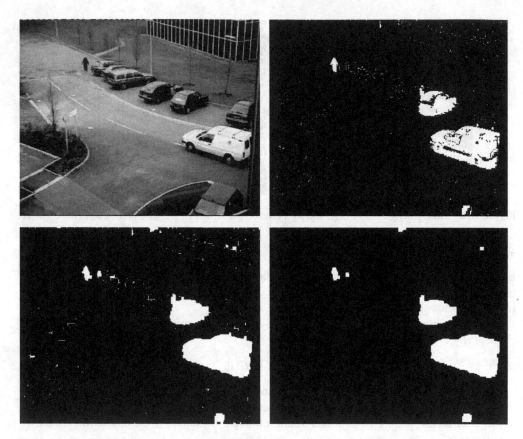

Figure 4.17   A binary image (top right) which has been determined through subtracting the current image (top left) from a background image, converting to grey-scale and thresholding. That binary image is closed to fill in holes and bridges small gaps (bottom left), and then is opened to remove small and narrow regions (bottom right). The original image (top left) is reproduced by permission of Dr. James Ferryman, University of Reading

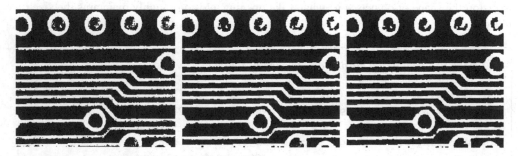

Figure 4.18   A binary image (top left) which has been closed to join close objects (middle) and then opened to break thin connections (right). Note that one of the tracks (bottom middle) of the printed circuit board has broken during the opening operation, which may indicate that there is a problem with the board

4.4.4   Grey-Scale and Colour Morphology

Morphological operations can be applied to grey-scale and colour images as well as to binary images. In these cases, each distinct grey-level on each channel is considered as a distinct set (i.e. all points that are greater than or equal to a particular grey-level). See Figure 4.19 for an illustration of how grey-scale erosion and dilation work, Figure 4.20 for an example of grey-scale opening and Figure 4.21 for a sample of colour opening.

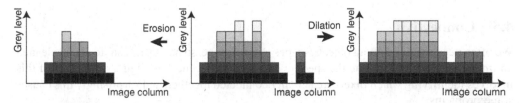

Figure 4.19   The bar chart in the centre shows 15 columns of a single row of an image with 7 grey-levels (0 to 6 inclusive) shown vertically. Each different grey-level is considered independently when performing morphological operations such as erosion (shown to the left) and dilation (shown to the right)

Figure 4.20   Example grey-scale 5×5 opening operation (centre) followed by binary thresholding (right)

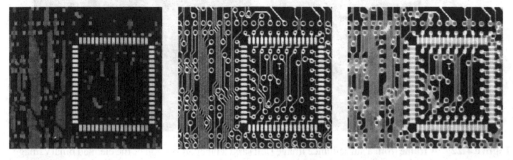

Figure 4.21   Example colour opening and closing operations. Original image is in the centre, with an opened version on the right and a closed version on the right (both created using an isotropic 5×5 structuring element)

In OpenCV, grey-scale and colour morphological operations are applied using exactly the same function calls that were used for binary images (i.e. by passing grey-scale or colour images as input instead of binary images).

Interestingly, grey-scale erosion and dilation are sometimes used to locate local maxima and minima in probability spaces (such as within template matching; see Section 8.1.4).

4.5   Connectivity

We often need to reason about objects/shapes within image, so having thresholded and cleaned an image we now try to locate the specific objects in the scene (see Figure 4.22). Part of this involves identifying which pixels are actually connected together, and surprisingly this causes some problems.

4.5.1   Connectedness: Paradoxes and Solutions

Figure 4.23 shows us some of the problems we face when trying to come up with a single interpretation for a scene (although note that only the problem on the right is relevant in the binary case).

There are two schemes that are commonly used when deciding which pixels are adjacent: 4-adjacency where only the North, South, East and West pixels are considered adjacent, and 8-adjacency where all directly surrounding pixels are considered adjacent. See Figure 4.24. In theory, we would like to use pixel adjacency to build contiguous regions (i.e. where, between any two points in the region, there is a continuous path of points belonging to the region). Such regions are often referred to as objects (with possible holes), against a background.

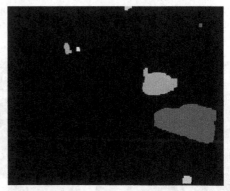

Figure 4.22   A frame from a surveillance image (left) and a labelled version of the cleaned binary image from Figure 4.17 (right). The original image (left) is reproduced by permission of Dr. James Ferryman, University of Reading

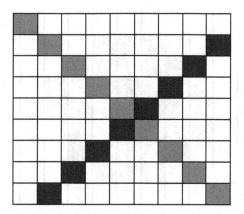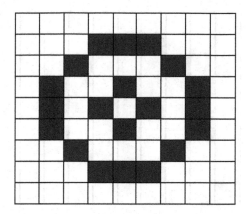

Figure 4.23 Two paradoxes. On the left two lines that cross and yet appear continuous. On the right two circles which appear continuous on a background which also appears continuous

However, if we apply either of the adjacency schemes in Figure 4.24 to the circles in Figure 4.23, we do not get the desired result (see Figure 4.25).

One way to overcome this problem is to use both 4-adjacency and 8-adjacency as follows:

- Treat outer background using 4-adjacency.
- Treat outer object using 8-adjacency.
- Treat holes using 4-adjacency.
- Treat objects in holes using 8-adjacency.

See Figure 4.26 for an example.

4.5.2   Connected Components Analysis

Having developed a solution to the paradoxes of connectedness we now need a practical algorithm to label pixels. The basic algorithm described here labels only the object pixels (not

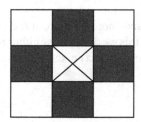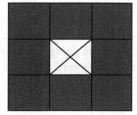

Figure 4.24   Pixel adjacency: 4-adjacency (left) where the centre pixel is considered to be adjacent to only the 4 shaded pixels, and 8-adjacency (right) where the centre pixel is considered to be adjacent to all 8 neighbouring pixels

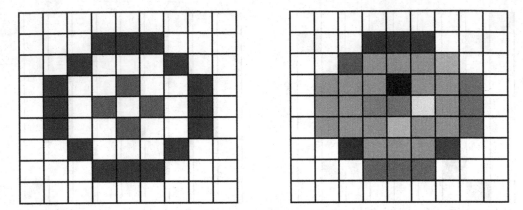

Figure 4.25 (left) 8-adjacency applied to the circles shown in Figure 4.23. Note that the background is fully connected as are the circles. (right) 4-adjacency applied to the same scene. In this case the circles are broken up as is the background

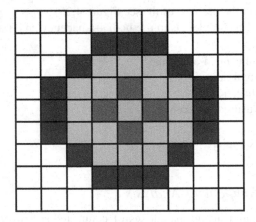

Figure 4.26 Alternate application of 8-adjacency and 4-adjacency to the circles and background in Figure 4.23

the background) within a binary image, and hence does not suffer from the connectedness problems described in the previous section. Because of this we can just use either 8-connectivity or 4-connectivity when assigning labels to each non-zero (object) pixel (based on the previous neighbouring pixels; see Figure 4.27).

Figure 4.27 Previous neighbouring pixels when using 8-adjacency or 4-adjacency respectively

Figure 4.28 Application of Connected Components Algorithm: Binary image (left), labelled regions after the first pass (centre left), equivalences identified during first pass (centre right), and after re-labelling in the second pass (right)

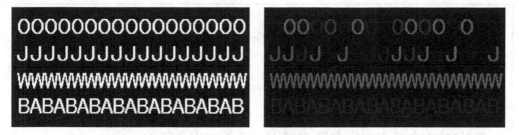

Figure 4.29 Application of Connected Components Algorithm using 8-adjacency on a test image

Algorithm 4.4

(See Figure 4.28 for an illustration and Figure 4.29 for an example)

1. Search image row by row and (within each row) column by column
   For each non-zero pixel:
      If all previous neighbouring pixels (see Figure 4.27) are background pixels
         Assign New Label to the current pixel
      Otherwise
         Pick any label for the current pixel from the previous neighbouring pixels
         If any other previous neighbouring pixels have different labels
            Note the equivalence of the labels.
2. Go through the entire image setting equivalent labels to the same label value.

In OpenCV, connected components is implemented using contour following techniques, so that the boundary points of the binary regions are described rather than labelling the individual member points. This is equivalent and arguably much more efficient. It is invoked as follows:

```
vector<vector<Point > contours;
vector<Vec4i> hierarchy;
findContours( binary_image, contours, hierarchy,
              CV_RETR_TREE, CV_CHAIN_APPROX_NONE );
```

where `contours` *is an array of lists of boundary points for the boundaries of the various binary regions in the image, and* `hierarchy` *is an array of indices which allows the contours to be considered in a hierarchical fashion (required as some contours representing holes in an object, for example, will occur inside other contours). The hierarchy provides a tree-like structure that indexes into the contours. Each contour has an associated entry in the hierarchy and this entry contains four indices (the next contour, the previous contour, the first child (i.e. enclosed) contour and the parent (i.e. enclosing) contour. Each index is set to a negative number if there is no contour to refer to.*

In OpenCV, to display the binary regions we can easily draw them as coloured regions based on the contour descriptions. Note that `CV_FILLED` *indicates that we want all pixels in the regions to be coloured in.*

```
for (int contour=0; (contour < contours.size());
                                        contour++)
{
   Scalar colour( rand()&0xFF,rand()&0xFF,rand()&0xFF );
   drawContours( contours_image, contours, contour, colour,
                        CV_FILLED, 8, hierarchy );
}
```

When we threshold an image, we are effectively segmenting the image into two distinct regions (with two labels: usually 0 and 255). Connected components analysis allows us to go further and label connected binary regions, of which there may be many in a binary image. It is worth noting that often we use labelled regions to describe both the object points and the background points. In this case we should use 8-adjacency for the objects and 4-adjacency for the background/holes.

5

Geometric Transformations

Geometric transformations (or operations) are used in image processing for a variety of reasons (Mundy and Zisserman, 1992). They allow us to bring multiple images into the same frame of reference so that they can be combined (e.g. when forming a mosaic of two or more images) or compared (e.g. when comparing images taken at different times to see what changes have occurred). They can be used to eliminate distortion (e.g. barrel distortion from a wide angle lenses) in order to create images with evenly spaced pixels. Geometric transformations can also simplify further processing (e.g. by bringing the image of a planar object into alignment with the image axes; see Figure 5.1).

An overview of the problem and how it is addressed is given in Section 5.1, followed by details of the most common linear transformations (affine transformations in Section 5.2 and perspective transformation in Section 5.3) and how more complex transformations are modelled (in Section 5.4). When applying any geometric transformation we must interpolate values for the output image from the pixels in the input image (see Section 5.5). The chapter finishes with details of how distortion in camera systems are modelled (see Section 5.6).

5.1 Problem Specification and Algorithm

Given a *distorted image* $f(i,j)$ and a *corrected image* $f'(i',j')$ we can model the geometric transformation between their coordinates as $i = T_i(i',j')$ and $j = T_j(i',j')$ that is given the coordinates (i',j') in the *corrected image*, the functions $T_i()$ and $T_j()$ compute the corresponding coordinates (i,j) in the *distorted image*.

Before we can apply the transformation to an image we must first somehow define the transformation. This may either be known in advance or can be determined through pairs of corresponding points between a sample *distorted image* and a corresponding sample *corrected image*. There are two main scenarios for determining the correspondences:

- Obtaining the *distorted* image by imaging a known pattern (such as in Figure 5.2) so that the *corrected image* can be produced directly from the known pattern.

A Practical Introduction to Computer Vision with OpenCV, First Edition. Kenneth Dawson-Howe.

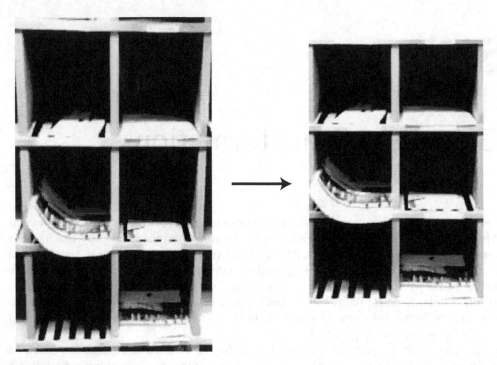

Figure 5.1   Example of a geometric transformation which corrects the perspective distortion introduced when viewing a planar object (e.g. the front of the postboxes above)

- Obtaining two images of the same object, where one image (referred to as the *distorted image*) is to be mapped into the frame of reference of the other image (referred to as the *corrected image*).

Once sufficient correspondences are determined between the sample *distorted* and *corrected images*, it is relatively straightforward to compute the geometric transformation function. Once the transformation is determined it can be applied to the *distorted* image and to any other images

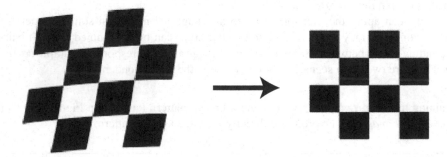

Figure 5.2   Correction of the image of a known pattern. The function to correct image distortion can be determined by viewing a known pattern such as that shown

that require the same 'correction' (e.g. all images from a camera with fixed settings will exhibit the same distortions).

A geometric transformation is applied as follows:

- For every point in the output/corrected image (i', j'):
  - Determine where it came from (i, j) using $T_i()$ and $T_j()$.
  - Interpolate a value for the output point from close neighbouring points in the input image, bearing in mind that $T_i()$ and $T_j()$ will compute real values and hence the point (i, j) is likely to be between pixels (see Section 5.5).

The transformation is defined and applied somewhat backwards. Normally in image processing we consider every point in the input image and compute a value for the corresponding output point. However, in this case if we take that approach it is possible that we will have points in the output image that do not have values (e.g. where we are expanding the image). By considering every output point (and finding out where it comes from) we can be confident that we will compute a value for each point.

The only downside to performing the computation in this manner is that we will be performing the interpolation within the distorted image domain (rather than in the corrected domain). Typically this is not a cause for concern, as it makes little difference.

5.2 Affine Transformations

Many common transformations can be described using the affine transform, which is defined as follows:

$$\begin{bmatrix} i \\ j \end{bmatrix} = \begin{bmatrix} a_{00} & a_{01} & a_{02} \\ a_{10} & a_{11} & a_{12} \end{bmatrix} \begin{bmatrix} i' \\ j' \\ 1 \end{bmatrix} \tag{5.1}$$

In OpenCV, linear transformations (such as the affine transformation) are described using floating point two-dimensional matrices such as:

```
Mat affine_matrix( 2, 3, CV_32FC1 )
```

in this case with two rows and three columns.

This transform is often used for simple regular transforms, such as change of scale, rotation, and so on (see Section 5.2.1). It can also be used to determine unknown transformations based on sample mappings (i.e. correspondences between points in the *distorted* and *corrected* images; see Section 5.2.2).

---

*In OpenCV the affine transformation is applied to an **image** (Mat) to generate a transformed **result** (Mat) using:*

```
warpAffine( image, result, affine_matrix, image.size() );
```

5.2.1   Known Affine Transformations

There are many examples of transformations that can be known in advance and a few of the more common ones are presented here:

5.2.1.1   Translation

$$\begin{bmatrix} i \\ j \end{bmatrix} = \begin{bmatrix} 1 & 0 & m \\ 0 & 1 & n \end{bmatrix} \begin{bmatrix} i' \\ j' \\ 1 \end{bmatrix} \tag{5.2}$$

Translation by m along the horizontal axis and n along the vertical axis.

5.2.1.2   Change of Scale (Expand/Shrink)

$$\begin{bmatrix} i \\ j \end{bmatrix} = \begin{bmatrix} a & 0 & 0 \\ 0 & b & 0 \end{bmatrix} \begin{bmatrix} i' \\ j' \\ 1 \end{bmatrix} \tag{5.3}$$

Change of scale a in the horizontal axis and b in the vertical axis. This is often required in order to normalise the size of objects in images.

5.2.1.3   Rotation

$$\begin{bmatrix} i \\ j \end{bmatrix} = \begin{bmatrix} \cos\phi & \sin\phi & 0 \\ -\sin\phi & \cos\phi & 0 \end{bmatrix} \begin{bmatrix} i' \\ j' \\ 1 \end{bmatrix} \tag{5.4}$$

Rotation by angle ϕ about the origin. This is sometimes required to align an image with the axes to simplify further processing. See Figure 5.3.

5.2.1.4   Skewing

$$\begin{bmatrix} i \\ j \end{bmatrix} = \begin{bmatrix} 1 & \tan\phi & 0 \\ 0 & 1 & 0 \end{bmatrix} \begin{bmatrix} i' \\ j' \\ 1 \end{bmatrix} \tag{5.5}$$

Skewing by angle ϕ. Often needed to remove nonlinear viewing effects such as those generated by a line scan camera. See Figure 5.3.

Figure 5.3   Rotation, followed by skewing, followed by panoramic distortion of an image

In OpenCV, the affine matrix can be defined directly as follows:

```
// Initialise to the identity matrix:
Mat affine_matrix = Mat::eye( 2, 3, CV_32FC1 );
// affine_matrix[0][1] Skewing:
*(((float*) (affine_matrix.data))+1) = 0.37;
// affine_matrix [0][2] Translate to the left:
*(((float*) (affine_matrix.data))+2) = -30.0;
// Apply transformation
warpAffine( image,result,affine_matrix,image.size() );
```

5.2.1.5 Panoramic Distortion

$$\begin{bmatrix} i \\ j \end{bmatrix} = \begin{bmatrix} a & 0 & 0 \\ 0 & 1 & 0 \end{bmatrix} \begin{bmatrix} i' \\ j' \\ 1 \end{bmatrix} \tag{5.6}$$

Panoramic distortion is in effect an incorrect aspect ratio. It appears in line scanners when the mirror rotates at an incorrect speed. See Figure 5.3.

5.2.2 Unknown Affine Transformations

On many occasions, the transformation required is not known in advance, but none the less can be described using the affine transformation. The problem then is to determine the six coefficients $a_{00} \dots a_{12}$ of the affine transform in order to be able to transform the image (or images). We can determine these coefficients from three observations (although generally the transformation will be more accurate if more observations are used): If the observed mappings are $(i_1, j_1) \leftrightarrow (i'_1, j'_1)$, $(i_2, j_2) \leftrightarrow (i'_2, j'_2)$, and $(i_3, j_3) \leftrightarrow (i'_3, j'_3)$ and given that

$$\begin{bmatrix} i \\ j \end{bmatrix} = \begin{bmatrix} a_{00} & a_{01} & a_{02} \\ a_{10} & a_{11} & a_{12} \end{bmatrix} \begin{bmatrix} i' \\ j' \\ 1 \end{bmatrix} \tag{5.7}$$

then we can reorganise as follows

$$\begin{bmatrix} i_1 \\ j_1 \\ i_2 \\ j_2 \\ i_3 \\ j_3 \end{bmatrix} = \begin{bmatrix} i'_1 & j'_1 & 1 & 0 & 0 & 0 \\ 0 & 0 & 0 & i'_1 & j'_1 & 1 \\ i'_2 & j'_2 & 1 & 0 & 0 & 0 \\ 0 & 0 & 0 & i'_2 & j'_2 & 1 \\ i'_3 & j'_3 & 1 & 0 & 0 & 0 \\ 0 & 0 & 0 & i'_3 & j'_3 & 1 \end{bmatrix} \begin{bmatrix} a_{00} \\ a_{01} \\ a_{02} \\ a_{10} \\ a_{11} \\ a_{12} \end{bmatrix} \tag{5.8}$$

Figure 5.4 Transformation of a license plate image using the affine transformation (top right) computed from correspondences for the top left, top right and bottom left corners of the license plate, and (bottom right) using the perspective transformation computed from correspondences for all four corners of the license plate

and can then solve for the coefficients by multiplying both sides by the inverse of the square matrix. Note that if there are more observations then the matrix will not be square and we must use the pseudo-inverse. A sample affine transformation based on three control points is shown in Figure 5.4.

> *In OpenCV computing the affine transformation from sample mappings is achieved as follows:*
>
> ```
> Point2f source [3], destination [3];
> // Assign values to source and destination points.
> affine_matrix = getAffineTransform (source,destination);
> ```

5.3 Perspective Transformations

Images acquired by most cameras are typically formed by perspective projection, as rays of light from the 3D world are projected onto the image plane through a single point (pinhole camera) or through a lens. If we view a planar surface that is not parallel to the image plane, then an affine transformation will not properly correct the view of that planar surface (see the bottom right corner of the affine corrected license plate in Figure 5.4). We must instead use a more complex model known as the perspective transformation:

$$\begin{bmatrix} i \cdot w \\ j \cdot w \\ w \end{bmatrix} = \begin{bmatrix} p_{00} & p_{01} & p_{02} \\ p_{10} & p_{11} & p_{12} \\ p_{20} & p_{21} & 1 \end{bmatrix} \begin{bmatrix} i' \\ j' \\ 1 \end{bmatrix} \qquad (5.9)$$

For this transformation, we require at least four observations of matching points and can solve for the coefficients as follows:

Noting that $i \cdot w = p_{00} \cdot i' + p_{01} \cdot j' + p_{02}$ and that $w = p_{20} \cdot i' + p_{21} \cdot j' + 1$.
Hence $i = p_{00} \cdot i' + p_{01} \cdot j' + p_{02} - p_{20} \cdot i \cdot i' - p_{21} \cdot i \cdot j'$.
A similar equation can be computed for $j = p_{10} \cdot i' + p_{11} \cdot j' + p_{12} - p_{20} \cdot j \cdot i' - p_{21} \cdot j \cdot j'$.

Figure 5.5 Perspective projection transformation to show the snooker table (left) from an aerial viewpoint (right). Note that the balls appear elongated in the corrected image because they sit above the plane for which the perspective transformation was computed

So using four observations ...

$$
\begin{bmatrix} i_1 \\ j_1 \\ i_2 \\ j_2 \\ i_3 \\ j_3 \\ i_4 \\ j_4 \end{bmatrix} =
\begin{bmatrix}
i'_1 & j'_1 & 1 & 0 & 0 & 0 & -i_1 i'_1 & -i_1 j'_1 \\
0 & 0 & 0 & i'_1 & j'_1 & 1 & -j_1 i'_1 & -j_1 j'_1 \\
i'_2 & j'_2 & 1 & 0 & 0 & 0 & -i_2 i'_2 & -i_2 j'_2 \\
0 & 0 & 0 & i'_2 & j'_2 & 1 & -j_2 i'_2 & -j_2 j'_2 \\
i'_3 & j'_3 & 1 & 0 & 0 & 0 & -i_3 i'_3 & -i_3 j'_3 \\
0 & 0 & 0 & i'_3 & j'_3 & 1 & -j_3 i'_3 & -j_3 j'_3 \\
i'_4 & j'_4 & 1 & 0 & 0 & 0 & -i_4 i'_4 & -i_4 j'_4 \\
0 & 0 & 0 & i'_4 & j'_4 & 1 & -j_4 i'_4 & -j_4 j'_4
\end{bmatrix}
\begin{bmatrix} p_{00} \\ p_{01} \\ p_{02} \\ p_{10} \\ p_{11} \\ p_{12} \\ p_{20} \\ p_{21} \end{bmatrix}
\tag{5.10}
$$

Hence, in a similar fashion to that employed for the affine transformation, we can determine the coefficients by multiplying both sides by the inverse of the square matrix.

Sample perspective projections are shown in Figure 5.4 and Figure 5.5.

In OpenCV the perspective transformation can be defined and applied as follows:

```
Point2f source [4], destination [4];
// Assign values to source and destination points.
perspective_matrix = getPerspectiveTransform( source, destination );
warpPerspective( image, result, perspective_matrix, result.size() );
```

5.4   Specification of More Complex Transformations

Both the affine transform and the perspective transform are linear transformations. There are circumstances in which more complex transformations are necessary (such as when aligning two medical images taken at different times or using different sensors).

These transformations are typically approximated with a polynomial with some predefined number of terms:

$$i = T_i(i',j') = a_{00} + a_{10}i' + a_{01}j' + a_{11}i'j' + a_{02}(j')^2 + a_{20}(i')^2 + a_{12}i'(j')^2 + a_{21}(i')^2 j'$$
$$+ a_{22}(i')^2(j')^2 + \dots \tag{5.11}$$

$$j = T_j(i',j') = b_{00} + b_{10}i' + b_{01}j' + b_{11}i'j' + b_{02}(j')^2 + b_{20}(i')^2 + b_{12}i'(j')^2 + b_{21}(i')^2 j'$$
$$+ b_{22}(i')^2(j')^2 + \dots \tag{5.12}$$

As in the cases of the affine and perspective transforms, in order to solve for the coefficients of the polynomials, it is necessary have a certain number of known correspondences between the distorted and the corrected image spaces. The minimum number required is defined by the order of the polynomial (i.e. it must be at least half the number of terms in the polynomial). The mathematics involved in solving these equations is similar to those from the affine and perspective transformations.

In order to compute the coefficients accurately:

* the corresponding points must be well distributed across the image;
* no incorrect correspondences should be included;
* as many corresponding points as possible should be used;
* the corresponding point locations should be specified to the greatest accuracy possible;
* the matrices must be manipulated very carefully when computing the inverse or pseudo inverse as there can be problems of numerical instability (large and small numbers are combined and the accuracy of the small numbers are essential to the solution).

If a geometric operation is too complex to be approximated by such a polynomial, it can instead be approximated by partitioning the image and determining a transformation for each partition.

5.5   Interpolation

As each point in the output image will map to real coordinates in the input (distorted) image, it is unlikely that the coordinates selected in the input image will correspond precisely to any one pixel. Hence we need to interpolate the value for the output point from the nearby surrounding pixels in the input image.

There are a variety of possible interpolation schemes and three of these will be detailed here.

Figure 5.6   Nearest neighbour interpolation when expanding an image 4-fold

5.5.1   Nearest Neighbour Interpolation

$$f'(i',j') = f(round(i), round(j)) \tag{5.13}$$

In nearest neighbour interpolation we simply round the real coordinates so that we use the nearest pixel value. This scheme results in very distinct blocky effects that are frequently visible (e.g. see Figure 5.6). Unfortunately, the error is perceptible on objects with straight line boundaries, which may appear step like after the transformation, and for this reason this simple technique is rarely used.

In OpenCV the interpolation scheme can be specified as follows:

```
int interpolation_scheme = INTER_LINEAR;
// Nearest neighbour interpolation: INTER_NEAREST
// Bilinear interpolation: INTER_LINEAR
// Bicubic interpolation: INTER_CUBIC
warpAffine( image, result, affine_matrix, result_size,
                                  interpolation_scheme );
warpPerspective( image, result, perspective_matrix,
                       result_size, interpolation_scheme );
```

5.5.2   Bilinear Interpolation

$$
\begin{aligned}
f'(i',j') = {} & (trunc(i) + 1 - i)(trunc(j) + 1 - j)f(trunc(i), trunc(j)) \\
& + (i - trunc(i))(trunc(j) + 1 - j)f(trunc(i) + 1, trunc(j)) \\
& + (trunc(i) + 1 - i)(j - trunc(j))f(trunc(i), trunc(j) + 1) \\
& + (i - trunc(i))(j - trunc(j))f(trunc(i) + 1, trunc(j) + 1) \tag{5.14}
\end{aligned}
$$

This interpolation scheme assumes that the brightness function is bilinear. The four closest neighbouring pixels $(f(trunc(i), trunc(j)), f(trunc(i) + 1, trunc(j)), f(trunc(i), trunc(j) + 1)$ and $f(trunc(i) + 1, trunc(j) + 1))$ are combined using a weighted average based on how close

Figure 5.7   Bilinear interpolation when expanding an image 4-fold

they are to the real point (i, j) averaged in proportion to their absolute distance from the desired point (between 0.0 and 1.0). Each of the pixels has two weights, which provide inverse measures of the distances from the real point (i, j) to the i and j integer coordinates of the point.

Linear interpolation overcomes the blocky effects causes by nearest neighbour interpolation, but can cause blurring and a slight effective decrease in resolution (as it is averaging the surrounding four pixels). See Figure 5.7.

5.5.3   Bi-Cubic Interpolation

Bi-cubic interpolation overcomes the step-like boundary problems seen in nearest neighbour interpolation and addresses the bilinear interpolation blurring problem. It improves the brightness interpolation by approximating locally using 16 neighbouring points on a bi-cubic polynomial surface. This function is very similar to the Laplacian, which is sometimes used to sharpen images (see Section 6.1.4).

Bi-cubic interpolation is frequently used in raster displays, which is why images will rarely appear blocky when blown up on your screen. See Figure 5.8 for an example.

5.6   Modelling and Removing Distortion from Cameras

This final section considers one of the common forms of geometric distortion and correction that is required in computer vision: that related to camera systems (i.e. camera and lenses).

Figure 5.8   Bi-cubic interpolation when expanding an image 4-fold

The simple pinhole camera model was described in Section 2.1.1. This provides a mapping from real world coordinates (x, y, z) to image coordinates (i, j). Unfortunately, many (if not most) real camera systems cannot be accurately modelled using the simple pinhole camera model and it is necessary to also model distortions caused by the physical setup and the lenses.

5.6.1 Camera Distortions

There are two forms of distortion that commonly appear in camera systems: (i) radial distortion and (ii) tangential distortion.

Radial distortion is distortion that is radially symmetric where the level of distortion is related to the distance from the optical axis of the camera (usually near the image centre). The distortion is in effect a change in magnification. If the magnification decreases as the distance from the optical centre increases, then the effect is referred to as *barrel distortion*. On the other hand, if it increases the effect is called *pincushion distortion*.

If we assume that the origin of the image $f(i, j)$ is at the optical axis then

$$i' = i(1 + k_1 r^2 + k_2 r^4 + k_3 r^6)$$
$$j' = j(1 + k_1 r^2 + k_2 r^4 + k_3 r^6) \tag{5.15}$$

Where $f'(i', j')$ is the corrected image, $r = \sqrt{i^2 + j^2}$ is the distance to the optical axis and k_1, k_2, k_3 are parameters describing the distortion.

Tangential distortion occurs when the lenses is not perfectly parallel with the image plane, and again results in uneven magnification but in this case the magnification will vary from one side of the image plane to the other.

Again assuming that the origin of the image is at the optical axis then tangential distortion may be modelled as

$$i' = i + (2p_1 ij + p_2(r^2 + 2i^2))$$
$$j' = j + (2p_2 ij + p_1(r^2 + 2j^2)) \tag{5.16}$$

where $r = \sqrt{i^2 + j^2}$ is the distance to the optical axis and p_1, p_2 are parameters describing the distortion.

In OpenCV the camera model can be determined using:

```
calibrateCamera( object_points, image_points,
    image_size, camera_matrix, distortion_coefficients,
    rotation_vectors, translation_vectors );
```

where object_points *and* image_points *are both vectors of vectors of 3D and 2D points respectively (which provide the locations of the grid points in 3D and 2D in each calibration image), the* camera_matrix *and* distortion_coefficients *are the model which is computed, and the* rotation_vectors *and* translation_vectors *specify the 3D pose of the camera for each calibration image.*

Note that camera calibration is quite complex and there are a large number of routines provided in OpenCV support it. For example a calcBoardCornerPositions () *routine is provided to locate the grid positions in an image, and a* computeReprojectionErrors () *routine is provided to determine how accurately the computed model represents the data in the calibration images. Please refer to the provided calibration code for further details.*

5.6.2   Camera Calibration and Removing Distortion

To determine the parameters of any distortions affecting an imaging system, it is necessary to calibrate it. Typically, this means determining the distortion parameters and the camera model simultaneously. This is achieved by repeatedly presenting a known calibration object (see Figure 5.9) to the imaging system at slightly different poses (positions and orientations). The model parameters can be extracted using mathematics similar to that employed when determining affine and perspective transformations from sample mappings. However, it is outside the scope of this text as we are primarily limiting ourselves to 2D image processing.

Once calibrated any distortions may be removed from images from this camera by simply transforming them according to the formulas.

In OpenCV distortion can be removed from a calibrated camera using:

```
undistort( camera_image, corrected_image,
                camera_matrix, distortion_coefficients );
```

If a camera parameters are unchanging then a camera need only be calibrated once and the camera model can be used repeatedly to remove distortion.

Figure 5.9   Image of a calibration grid with the located corners marked in various colours

6

Edges

The segmentation of an image is the process of dividing the image into pieces such that different objects or parts of objects are separated. This is an essential processing step in image understanding (where the goal is to understand the content of the images). There are two main ways of addressing the segmentation of images:

1. Edge processing, where we identify the discontinuities (the edges) in images.
2. Region processing, where we look for homogeneous regions (or sections) of the images. Binary vision is a very simple example of region processing and much more complex approaches to this problem exist (although this is not a topic considered in this text).

These representations can or should be complementary, with the edges delineating the homogeneous regions. Unfortunately it is very difficult to decide where the edges are (and hence to get a unique edge image) and it is equally hard to make a unique interpretation of an image in terms of regions. There are many techniques in both edge-based vision and region-based vision, all of which have the goal of determining the best representation of the scene in terms of edges or regions. For most images there is no absolute correct answer as the answer is typically subjective (it will depend on the observer and will depend upon the purpose of the segmentation).

This chapter looks at basic edge detection techniques for determining which pixels should be considered to be edge pixels (see Section 6.1), how these edges points can then be processed (e.g. using contour following techniques for joining up the edge points; see Section 6.2), and finally looks at a technique (the Hough transform; see Section 6.3) for locating defined edge shapes in images.

6.1 Edge Detection

Edge detection was developed and is normally presented for single channel (grey-scale) images. Edges are the locations where brightness changes abruptly and hence are often considered from a point of view of 2D derivatives (i.e. rates of changes). Because we perform our processing

A Practical Introduction to Computer Vision with OpenCV, First Edition. Kenneth Dawson-Howe.
© 2014 John Wiley & Sons, Ltd. Published 2014 by John Wiley & Sons, Ltd.

Figure 6.1   A grey-scale image of a church (left), the Sobel edge gradient magnitude (centre left), a thresholded version of the gradient magnitude (centre right) and the corresponding Sobel orientations (right)

in a discrete domain we typically represent the locations where brightness changes abruptly as edge pixels (although the brightness change will often be between pixels rather than on them). An example of Sobel edge detection is shown in Figure 6.1.

An edge pixel has a gradient (rate of change) and a direction/orientation (which is taken to be the direction of the largest growth). For example, see Figure 6.2.

Typically edge detection is performed using either first derivative or second derivative operators (or some combination of the two). A first derivative operator results in a local maximum at an edge (where the rate of change is highest). The second derivative results in a 'zero-crossing' at an edge (where the function changes from +ve to −ve or vice versa). See Figure 6.3.

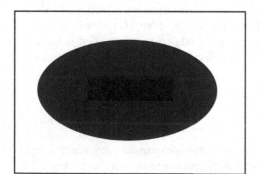
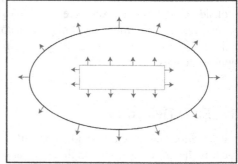

Figure 6.2   Simple image (left) and simulated sample edge gradients and orientations (right). Gradient magnitude is proportional to the length of the vectors shown (the transition from dark grey to white is much stronger than that from dark grey to black). The orientations are drawn for some sample points. Note that a dark to bright transition will give the opposite orientation as a bright to dark transition

Figure 6.3 A simple grey-scale image (left), together with the intensity magnitude (centre left), the first derivative function (centre right) and the second derivative function (right)

At this point, it is worth pointing out that derivatives work on continuous functions, whereas the images we are processing are in the discrete domain. To approximate the derivates (both first and second derivatives), differences between image pixels are used.

6.1.1 First Derivative Edge Detectors

First derivative edge detectors compute two partial derivatives (see Sections 6.1.1.1 and 6.1.1.2) and then combine these to determine gradient and orientation values for each edge point (see Section 6.1.1.3). The resulting gradients must then be non-maxima suppressed (see Section 6.1.1.5) and thresholded (see Section 6.1.1.4).

Note that there are a large number of first derivative edge detectors which may be used to compute the partial derivatives, but the results of these do not vary significantly so, as examples, we just consider Roberts, and the compass edge detectors, Sobel and Prewitt.

6.1.1.1 Roberts Edge Detector

The two partial derivatives are used by Roberts consider the diagonal differences between pixels:

$$\delta_1(i,j) = f(i,j) - f(i+1,j+1) \tag{6.1}$$

$$\delta_2(i,j) = f(i+1,j) - f(i,j+1)$$

Such functions are often presented in terms of the filters which would have to be convolved with an image in order to compute the function over the entire image (i.e. the convolution filter is moved to every possible position in the image and then convolved/multiplied by the corresponding pixels):

$$\delta_1(i,j) = \begin{bmatrix} 1 & 0 \\ 0 & -1 \end{bmatrix} \qquad \delta_2(i,j) = \begin{bmatrix} 0 & 1 \\ -1 & 0 \end{bmatrix} \tag{6.2}$$

The overall gradient is computed as the RMS (see Section 6.1.1.3) of the two partial derivatives or sometimes as the sum of the absolute differences. The orientation is computed

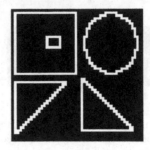

Figure 6.4   Roberts edge detection (right) as applied to a binary image (left)

using the inverse tan function (again, see Section 6.1.1.3). Figure 6.4 and Figure 6.5 show the Roberts operator as applied to a binary image and a grey-scale image respectively.

In the case of the binary image (Figure 6.4) the result of applying the Roberts operator is extremely good. It is very clean (points are either edge points or not), and edges are only one pixel wide. In fact, this is arguably the only first derivative edge detector of those presented in this text that should/can be used with binary images.

In the case of the grey-scale image (Figure 6.5) the result of applying the Roberts operator seems poor. This is largely because in real images edges do not occur sharply (i.e. between two pixels) but rather change over a few pixels, whereas the Roberts operator is based on adjacent points. In addition, the partial derivative calculations are severely affected by any noise in the image.

Before leaving Roberts it is worth pointing out that the edge gradients computed are actually $^1/_2$ a pixel out along both the I and J axes – where the halfway point is between the two partial

Figure 6.5   Roberts edge detection (right) as applied to a grey-scale image (left)

derivatives. In fact, because of how the partial derivatives intersect, the Roberts operator is often referred to as the Roberts cross-operator.

6.1.1.2 Compass Edge Detectors

The compass edge detectors, of which the two best known examples are **Sobel** and **Prewitt** (Prewitt, 1970), each have eight partial derivatives defined. The eight partial derivatives for Prewitt are shown here:

$$h_1(i,j) = \begin{bmatrix} 1 & 1 & 1 \\ 0 & 0 & 0 \\ -1 & -1 & -1 \end{bmatrix} \quad h_2(i,j) = \begin{bmatrix} 0 & 1 & 1 \\ -1 & 0 & 1 \\ -1 & -1 & 0 \end{bmatrix} \quad h_3(i,j) = \begin{bmatrix} -1 & 0 & 1 \\ -1 & 0 & 1 \\ -1 & 0 & 1 \end{bmatrix}$$

$$h_4(i,j) = \begin{bmatrix} -1 & -1 & 0 \\ -1 & 0 & 1 \\ 0 & 1 & 1 \end{bmatrix} \quad h_5(i,j) = \begin{bmatrix} -1 & -1 & -1 \\ 0 & 0 & 0 \\ 1 & 1 & 1 \end{bmatrix} \quad h_6(i,j) = \begin{bmatrix} 0 & -1 & -1 \\ 1 & 0 & -1 \\ 1 & 1 & 0 \end{bmatrix} \quad (6.3)$$

$$h_7(i,j) = \begin{bmatrix} 1 & 0 & -1 \\ 1 & 0 & -1 \\ 1 & 0 & -1 \end{bmatrix} \quad h_8(i,j) = \begin{bmatrix} 1 & 1 & 0 \\ 1 & 0 & -1 \\ 0 & -1 & -1 \end{bmatrix}$$

Of these eight partial derivatives, only two orthogonal ones are really needed – and h_1 and h_3 are typically used. See Figure 6.6 for an example of the partial derivatives, noting that the values returned are both positive and negative.

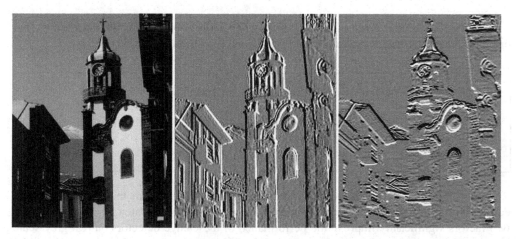

Figure 6.6 An image (a) together with the horizontal (b) and vertical (c) partial derivatives. Note that as the partial derivatives can be positive or negative, 0 is represented by grey, the maximum positive value is represented by white and the maximum negative value is represented by black

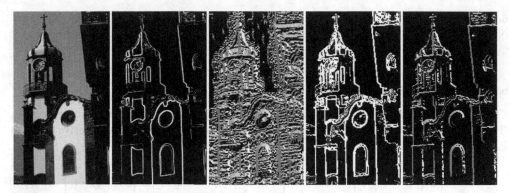

Figure 6.7 A grey-scale image of a church (a), the Sobel gradient magnitude (b), the complete orientation image (c) a thresholded version of the gradient magnitude (c) and the corresponding Sobel orientations (d). Note that the orientation image in (c) is a typical orientation image where an orientation value is presented for all points in the image. This type of image is confusing though, as many points in the corresponding gradient image (b) have no noticeable gradient response (i.e. appear black) and hence the orientation information is unreliable (effectively noise). To make the orientation image easier to understand, we have selected those points from the gradient image above a particular threshold (d) and then just displayed the orientations corresponding to those points in (e). When looking at orientation images, bear in mind that the representation is circular (0° which is black is only 1 ° from 359 ° which is white)

For Sobel, the relevant partial derivatives are:

$$h_1(i,j) = \begin{bmatrix} 1 & 2 & 1 \\ 0 & 0 & 0 \\ -1 & -2 & -1 \end{bmatrix} \qquad h_3(i,j) = \begin{bmatrix} -1 & 0 & 1 \\ -2 & 0 & 2 \\ -1 & 0 & 1 \end{bmatrix} \qquad (6.4)$$

The two partial derivatives (for Sobel or Prewitt) can be used to compute the gradient and orientation as described in Section 6.1.1.3. See Figure 6.7 for an example.

In OpenCV, the Sobel partial derivatives can be computed as follows:

```
Mat horizontal_derivative, vertical_derivative;
Sobel( gray_image, horizontal_derivative, CV_32F ,1,0 );
Sobel( gray_image, vertical_derivative, CV_32F,0,1 );
```

Both Sobel and Prewitt effectively incorporate smoothing within the partial derivative convolution masks. They also consider points that are slightly separated, and together these two factors significantly improve the performance of these edge detectors on real grey-scale images (in comparison to the performance of the Roberts operator). In both cases the partial derivatives are centred on a particular pixel and hence no shift is caused in the position of the determined edges (whereas the Roberts operator causes a $1/2$ pixel shift).

The only difference between Sobel and Prewitt is the weighting of the smoothing filter on each side of the partial derivative. Hence, the difference in results between the two operators is not significant.

6.1.1.3 Computing Gradient and Orientation

First derivative edge detectors compute the gradient of the edge as a combination (typically Root-Mean-Square, also referred to as the l^2-*norm*) of two orthogonal partial derivatives:

$$\nabla f(i,j) = \sqrt{\left(\frac{\delta f(i,j)}{\delta i}\right)^2 + \left(\frac{\delta f(i,j)}{\delta j}\right)^2} \tag{6.5}$$

For speed reasons this is sometimes approximated using the sum of the absolute partial derivatives:

$$\nabla f(i,j) = \left|\frac{\delta f(i,j)}{\delta i}\right| + \left|\frac{\delta f(i,j)}{\delta j}\right| \tag{6.6}$$

The orientation of the edge is computed from the two orthogonal partial derivatives using the inverse tangent function with two arguments (to allow all 360° to be distinguished):

$$\phi(i,j) = \arctan\left(\frac{\delta f(i,j)}{\delta j}, \frac{\delta f(i,j)}{\delta i}\right) \tag{6.7}$$

In OpenCV, given the two partial derivatives we may compute the absolute gradient and the l^2-norm (gradient) and orientation as follows:

```
abs_gradient = abs(horizontal_derivative) + abs(vertical_derivative);
cartToPolar(horizontal_derivative,vertical_derivative,
                              l2norm_gradient, orientation);
```

6.1.1.4 Edge Image Thresholding

Edge image thresholding is simply binary thresholding applied to a gradient image. Unfortunately, edges typically result in gradient responses which are several pixels wide and as a result edge image thresholding normally results in multiple responses across the edges. See Figure 6.8.

To address this issue, we need to add an additional stage prior to edge image thresholding in which all gradient responses outside the central maximum (for any given edge point) are suppressed. This technique is referred to as non-maxima suppression.

Figure 6.8 An edge gradient image (a) together with three thresholded versions (b), (c) and (d) thresholded at 120, 160 and 200 respectively

6.1.1.5 Non-maxima Suppression

This technique uses the gradient and orientation information to determine which edge points are the central ones (i.e. the main response at each point along an edge contour). It does this by using the orientation information from each point to determine which points are to each side of the current edge point, and then suppresses the current point if its gradient is less than either of its two neighbours. See Figure 6.9 for an example and Figure 6.10 for an illustration of the technique.

Algorithm 6.1

- Quantise edge orientations (into eight directions as there are only eight bordering points which can be considered)

Figure 6.9 An image (left) together with the derived gradients (centre) and the non-maxima suppressed gradients (right)

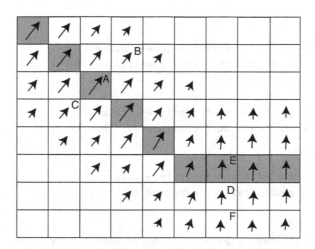

Figure 6.10 An edge image where each edge orientation is represented by the direction of the arrows and gradient is represented by the length of the arrows. The centre of the edge contour is highlighted in grey. The gradient of pixel A is greater than the gradients in both pixels B and C and hence is not suppressed. Pixel D will be suppressed as its gradient is less than pixel E

- For all points (i,j)
  - Look at the two points orthogonal to edge
  - if gradient(i,j) < gradient of either of these two points
    - output$(i,j)=0$
    - else output(i,j) = gradient(i,j).

In OpenCV, oddly no non-maxima suppression routine is provided. An efficient implementation is provided in the resources associated with this text. This is an inefficient implementation (for ease of understanding):

```
nms_result = gradients.clone();
for (int row=1; row < gradients.rows-1; row++)
for (int column=1; column < gradients.cols-1; column++)
{
    float curr_gradient = gradients.at <float>(row,column);
    float curr_orientation = orientations.at<float>(row,column);
    // Determine which neighbours to check
    int direction = (((int) (16.0*(curr_orientation)/(2.0*PI))+15)%8)/2;
    float gradient1 = 0.0, gradient2 = 0.0;
    switch(direction)
    {
    case 0:
        gradient1 = gradients.at<float>(row-1,column-1);
        gradient2 = gradients.at<float>(row+1,column+1);
```

```
      break;
   case 1:
      gradient1 = gradients.at<float>(row-1,column);
      gradient2 = gradients.at<float>(row+1,column);
      break;
   case 2:
      gradient1 = gradients.at<float>(row-1,column+1);
      gradient2 = gradients.at<float>(row+1,column-1);
      break;
   case 3:
      gradient1 = gradients.at<float>(row,column+1);
      gradient2 = gradients.at<float>(row,column-1);
      break;
   }
   if ((gradient1 > curr_gradient) || (gradient2 > curr_gradient))
      nms_result.at<float>(row,column) = 0.0;
}
```

6.1.2   Second Derivative Edge Detectors

Second derivative edge detectors look at the rate of change of the rate of change (see Figure 6.3) and are computed in the discrete domain using a single convolution filter. Probably the most common second derivative filter is the **Laplacian**, two discrete approximations of which are:

$$h(i,j) = \begin{bmatrix} 0 & 1 & 0 \\ 1 & -4 & 1 \\ 0 & 1 & 0 \end{bmatrix}$$
(6.8)

or alternatively

$$h(i,j) = \begin{bmatrix} 2 & -1 & 2 \\ -1 & -4 & -1 \\ 2 & -1 & 2 \end{bmatrix}$$
(6.9)

In these approximations it is notable that the centre pixel has a significant weighting and this causes problems in the presence of noise. Hence, Laplacian filtering is normally preceded by some type of smoothing.

Second derivative edge detectors may be used to determine gradient magnitude and location, but unfortunately cannot be used to determine gradient orientation. For gradient magnitude, the slope of the second derivative function at the zero crossing must be determined. This is a little complicated, and hence often the gradient magnitude from the first derivative function is used. At this point it is reasonable to ask what the purpose of the second derivative edge operators actually is, and the answer is simply that they are excellent at determining the edge location to high precision.

Two practical implementations of second derivative edge detection will be considered here: the Laplacian of Gaussian and the Canny edge detectors.

6.1.2.1   Laplacian of Gaussian

The Laplacian of Gaussian is a second derivative edge detector developed by Marr and Hildreth, and is still one of the most widely used. As previously noted, second derivative edge detectors are susceptible to noise, so to detect edges robustly we need to reduce the level of noise by smoothing before applying the edge detector. The smoothing filter has to satisfy two criteria: (i) that it is smooth and band limited in the frequency domain (i.e. it must limit the frequencies of edges in the image) and (ii) that it exhibits good spatial localisation (i.e. the smoothing filter must not move the edges or change their spatial relationships). The optimal solution to this problem is to use Gaussian smoothing where σ^2 indicates the width of the Gaussian function:

$$G(i,j) = e^{-\frac{i^2+j^2}{2\sigma^2}} \tag{6.10}$$

To compute the second derivative, then, the Gaussian smoothing operator should be applied to the image first and then the Laplacian operator should be applied. See Figure 6.11 for an example. However it is possible to combine these two operators and apply them simultaneously

Figure 6.11   Grey-scale image of a sign (top left), smoothed by a Gaussian smoothing filter (top right), convolved with the Laplacian operator (bottom left), and a binary version showing zero crossing located in a simple (i.e. inaccurate) manner (bottom right)

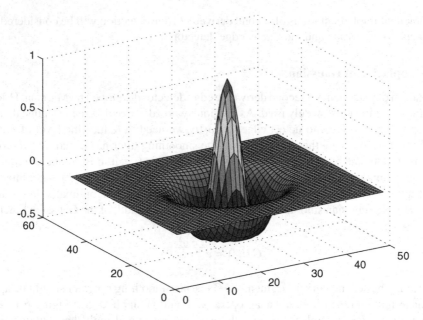

Figure 6.12   The Laplacian of Gaussian (Mexican hat) filter

to the image as a single 'Laplacian of Gaussian' operator. The convolution filter for this operator is defined as follows:

$$h(i,j) = \frac{1}{\pi\sigma^4}\left(\frac{i^2+j^2}{2\sigma^2}-1\right)e^{-\frac{i^2+j^2}{2\sigma^2}} \tag{6.11}$$

The shape of this convolution mask is positive in the centre and negative surrounding that returning to zero further from the centre. As a result it is often referred to as the Mexican hat filter. See Figure 6.12.

In OpenCV, we apply 5x5 Gaussian blurring (with a σ of 1.5) and then apply the Laplacian as follows:

```
Mat laplacian;
Mat blurred_image1_gray;
GaussianBlur(gray_image, blurred_image, Size (5,5), 1.5 );
Laplacian(blurred_image, laplacian, CV_32F, 3 );
```

One advantage of this filter is that it can take a much larger area into account (when compared to normal edge operators) when computing edges. This is not always a good thing though – say if a number of edges are present within that area. In addition, it sometimes does too much smoothing – losing fine details such as corners. Another frequently postulated advantage is that the Laplacian of Gaussian operator gives guaranteed closed loops of edges – which was presented as an important benefit but causes problems for some applications (or more to the point certain types of post-processing). It has been shown using neuro-physiological experiments that the human vision system (in the form of ganglion cells) performs operations which are very similar to Laplacian of Gaussian.

To practically employ this filter, the vision community needed to come up with efficient ways of applying it, as the filter mask is typically very large (depending on the value of sigma). It was found that the 2D Laplacian of Gaussian function can be separated into four 1D convolutions which are much faster to compute. In addition, the Laplacian of Gaussian is often approximated by the Difference of Gaussians (the difference between two images that have been smoothed with different values of sigma).

To find zero crossings within the second derivative image is not simple. We cannot just look for zeros (as the domain is not continuous). We can just mark points as being zero crossing if their sign (+ve or −ve) is different from the sign of the previous point on that row or the previous point in that column. However, if we do this, we are discarding one of the major advantages of the second derivative (i.e. the high precision to which we can determine the edge position).

> In OpenCV, no implementation is provided for locating zero-crossings.

6.1.2.2 Multiple Scales

Many image processing techniques work locally using individual pixels or more frequently pixels from a local area. A major problem is knowing what size of neighborhood to use and the 'right' size depends on the size of the objects under investigation. This is effectively a problem of scale within the image. Knowing what the objects are assumes that it is clear how the image should be interpreted, which is acceptable for industrial applications but for general vision seems intractable (a chicken and egg type problem). One proposed solution to this is to study the image under different resolutions (scales) simultaneously. We create models at multiple resolutions and then study the way in which the model changes at different resolutions to obtain meta-knowledge which is unavailable at one scale.

In the case of Laplacian of Gaussian edge detection one possibility proposed by David Marr (Marr, 1982) is that the image should be smoothed with different Gaussians. Correspondences across multiple scales can be used to identify significant discontinuities. See Figure 6.13 for an example of an image processed at two scales.

6.1.2.3 Canny Edge Detection

The Canny edge detector (Canny, 1986) combines first derivative and second derivative edge detection to compute both edge gradient and orientation. It was designed to optimise the following three criteria:

1. Detection – edges should not be missed.
2. Localisation – distance between actual and located edges should be minimised.
3. One response – minimises multiple responses to a single edge.

Figure 6.13 The zero crossing determined using two different Laplacian of Gaussian filters ($\sigma = 0.5$ top right and $\sigma = 2.0$ bottom right). The images as smoothed by the two different Gaussian filters are shown to the left

Algorithm 6.2

1. Convolve with Gaussian with some standard deviation σ.
2. Estimate the edge normal direction (i.e. orientation) using the first derivative of the Gaussian convolved image.
3. Find the edges, suppressing non-maxima values. This is done by searching for zero-crossings in the directional second derivative of the Gaussian convolved image, where those derivatives are taken with respect to the edge orientations which were computed in the previous step.
4. The edge gradient is computed based on the first derivative of the Gaussian convolved image.
5. Thresholding edges with hysteresis. The idea here is that edge points are considered in contours of connected points. Two thresholds are used – a high gradient threshold over which all points are definitely classified as edge points and a low threshold over which points which are connected to definitive edge points are considered edge points. This attempts to get over the problem of edge contours which break up into unconnected segments, due to the use of a simple threshold.
6. Similar to Marr's detector we can do this processing for multiple scales (using different Gaussians) and then use 'feature synthesis' to combine edges from different scales.

Figure 6.14 Canny edge detection. The three Canny images all use the same smoothing filter but various low and high gradient thresholds (7 and 236 – top right, 7 and 100 – bottom left, 1 and 1 – bottom right). The bottom right image shows all possible edges and the other two show some of the effects of the thresholds

Examples of Canny edge images are shown in Figure 6.14.

In OpenCV, a function to compute Canny, which requires the low and high thresholds, is provided. Note that this can only process grey-scale images:

```
Canny(gray_image, binary_edges, 100, 200 );
```

6.1.3   Multispectral Edge Detection

The application of edge detection to colour imagery is not as straightforward as it might seem. If images are converted to grey-scale and then edge detection is applied, it is possible that some edges will not be located (where the grey-scales of two different adjacent colours are similar). See Figure 6.15. In this figure some significant edges are not present in the edge image derived from the grey-scale image. Note, though, that this is not typical of most images and, in fact, it took a little searching to find an appropriate image to use to illustrate this problem. For this reason, many developers in vision just use grey-scale edge detection.

Colour edge detection (Koschan & Abidi, 2007) can be approached in a variety of ways:

1. Vector methods. In these methods colours are treated as vectors. Median vectors and the distance between vectors can be computed and these can be used to measure the gradient (and orientation). In effect, each colour is treated as a single entity (rather than three separate dimensions).

Figure 6.15 A colour image (left), in grey-scale (centre left), the Canny edges detected in the grey-scale image (centre right) and the Canny edges detected from the three (RGB) channels of the colour image (right). It is notable that many edges in this image appear in only one of the RGB channels. All Canny detectors used the same thresholds (100 and 200)

2. Multidimensional gradient methods. The gradient and orientation are computed based on data from all channels, typically using relatively complex formula.
3. Output fusion methods. Gradients and orientations are computed separately for all channels and then combined into a single result, typically using a weighted sum or a maximum value.

Note that the choice of colour space can be quite important for colour edge detection.

6.1.4   Image Sharpening

It is possible to use the second derivative to sharpen images, by simply subtracting a fraction (e.g. 3/10) of the second derivative from the original image. This has the effect of lengthening the edges (see Figure 6.16). An example of the application of this technique is shown in Figure 6.17.

In OpenCV, image sharpening by subtracting the Laplacian is quite straightforward:

```
image.convertTo( image_32bit, CV_32F );
Laplacian( image, laplacian, CV_32F, 3 );
Mat sharp_image_32bit = image_32bit - 0.3*laplacian;
sharp_image_32bit.convertTo( sharp_image, CV_8U );
```

Figure 6.16 A simple image (left), its intensity magnitudes (centre left), its second derivative (centre right) and the sharpened image intensity magnitudes (right) which were computed by subtracting a small fraction of the second derivative from the original image magnitudes. The edges have effectively been extended somewhat

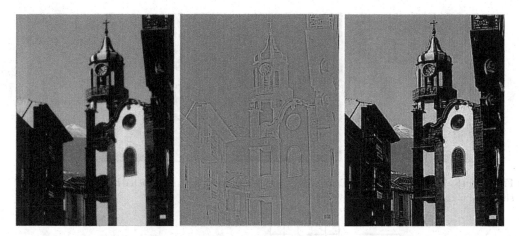

Figure 6.17   An original image (left), the second derivative (Laplacian) of that image (centre) and the sharpened image (right) which was computed by subtracting 0.3 times the second derivative from the original image

6.2   Contour Segmentation

Unfortunately, extracting an edge image is not sufficient for most applications. We need to extract the information contained in the edge image and represent it more explicitly so that it can be reasoned with more easily. The extraction of edge data involves firstly deciding on which points are edges (as most have a non-zero gradient). This is typically achieved by edge image thresholding and non-maxima suppression (or through the use of Canny). The edge data then needs to be extracted from the image domain (e.g. using graph searching, border refining and so on) and represented in some fashion (e.g. BCCs, graphs, sequences of straight line segments and other geometric representations).

Obtaining a consistent representation from the image is made harder by contours that are not closed and by contours with T junctions or cross-roads.

6.2.1   Basic Representations of Edge Data

There are many ways in which edge image data can be represented outside of the image domain. Here we will present two of the simplest: boundary chain codes and directed graphs.

6.2.1.1   Boundary Chain Codes

A boundary chain code (BCC) (Freeman, 1961) consists of a start point and a list of orientations to other connected edge points (i.e. a chain of points). See Figure 6.18 for the BCCs extracted from a real image.

The start point is specified by the (row,column) pair, and then the direction to the next point is repeatedly specified simply as a value from 0 to 7 (i.e. the eight possible directions to a neighbouring pixel). See Figure 6.19.

If considering this as a shape representation then we have to consider how useful it will be for further processing (e.g. shape/object recognition). BCCs are orientation dependant in that

Figure 6.18   An image (left), the Canny edges detected (centre) and the extracted boundary chain codes shown in a variety of colours (right)

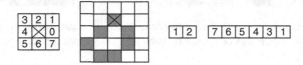

Figure 6.19   The eight possible directions from a pixel (left), a sample image, the start point (1,2) which is marked by an cross in the image and the list of orientations (following a clockwise direction)

if the orientation of the object/region changes then the representation will change significantly. The representation will also change somewhat with object scale. It is only position dependent to the extent of the start point, although it should be noted that the start point is somewhat arbitrary for a closed contour.

In OpenCV, we can extract the contours from a binary edge image as follows:

```
vector<vector<Point>> contours;
vector<Vec4i> hierarchy;
findContours( binary_edge_image, contours, hierarchy,
                  CV_RETR_CCOMP, CV_CHAIN_APPROX_NONE );
```

In OpenCV, each individual contour is stored as a vector of points, and all the contours are stored as a vector of contours (i.e. a vector of vectors of points).

The boundary can be smoothed to reduce noise, although it will need to be done carefully so that the shape isn't deformed.

6.2.1.2   Directed Graphs

A directed graph is a general structure consisting of nodes (which correspond to edge pixels in this case) and oriented arcs (connections between bordering pixels/nodes). See Figure 6.20.

To create this type of graph, we add all edge pixels to the graph as nodes if their gradient values $s(x_i)$ are greater than some threshold (T). To decide on which nodes are then connected

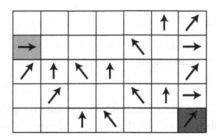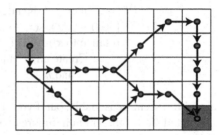

Figure 6.20   An edge orientation image (left) with the orientation vector for each edge point shown. Possible source and destination edge points are shown in green and red respectively. The corresponding directed graph is also shown (right) with the nodes (which correspond to the edge pixels) shown as red dots and the oriented arcs (the allowed connections between nodes) shown as arrows between nodes

by arcs, we look at the orientation $s(x_i)$ associated with each node n_i to determine which neighbouring pixels x_j could be connected. The orientation vectors as shown in Figure 6.20a, which have been quantised to eight possible directions, are orthogonal to the edge contours and hence the most likely next pixel will be to the side of the point (and hence is a possible arc). We also allow pixels on either side of this pixel (i.e. $\pm 45°$) to be considered to be connected via an arc. If any of these pixels have an associated node n_j then we add in a directed arc from n_i to n_j if the difference in orientation between the two corresponding pixels is less than $\pi/2$.

In OpenCV, to draw contours we simply loop through the contours, picking a (random) colour for each contour and drawing them to some `display_image`:

```
for (int contour_number=0;
        (contour_number<contours.size()); contour_number++)
{
    Scalar  colour( rand()&0xFF, rand()&0xFF, rand()&0xFF );
    drawContours( display_image, contours, contour_number,
                                colour, 1, 8, hierarchy );
}
```

Algorithm 6.3

Algorithm 6.3 for graph creation:

> Given an edge image where every pixel x_i has an associated gradient $s(x_i)$ and orientation $s(x_i)$
> For all pixels x_i
>> If the gradient $s(x_i)$ is greater than a threshold T
>>> Create a corresponding node n_i
> For all nodes n_i
>> For all neighbouring nodes n_j

If (x_j is in one of the allowed the directions
[$s(x_i) - 3\pi/4$, $s(x_i) - \pi/2$, $s(x_i) - \pi/4$]
relative to x_i) AND ($| s(x_i) - s(x_j) | < \pi/2$)
Create an oriented arc joining n_i
and n_j.

This algorithm seems reasonable, but if you consider the arc which goes diagonally upwards on the right-hand side of the graph in Figure 6.20b, you will see that we should probably have taken into account the relative positions of the edge pixels when deciding which orientations to permit in a successor node.

6.2.2   Border Detection

Border detection is either addressed as a search for the optimal path between a source and destination (see Section 6.2.2.1), or as a search for a best representation of all edge points in the image (see Section 6.2.2.4). In the first case we are typically addressing applications where there is a good amount of *a priori* knowledge (e.g. in PCB inspection) and hence the locations of the source and destination can be at least approximately known in advance. In the second case we are typically trying to extract a general representation of all the edge contours in the scene for further processing.

6.2.2.1   A-algorithm Graph Search (for the Optimal Path)

Having created a directed graph (see Section 6.2.1.2) we must now search within the graph for the optimal path from source node to destination node.

When performing graph search we maintain an OPEN list of nodes being considered where each node n_i in the open list has an associated accumulated cost $f(n_i)$. We initialise this list by adding the source node to it with an accumulated cost of 0. While the list is not empty and the destination hasn't been reached we repeatedly expand the node from the OPEN list which has the lowest cost. Expanding the node means replacing that node in the list with all possible successors (i.e. other nodes which are connected by an arc from the node in question). We will terminate either when we reach the destination or find there is no possible path.

Algorithm 6.4

Algorithm 6.4 for graph search:

Given a source node n_A and a destination node n_B together with the graph structure
    containing them
Put n_A in the list of open nodes (OPEN) with accumulated cost $f(n_A)=0$
While ((OPEN $\neq \emptyset$) AND ($n_B \notin$ OPEN))
        Choose the node n_y in OPEN with the lowest cost $f(n_y)$
        Expand n_y by removing it from OPEN and putting all its successors
            into OPEN with the their associated accumulated costs.
If ($n_B \in$ OPEN)
        Optimal path from n_A to n_B has been found
Otherwise No path is possible.

There are problems with this approach, such as the possibility of an infinite loop if the graph has any circular loops in it. This can be prevented by labelling nodes once they have been included in the OPEN list so that they will not be considered (i.e. included in the OPEN list) again.

There is also a significant problem with the approach in that it expands nodes in all directions taking no account of where the destination node is. This is addressed by a modification to the approach called the 'Gradient Field Transform' which for each node in the OPEN list considers both the accumulated cost and the cost to the destination.

6.2.2.2 Cost Function

For the A algorithm or Gradient Field Transform to work we need to be able to determine costs for nodes in the OPEN list (effectively this means costs for paths from the source node to each node in the OPEN list and costs for paths from each node in the OPEN list to the destination node). There are only a limited range of possibilities:

1. The strength of edges (i.e. the gradient). The additional cost of adding node n_i to a path in the OPEN list is $(Max_{image}\ s(x_k)) - s(x_i)$. In this case, the edge points with the strongest gradient would add no cost onto a PATH, and ones with smaller gradients would add more cost. This approach seems reasonable and appears frequently to give good results, but one should consider how much sense it makes as all edge points in the graph structure have already been compared with a threshold and hence considered significant enough to be included in the graph.
2. The border curvature. The additional cost of adding node n_j to a path in the OPEN list ending in n_i is $| s(x_i) - s(x_j) |$. This function penalizes changes in orientation, which seems reasonable. However, it might be even better to look at the relative position of pixels (and the orientations) to determine a measure of continuity and calculate the cost as the inverse of the continuity.
3. Distance to an approximate (expected) border. This would be a useful measure of cost as long as an approximate border was known – either from knowledge about what is expected in the image *a priori* or from previous processing at a lower resolution (which is done in many applications in order to reduce computational cost).
4. Distance to the destination. In the absence of an approximate border the only practical way to estimate the cost to the destination is to measure the Euclidean distance from each node to the destination node.

6.2.2.3 More Efficient Search

There are a number a ways which have been suggested to improve the efficiency of the graph search some of which are listed here:

1. Multi-resolution processing. Determine the approximate boundary first in a lower resolution image. This assumes the boundary can be detected in the lower resolution image.
2. Depth first search. Reduce the likelihood that poor edges will be expanded by reducing the cost of all expanded nodes by the cost of the best successor (whose cost as result will be 0 – hence guaranteeing that this node will be expanded again immediately).

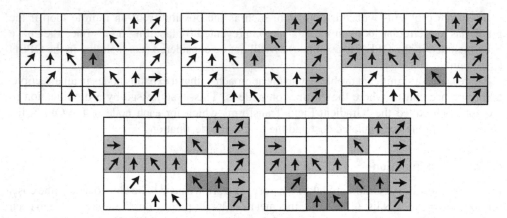

Figure 6.21 An edge image is shown (top left) with the strongest unused edge point highlighted in grey and the edge points shown with their orientations. The strongest edge point is expanded forwards until it can go no further (top centre) and then backwards (top right). The next strongest edge point is expanded forwards (bottom left) and backwards (bottom right) at which point there are no further unused edge points

3. Incorporation of higher level knowledge. For example, distance to an expected boundary.
4. Pruning the solution tree. Delete paths which have too high an average cost per unit length.
5. Maximum cost. Determine a maximum cost for paths and hence stop searching once the minimum cost in the OPEN list is greater than this maximum.

6.2.2.4   Heuristic Search for All Image Borders

The purpose of this algorithm is to represent all edge points in an image in the best way possible.

This technique attempts to extract chains of edge points which can be represented using boundary chain codes (described earlier in this chapter). See Figure 6.18 and Figure 6.23 for examples of the BCCs extracted. It does so by repeatedly starting with the strongest unused edge point and building a chain of edge points forwards and (if the edge points don't form a loop) backwards until all edge points are used. See Figure 6.21.

Note that similar rules to those employed in the creation of a graph earlier in this chapter should be used when deciding which edge points can be joined together. When there is more than one edge point, the best one (the one which is most similar or most continuous) should be chosen.

The basic technique is followed by a post-processing stage which is intended to clean up the resulting contours, to get thin edges, to remove changes in lighting, and to fill in small gaps (note: more complicated systems are sometimes used to fill in the gaps).

Algorithm 6.5

Given an edge image which has been non-maxima suppressed and semi-thresholded (so that all edge points below a certain threshold are set to 0).

While there are unused edge point in the image
Search for the strongest edge point in the image.

Figure 6.22   An edge contour (in black) together with a straight line approximation (in red). The bounds of the error are shown with green lines which are *t* pixels from the straight line approximation

Expand the edges 'in front of' the specified edge point
Expand the edges 'behind' the specified edge point
If the edge chain is greater than three pixels in length, store it.
Modify edge chains according to these rules:
Remove any edge chains which are parallel to larger ones
Remove all edge chains where there are multiple parallel chains
Join any edge chains which are in line with each other but are
separated by a single (missing) point.

6.2.3   Extracting Line Segment Representations of Edge Contours

Particularly with manmade objects, we frequently represent edge contours using straight line segments. These segments summarise quite a large amount of edge image data (depending on how long they are) as they can be represented just by the locations of the start and end points of the segments.

Contours in images, however, are rarely perfectly straight and hence when extracting edge segments it is necessary to specify some tolerance (*t*) for the maximum distance permitted between the contour and the segments that approximate it. See Figure 6.22 and Figure 6.23. There are two common approaches to this problem: recursive boundary splitting (see Section 6.2.3.1) and the divide and conquer technique (see Section 6.2.3.2).

6.2.3.1   Recursive Boundary Splitting

Recursive boundary splitting (Ramer, 1972) splits a contour into multiple sections using the data to drive the locations of the splits.

Given an edge contour, approximate it with a single straight line segment (from the start of the contour to the end). Split the segment in two at the point on the edge contour which is furthest from the straight line segment. Keep doing this until all straight line segments are no

Figure 6.23   An image (left), the boundary chain codes extracted (centre left) using heuristic search, and the straight line segments extracted (centre right) and (right) with a maximum distance of 3 and 6 respectively

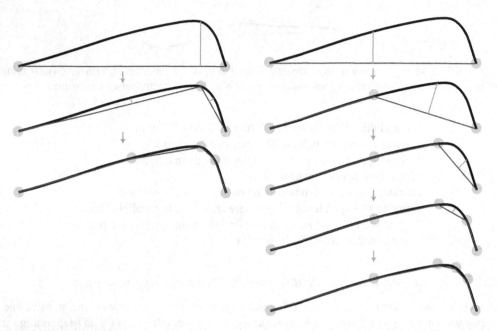

Figure 6.24   Line segment extraction for a contour using recursive boundary splitting (left) and divide and conquer (right). The blue lines show how the points for splitting were located

further from the contour than a preset tolerance. See Figure 6.24 for an illustration and Figure 6.23 (c) and (d) for two real examples using different values for the tolerance.

In OpenCV, line segments are identified using the `approxPolyDP` *function which implements an algorithm akin to recursive boundary splitting. Assuming we have to process all of the edge contours (which were extracted as detailed in Section 6.2.1.1):*

```
vector<vector<Point>> approx_contours(contours.size());
for (int contour_number=0;
        (contour_number<contours.size()); contour_number++)
    approxPolyDP( Mat(contours[contour_number]),
              approx_contours[contour_number], 3, true );
```

In OpenCV, the `approxPolyDP` *function represents the line segments within a vector of points structure, just with fewer points than previously. To be able to process the segments more efficiently we extract their end points and store them explicitly:*

```
vector<Vec4i> line_segments;
for (int contour_number=0;
      (contour_number<contours.size()); contour_number++)
```

```
for (int segment_num=0; (segment_num <
              approx_contours[contour_number].size()-1);
                                         segment_num++)
  line_segments.push_back( Vec4i(
    approx_contours[contour_number][segment_num].x,
    approx_contours[contour_number][segment_num].y,
    approx_contours[contour_number][ segment_num+1].x,
    approx_contours[contour_number][segment_num+1].y));
```

6.2.3.2 Divide and Conquer

Divide and conquer considers the same tolerance value and if the contour is too far from a straight line segment then the segment is split in the middle. The contour point (v_n) chosen to split the segment is that which is further from the current segment along the line which is orthogonal to the current segment (v_1, v_2), and which goes through the middle of the segment, is used as a new vertex giving two segments (v_1, v_n) and (v_n, v_2). This is done until all line segments are within the tolerance. See Figure 6.24.

6.2.3.3 Comparison

It is arguable that the recursive boundary splitting technique is better as it attempts to create segments that better represent the data, although there is a slight increase in computational cost.

For a curve, such as that shown in Figure 6.24, both techniques have the straight line segments to one side of the edge data as the start and end points are on the edge contours. This clearly is not the best possible approximation to the edge data.

6.2.3.4 Curved Segments

Some manmade (and natural) objects are better described using curves than straight lines. However, the use of curves poses an immediate question. What order of curves should we use? Should we use curves of constant curvature, second order polynomials (circles, ellipses, parabolas), and so on? Also, where does one curve end and the next start? The possibilities for multiple interpretations (all equally valid) are significantly increased. Due to these issues, the most frequently used segment representation is the straight line segment.

While dealing with curves it is worth pointing out how curvature should be computed for a contour (of edge points). Typically, we cannot rely on the orientation values (i.e. just compute the rate of change of orientation from point to point). Nor can we compute curvature for a pixel based on its two nearest neighbours on the contour. Instead, to compute the curvature at point x along a contour, we look at a point on the contour n points before x and another point n points after x and then compute the curvature from these three points. This will give an increasing value as we approach a 'corner' and a decreasing value after the corner, so important feature points along such a contour would be located by looking for local maxima in the curvature value along the contour (see Figure 6.25).

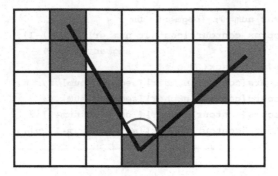

Figure 6.25 Diagram showing how curvature is computed for a point along a contour by looking at the points which are a number of points (n) away in each direction along the contour. In this example $n = 4$

6.3 Hough Transform

The Hough transformation (Illingworth & Kittler, 1988) is a very elegant transformation that directly maps from image space to the probability of the existence of some features (such as lines, circles or generalised shapes) (see Figure 6.26).

The Hough transform is capable of detecting partial objects. In these cases the amount of evidence is reduced (as compared to a complete object).

Note that perhaps the greatest issue for the Hough is the speed at which it can be computed. It is an expensive operation, so methods for reducing the computational cost of the operation are always sought. For example, if reliable edge orientation information is available and the edges are smooth, then edge orientation can be used to restrict the Hough space which is mapped into by any edge point. Also, many applications of the Hough start processing at a small resolution and then after finding the local maxima which represent the located shapes, generate new small higher resolution Hough spaces to obtain the local maxima (and hence the locations of the shapes) to higher accuracy.

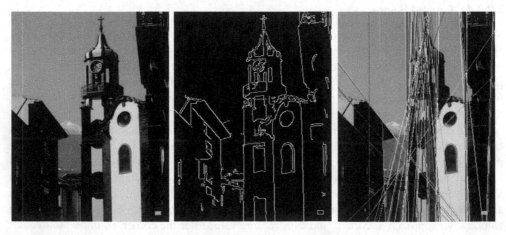

Figure 6.26 The Hough transform for straight lines. The original image (left), edges computed using the Canny operator (centre) and the located edges (right)

6.3.1   Hough for Lines

For lines (Risse, 1989), the most familiar equation is $j = mi + c$ (usually presented as $y = mx+c$) where m indicates the slope of the line. Unfortunately, this line equation cannot represent some lines (i.e. $i = p$ where p is any constant) so an alternative form of the line equation must be used:

$$s = i.\cos(\vartheta) + j.\sin(\theta) \qquad (6.12)$$

where s is orthogonal distance of the line to the origin and ϑ is the angle between that line and the I axis. To find lines in image space, we transform from image space to Hough space where the axis in this case will be s and ϑ. For each edge point in the binary edge image of the scene, we increment the cells in the Hough space which correspond to every possible line through the edge point. See Figure 6.27 for an example of the mapping from image space to Hough space.

Algorithm 6.5

- Initialise all cells (s, θ) in the Hough space accumulator to 0
- For every edge point in image space (i,j)
  - Increment cells in the Hough space accumulator corresponding to all possible lines through the point as determined using $s = i.\cos(\vartheta) + j.\sin(\theta)$. In practical terms i and j are known and hence we can simply compute a value of s for every possible value of θ. Care must be taken to ensure the evidence for a given image point is continuous in Hough space.
- Search for local maximums in the Hough space accumulator. This means identifying any cells (s, θ) in the accumulator whose value is greater than or equal to each of the neighbouring cells.

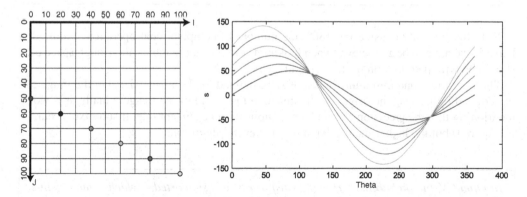

Figure 6.27   Example showing the mapping of six collinear points from image space (i,j) on the left to Hough space (s, θ) on the right. Note that each coloured point in image space corresponds to a sinusoidal curve of the same colour in Hough space, where each point on the curve represents a line through the point in image space at a different angle. The curves intersect twice as a full 360 ° has been considered (and lines which are 180° apart are effectively the same)

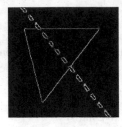

Figure 6.28 The Hough transform for lines as applied to a simple image. The simple image (left), the resultant non-maxima suppressed thresholded gradient image (centre left), the lines found (centre right), and the Hough space (right) in which the vertical axis is the s and the horizontal is θ from 0–180°

Hough space for lines, if computed for all 360°, actually represents each line twice. This can be handy, though, as it allows discrimination of (black to white) vs. (white to black) lines, but in many applications this is unnecessary so instead only the first 180° on Hough space is considered. See Figure 6.28 for an example.

In OpenCV, the Hough for lines is computed using the `HoughLines` *routine, taking the distance resolution (e.g. 1), the orientation resolution (e.g. PI/200.0) and a minimum evidence threshold for a line (e.g. 60). It computes a vector of lines (each represented by two floating point numbers (s and ϑ):*

```
vector<Vec2f> hough_lines;
HoughLines( binary_edge_image, hough_lines, 1, PI/200.0,
                                                    60);
```

Note that by only considering 180°, the number of computational operations required is halved. We have to be a bit clever when looking for maxima, though, as the Hough space then should be wrapped back on itself in an odd fashion.

The maximum and minimum values of s are defined by the image size, but the range can be reduced by moving the origin on the image to the centre of the image. Finally, it is worth mentioning that the precision of s and θ are application dependent (e.g. if sub-pixel accuracy is required) but the higher the precision the slower the algorithm.

In OpenCV, the probabilistic Hough transform is also supported – which computes line segments rather than lines:

```
vector<Vec4i> line_segments;
HoughLinesP( binary_edge_image, line_segments, 1.0, PI/200.0, 20, 20, 5);
```

Figure 6.29 Hough for circles. Original image (top left), a derived Canny edge image (top right), and located circles (bottom left and right) with only slightly different parameters (for the Canny edge threshold and the required number of points of evidence for a circle)

6.3.2 Hough for Circles

The equation of a circle is $(i - a)^2 + (j - b)^2 = r^2$ where r is the radius of the circle, and (a, b) is the centre of the circle. If we assume constant radius r then to specify a circle all we need to determine is the circle centre (a, b). Using the Hough transform, then, we want to transform from image space (i, j) to Hough space (a, b), representing the likelihood of a particular circle being present (Yuen, et al., 1990). See Figure 6.29 for an example.

We use the algorithm that was presented in the previous section, but we use the circle equation $(i - a)^2 + (j - b)^2 = r^2$ rather than the line equation and the parameters of the Hough accumulator are a and b rather than s and θ.

As the Hough transform is capable of detecting partial objects, the Hough for circles can detect circles whose centre is outside the image space. In theory, such circles could be up to the radius r outside the image space and hence the Hough space should actually be $2*r$ larger than the image space in both i and j.

In addition, as we are using evidence from all points on the circle we can detect the circle centre to a higher precision (i.e. sub-pixel accuracy). Again, this means increasing the resolution of the Hough space (to represent points between pixels).

> *In OpenCV, the Hough for circles is applied (somewhat strangely) directly to a grey-scale image. Circles are stored in a vector where each element is three floating point numbers (centre column, centre row and radius):*
>
> ```
> vector<Vec3f> circles;
> HoughCircles( gray_image,circles,CV_HOUGH_GRADIENT,2,20,300,20,5,15 );
> ```

One major issue for the Hough for circles is if the size of the circle isn't known in advance. We are then faced with needing a 3D accumulator (the third dimension being for the radius) which increases the computations by an order of magnitude.

6.3.3   Generalised Hough

It is possible to use the Hough transform to locate any shape (i.e. not just those for which simple parametric equations exist) (Ballard, 1981). To do this we need to learn the shape to be located in a training phase (in which a sample of the shape must be provided). The shape is stored in a representation called an R-table. Once determined, we can use the R-table to search for the shape in other images (during the recognition phase). This will work for any shape and doesn't even require the edge points of the shape to be connected.

Given a training image of the shape, we first must define an arbitrary reference point X^R with respect to which the shape will be defined (see Figure 6.30). This reference point can be anywhere (either inside or outside the shape) although generally the centre of the shape is used. Once this has been done, every single edge point from the shape must be represented in terms of where it is with respect to this reference point. This information is stored in the R-table (see Figure 6.31). The R-table consists of an array of pointers (one for each possible edge orientation ϕ) each of which points to a linked list of (r, α) pairs, where r is the distance from the reference point to the one of the edge points and α is the angle of the line between the edge point and the reference point. The edge orientations have to be quantised into a discrete number of possible orientations. For example, in Figure 6.31 the orientation has been quantised into 4 bits (16 possibilities).

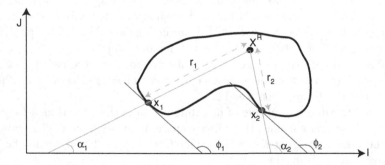

Figure 6.30   Definition of an arbitrary shape with respect to a reference point X^R. Each point (x) on the boundary is defined in terms of the distance (r) from the reference point, the angle between the line from the reference point through x and the i axis (α) and the angle between the tangent at x and the i axis (ϕ). The lines and angles are shown for two points – which happen to have the same tangent

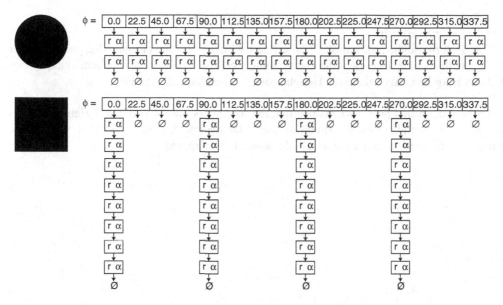

Figure 6.31   Two shapes and their associated R-tables. The edge orientations have been quantized quite coarsely into 16 possibilities. In the case of the circle which has 32 boundary edge points each orientation has two (r,α) pairs due to two of the points being quantised to each orientation. In the case of the square again we are assuming 32 edge points and hence there are 8 (r,α) pairs in four orthogonal locations and no (r,α) pairs in the other orientations

Algorithm 6.6

Training phase algorithm 6.6 (build up an R-table):

- For each edge point x
  - Determine the distance r of the edge point x from the reference point X^R.
  - Determine the orientation ϕ of the edge point x (i.e. the orientation of the tangent). Note that multiple points can have the same orientation (as shown in the diagram).
  - Determine the orientation α of the line from the reference point X^R through the edge point x.
  - Add a link to the linked list for orientation ϕ in the R-table with the pair (r,α) as values.

To recognise the shape defined in an R-table, we accumulate evidence for it in terms of the likelihood of the shape being present relative to the reference point in a Hough space as follows:

Algorithm 6.7

Recognition phase algorithm 6.7

- Create an accumulator for the coordinates of X^R and initialise all cells to 0.
- For every edge point
  - Determine its orientation ϕ

o Select the appropriate linked list of (r,α) pairs from the R-table
o For each (r,α) pair
   ■ Determine the position of X^R based on the position of the current edge point together with r and α. Increment the corresponding cell in the Hough Space (accumulator).
• Search for local maxima in the Hough space (accumulator) to find the shape

In the recognition phase, we assume that the size and orientation are fixed. Hence we get a simple 2D accumulator for the Hough space. If the overall size and orientation of the shape were allowed to vary, then a 4D accumulator would be required.

7

Features

Given an edge image, it is often impossible to determine locally the movement of the edge from one frame to the next frame in an image sequence (see Figure 7.1). This is caused to a large extent by the ambiguity of the match (i.e. it is not apparent which edge point in the next image the current edge point maps to), but there are many different reasons why it is difficult to associate edge points from one frame to the next. Even in the simple example shown there are many different possible interpretations. The red object could be expanding in size or equally it could be moving in a variety of directions as illustrated. For real imagery we have extra possibilities caused by the objects being three-dimensional with a whole variety of different rotations, translations and deformations possible.

To overcome this problem, a common approach in computer vision is to instead make use of corners, image features or interest points (these terms are used almost interchangeably). Technically a corner is the intersection of two edges, whereas an interest point is any point that can be located robustly, which includes corners but also includes such features as small marks. This use of features significantly reduces the number of points that are considered from frame to frame and each of these points is more complex (than an edge point). Both of these factors make it much easier to establish reliable correspondences from frame to frame. See Figure 7.2.

Unfortunately corner/feature detection is often not particularly robust/repeatable: the location of corner points can vary quite a bit from frame to frame, as well as some corners disappearing in some frames while new corners simultaneously appear.

In this chapter, we present a number of different corner/feature detectors:

- Moravec corner detector (see Section 7.1) – which was one of the first and simplest corner detectors.
- Harris/Plessey corner detector (see Section 7.2) – which uses eigenvalues in the computation of cornerness (see Figure 7.3).
- FAST corner detector (see Section 7.3) – which is simpler and faster than all other detectors described here (see Figure 7.3).
- SIFT feature detector (see Section 7.4) – which is much more complex in what it aims to represent (see Figure 7.3).

A Practical Introduction to Computer Vision with OpenCV, First Edition. Kenneth Dawson-Howe.
© 2014 John Wiley & Sons, Ltd. Published 2014 by John Wiley & Sons, Ltd.

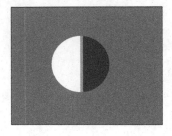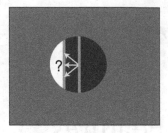

Figure 7.1 The Aperture Problem exemplifies the problem of local processing. In the images shown we are considering just the pixels inside the hole in the grey area. Two images are shown from a synthetic image sequence (left) and (centre) with the edge points marked in green, along with some of the possible linkages for one of the (green) edge points (right)

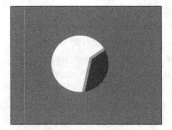

Figure 7.2 Two images from an image sequence (left) and (centre) with the edge points marked in green, the only reasonable linkage for the corner (right) assuming that the same feature has remained visible

Figure 7.3 Corners/features detected from Harris (centre left), FAST (centre right), SIFT (right) from a greyscale version of the image on the left

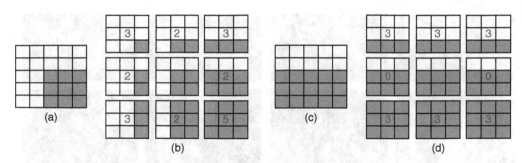

Figure 7.4 Idea underlying the Moravec corner detector. Images of a corner and an edge are shown (a) and (c) together with the various patches used by the Moravec corner detector (b) and (d). Each of the patches with which the central patch is compared is annotated with the cornerness values (assuming that the binary pixels have values 0 or 1). As the minimum difference is used, in the case of the edge the value computed is 0 whereas in the case of the corner the minimum computed is 2

Most algorithms for corner detection follow a similar serious of steps, which are presented here.

1. Determine cornerness values. For each pixel in the image, compute a cornerness value based on the local pixels. This computation is what distinguishes most corner detectors. The output of this stage is a cornerness map.
2. Non-maxima suppression. Suppress all cornerness values which are less than a local neighbour (within n pixels distance; e.g. $n = 3$) in order to avoid multiple responses for the same corner.
3. Threshold the cornerness map. Finally, we need to select those cornerness values which remain and are significant and this is typically done using thresholding (i.e. the cornerness value must be above some threshold T in order to be considered a corner).

7.1 Moravec Corner Detection

The Moravec corner detector (Moravec, 1980) looks at the local variation around a point by comparing local images patches and computing the un-normalized local autocorrelation between them. In fact, for each pixel it compares a patch centred on that pixel with eight local patches which are simply shifted by a small amount (typically one pixel in each of the eight possible directions) from the current patch. It compares the patches using the following sum of squared differences formula and records the minimum of these eight values as the cornerness for the pixel. See Figure 7.4 for an illustrative (binary) example of the technique used.

$$V_{u,v}(i,j) = \sum_{\forall a,b \in Window} (f(i+u+a,j+v+b) - f(i+a,j+b))^2 \qquad (7.1)$$

where $(u,v) \in \{ (-1,-1), (-1,0), (-1,1), (0,-1), (0,1) (1,-1), (1, 0), (1,1,) \}$ and the Window is typically 3x3, 5x5 or 7x7.

Figure 7.5 Two different images are shown (left) together with their Moravec cornerness maps (centre left), the Moravec corners detected (centre right) and the Harris corners detected (right)

See Figure 7.5 for examples. The Moravec corner detector has two flaws which have motivated the development of different detectors:

1. Anisotropic response. If you consider the road sign in Figure 7.5 it is apparent that the Moravec corner detector responds quite strongly to diagonal lines (whereas it does not respond in the same way to vertical or horizontal lines). Hence the response of the operator is not isotropic. The anisotropic response can be reduced by smoothing in advance of applying the corner detector.
2. Noisy response. The Moravec detector is also quite sensitive to noise. This response to noise can be lessened by using a larger area or by smoothing before applying the corner detector.

7.2   Harris Corner Detection

The Harris corner detector (Harris and Stephen, 1988) differs from the Moravec detector in how it determines the cornerness value. Rather than considering the sum of squared differences. it makes use of partial derivatives, a Gaussian weighting function and the eigenvalues of a matrix representation of the equation.

Consider the intensity variation (sum of squared differences) of an image patch W for a small shift $(\Delta i, \Delta j)$:

$$SSD_W(\Delta i, \Delta j) = \sum_{(i,j)\in W} (f(i,j) - f(i - \Delta i, j - \Delta j))^2 \qquad (7.2)$$

The second term can be approximated as

$$f(i - \Delta i, j - \Delta j) \approx f(i,j) + \left[\frac{\delta f(i,j)}{\delta i} \quad \frac{\delta f(i,j)}{\delta j} \right] \begin{bmatrix} \Delta i \\ \Delta j \end{bmatrix} \qquad (7.3)$$

Hence, the equation can be rewritten as

$$SSD_W(\Delta i, \Delta j) = \sum_{(i,j)\in W} \left(f(i,j) - f(i,j) - \left[\frac{\delta f(i,j)}{\delta i} \quad \frac{\delta f(i,j)}{\delta j} \right] \left[\begin{matrix} \Delta i \\ \Delta j \end{matrix} \right] \right)^2$$

$$SSD_W(\Delta i, \Delta j) = \sum_{(i,j)\in W} \left(\left[\frac{\delta f(i,j)}{\delta i} \quad \frac{\delta f(i,j)}{\delta j} \right] \left[\begin{matrix} \Delta i \\ \Delta j \end{matrix} \right] \right)^2$$

$$SSD_W(\Delta i, \Delta j) = \sum_{(i,j)\in W} \left(\left[\Delta i \quad \Delta j \right] \left(\left[\begin{matrix} \frac{\delta f(i,j)}{\delta i} \\ \frac{\delta f(i,j)}{\delta j} \end{matrix} \right] \left[\frac{\delta f(i,j)}{\delta i} \quad \frac{\delta f(i,j)}{\delta j} \right] \right) \left[\begin{matrix} \Delta i \\ \Delta j \end{matrix} \right] \right)$$

$$SSD_W(\Delta i, \Delta j) = \left[\Delta i \quad \Delta j \right] \left(\sum_{(i,j)\in W} \left[\begin{matrix} \frac{\delta f(i,j)}{\delta i} \\ \frac{\delta f(i,j)}{\delta j} \end{matrix} \right] \left[\frac{\delta f(i,j)}{\delta i} \quad \frac{\delta f(i,j)}{\delta j} \right] \right) \left[\begin{matrix} \Delta i \\ \Delta j \end{matrix} \right]$$

$$SSD_W(\Delta i, \Delta j) = \left[\Delta i \quad \Delta j \right] \left[\begin{matrix} \sum_{(i,j)\in W} \left(\frac{\delta f(i,j)}{\delta i} \right)^2 & \sum_{(i,j)\in W} \frac{\delta f(i,j)}{\delta i} \frac{\delta f(i,j)}{\delta j} \\ \sum_{(i,j)\in W} \frac{\delta f(i,j)}{\delta i} \frac{\delta f(i,j)}{\delta j} & \sum_{(i,j)\in W} \left(\frac{\delta f(i,j)}{\delta j} \right)^2 \end{matrix} \right] \left[\begin{matrix} \Delta i \\ \Delta j \end{matrix} \right] \quad (7.4)$$

This matrix equation then allows the computation of the eigenvalues (λ_1, λ_2) of the central matrix. If both eigenvalues are high then we have a corner (changes in both directions). If only one is high then we have an edge, and otherwise we have a reasonably constant region. Based on this, Harris and Stephens proposed the following cornerness measure:

$$C(i,j) = \det(M) - k(trace(M))^2 \quad (7.5)$$

where k is a constant empirically determined to be in the range 0.04 to 0.06 and

$$M = \left[\begin{matrix} \sum_{(i,j)\in W} \left(\frac{\delta f(i,j)}{\delta i} \right)^2 & \sum_{(i,j)\in W} \frac{\delta f(i,j)}{\delta i} \frac{\delta f(i,j)}{\delta j} \\ \sum_{(i,j)\in W} \frac{\delta f(i,j)}{\delta i} \frac{\delta f(i,j)}{\delta j} & \sum_{(i,j)\in W} \left(\frac{\delta f(i,j)}{\delta j} \right)^2 \end{matrix} \right] = \left[\begin{matrix} A & B \\ B & C \end{matrix} \right] \quad (7.6)$$

$$\det(M) = \lambda_1 \lambda_2 = AC + B^2$$

$$\text{trace}(M) = \lambda_1 + \lambda_2 = A + C$$

The summation over the image patch W is actually weighted in order to put more weight on measurements that are made closer to the centre of the window. It is calculated using the Gaussian function. For example, for a 3x3 window the weights are shown in Figure 7.6.

Sample results from the Harris corner detector are shown in Figure 7.5 and Figure 7.7. The Harris corner detector is significantly more expensive computationally than the Moravec

0.04	0.12	0.04
0.12	0.36	0.12
0.04	0.12	0.04

Figure 7.6   Gaussian weights for a 3×3 window as used in the Harris corner detector

corner detector. It is also quite sensitive to noise and does have somewhat of an anisotropic response (i.e. the response changes depending on the orientation). For all this, the Harris detector is one of the most commonly used corner detectors – mainly due to two factors. It has a very repeatable response, and it has a better detection rate (i.e. taking into account true positives, false positives, true negatives and false negatives) than the Moravec detector.

In OpenCV, to efficiently determine Harris corners we use a `GoodFeaturesToTrackDe-tector` *(note it can be done using* `FeatureDetector` *but that implementation seems significantly slower). Note that this can only process grey-scale images:*

```
GoodFeaturesToTrackDetector harris_detector( 1000, 0.01, 10, 3, true );
vector<KeyPoint> keypoints;
cvtColor( image, gray_image, CV_BGR2GRAY );
harris_detector.detect( gray_image, keypoints );
```

To draw the keypoints (in red) on the original colour image:

```
Mat display_image;
drawKeypoints( image, keypoints, display_image, Scalar( 0, 0, 255 ) );
```

Figure 7.7   The Harris/Plessy corner detector. The grey-scale image (left) was processed to obtain the cornerness map (centre) which in turn was analysed to extract the corners (right)

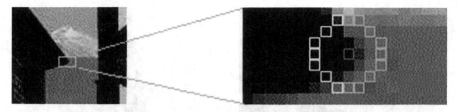

Figure 7.8 The FAST corner detector. The pixels highlighted in yellow and blue are those considered when evaluating whether the centre pixel highlighted in red is a corner pixel. A contiguous arc of 9 of these points (such as that shown in blue) must be found which are all brighter (or all darker) than the centre point

7.3 FAST Corner Detection

The FAST (Features from Accelerated Segment Test) corner detector was developed by Rosten et al. (Rosten, 2006). This detector is somewhat different from the preceding ones as it does not compute a cornerness metric. Instead it looks at a circle of points (normally of radius 3, mapping to 16 pixels) around the current pixel being considered. The current pixel p is a corner if there is a contiguous arc of at least 9 pixels around the circle which are all brighter or all darker than the nucleus (the current point or an average of the current point and its close neighbours) by some predefined threshold t. The value 9 is chosen to exclude edges and has been shown to give the best results, although it should be clear that some false responses will be generated at such a level. In fact a value of 12 was suggested in the original work. See Figure 7.8.

As the FAST detector does not compute a cornerness response, in order to be able to use non-maxima suppression (to ensure only a single response per corner), the corner strength is defined as the maximum of value of the threshold t which classifies p as a corner.

The FAST detector, as its name suggests, is much faster than the other detectors. In comparison to some of the other detectors in this chapter (as implemented in OpenCV), Harris was around 5–10 times slower while SIFT (see Section 7.4) was around 50 times slower. See Figure 7.9 for sample FAST images features.

In OpenCV, to locate FAST corners we make use of the `FeatureDetector` *class which provides a common interface for most feature detectors in OpenCV:*

```
Ptr<FeatureDetector> feature_detector =
                    FeatureDetector::create("FAST");
vector<KeyPoint> keypoints;
cvtColor( image, gray_image, CV_BGR2GRAY );
feature_detector->detect( gray_image, keypoints );
```

However, an implementation which is around 5 times faster is available by using the `FASTX` *routine:*

```
FASTX( gray_image, keypoints, 50, true,
                    FastFeatureDetector::TYPE_9_16 );
```

Figure 7.9   Sample FAST image features

7.4   SIFT

SIFT (or Scale Invariant Feature Transform) was developed by David Lowe (Lowe, 2004) in order to provide repeatable and robust features for tracking, recognition, panorama stitching, and so on. Most impressively it is invariant to scaling and rotation and partly invariant to illumination and viewpoint changes. When contrasted with typical corner detectors (such as Moravec, Harris and FAST) it represents a significant step forward (see Figure 7.10).

Figure 7.10   Sample SIFT image features

SIFT features are extracted in a number of stages which we will consider in the sections that follow:

1. Scale space extrema detection.
2. Accurate keypoint location.
3. Keypoint orientation assignment.
4. Keypoint descriptors.

In addition, we require the ability to match features (from image to image), including identifying and dropping any matches which are ambiguous.

7.4.1   Scale Space Extrema Detection

In order to provide features which are invariant to the scale of the object viewed, the image is considered at a number of scales simultaneously and extrema (maxima or minima) are located within these scaled images. To achieve this, the image is convolved with a number of Gaussians $L_n(i, j, k, \sigma) = G(i, j, k^n \sigma)^* f(i, j)$ where $n = 0, 1, 2, 3, \ldots$ See Figure 7.11. In addition, this is done in a number of octaves of scale space where each octave corresponds to a doubling of the standard deviation (σ).

To find potential stable keypoint locations we then consider the Difference of Gaussian (DoG) functions across the various scale spaces (i.e. $D_n(i, j, k, \sigma) = L_{n+1}(i, j, k, \sigma) - L_n(i, j, k, \sigma)$). See Figure 7.12.

Figure 7.11   Scale images considered in the determination of SIFT features. Three octaves of scale space are shown where each octave corresponds to a doubling of the standard deviation (σ) which is applied to the left most image. The images in each octave are convolved with a number of Gaussians $\mathbf{L_n}(\mathbf{i}, \mathbf{j}, \mathbf{k}, \sigma) = \mathbf{G}(\mathbf{i}, \mathbf{j}, \mathbf{k^n}\sigma)^* \mathbf{f}(\mathbf{i}, \mathbf{j})$ where $\mathbf{n} = 0, 1, 2, 3, \ldots$

Figure 7.12 Difference for Gaussian images (bottom) derived from the various Gaussian smoothed images shown above

---

In OpenCV, to locate SIFT features we can again make use of the `FeatureDetector` *class:*

```
Ptr<FeatureDetector> feature_detector =
                    FeatureDetector::create("SIFT");
vector<KeyPoint> keypoints;
cvtColor( image, gray_image, CV_BGR2GRAY );
feature_detector->detect( gray_image, keypoints );
```

To then find extrema, we consider multiple DoG images and locate points which are greater (or less) than all their neighbours both in the current scale and in the neighbouring scales (higher and lower). See Figure 7.13.

7.4.2 Accurate Keypoint Location

Originally the location and scale were taken from central point, but it was determined that this was inaccurate, and so in order to locate keypoints more precisely the data is modelled locally using a 3D quadratic and the interpolated maximum/minimum can then be found.

In addition it was determined that many of the located keypoints were not sufficiently robust, so two tests are performed to select more reliable keypoints. The first test considers the local contrast in the area around the keypoint, by simply checking the curvature of the quadratic at

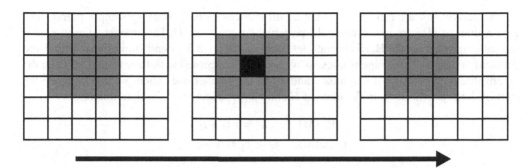

Figure 7.13 Consider an image at three different scales. If we consider the black point in the centre image it must either be greater than (or less than) all of the neighbours in that image and all of neighbours in the higher and lower scale images. That is, the black point must be compared with all the grey points before it can be declared an extrema

the keypoint. If the curvature is low then this indicates that the contrast is low and hence the keypoint should be discarded. See Figure 7.14.

The second test which is performed is to check the localisation of the keypoint (e.g. whether it is on an edge rather than at a distinguishable feature). A poorly defined peak (i.e. a ridge) in the difference-of-Gaussian function will have a large principal curvature across the edge but a small one in the perpendicular direction. The principal curvatures can be computed from a 2x2 Hessian matrix, H, computed at the location and scale of the keypoint:

$$H = \begin{bmatrix} A & B \\ B & C \end{bmatrix} = \begin{bmatrix} \displaystyle\sum_{(i,j) \in W} \frac{\delta^2 D_n(i,j,k,\sigma)}{\delta i^2} & \displaystyle\sum_{(i,j) \in W} \frac{\delta D_n(i,j,k,\sigma)}{\delta i} \frac{\delta D_n(i,j,k,\sigma)}{\delta j} \\ \displaystyle\sum_{(i,j) \in W} \frac{\delta D_n(i,j,k,\sigma)}{\delta i} \frac{\delta D_n(i,j,k,\sigma)}{\delta j} & \displaystyle\sum_{(i,j) \in W} \frac{\delta^2 D_n(i,j,k,\sigma)}{\delta j^2} \end{bmatrix}$$

$$(7.7)$$

Figure 7.14 Scale invariant keypoints (left), after discarding low contrast keypoints (centre) and after discarding poorly localized keypoints (right)

The derivatives are estimated by taking differences of neighbouring sample points. The eigenvalues of H are proportional to the principal curvatures of D. This mathematics is similar to that employed by the Harris corner detector (see Section 7.2) and similarly we can avoid explicitly computing the eigenvalues, as we are only concerned with their ratio. Let λ_1 be the eigenvalue with the largest magnitude and λ_2 be the smaller one. Then, we can compute the sum of the eigenvalues from the trace of H and their product from the determinant.

$$\det(M) = \lambda_1 \lambda_2 = AC + B^2$$
$$\text{trace}(M) = \lambda_1 + \lambda_2 = A + C$$

We let r be the ratio between the largest magnitude eigenvalue and the smaller one, so that $\lambda_1 = r\lambda_2$. r depends only on the ratio of the eigenvalues rather than their individual values. If we consider the trace squared, divided by the determinant, we can determine that this is equivalent to $(r+1)^2/r$:

$$\frac{trace(H)^2}{\det(H)} = \frac{\left(\lambda_1 + \lambda_2\right)^2}{\lambda_1 \lambda_2} = \frac{\left(r\lambda_2 + \lambda_2\right)^2}{r\lambda_2^2} = \frac{(r+1)^2}{r} \tag{7.8}$$

This value is at a mimimum when the two eigenvalues are equal and increases with r. As we have already discarded keypoints with low curvature we need only now consider the ratio of the curvature and ensure that the ratio is below some fixed (threshold) value of r (T_r):

$$Tr(H)^2 \big/ Det(H) < (T_r + 1)^2 \big/ T_r \tag{7.9}$$

All features not satisfying this test are discarded. See Figure 7.14 and in particular note the removal (in the rightmost image) of a large number of features along some of the vertical edges.

7.4.3   Keypoint Orientation Assignment

We have now effectively located scale invariant features in the image. However, we also need to make the features rotation invariant. To do this we assign each feature a specific (principal) orientation. The scale of the keypoint is used to select the Gaussian smoothed image, L_n, with the closest scale, so that all computations are performed in a scale-invariant manner. For each image sample, $L_n(i,j,k,\sigma)$, at this scale, the gradient magnitude, $\nabla f(i,j)$, and orientation, $\phi(i,j)$, is computed:

$$\nabla f(i,j) = \sqrt{\left(L_n(i+1,j,k,\sigma) - L_n(i-1,j,k,\sigma)\right)^2 + \left(L_n(i,j+1,k,\sigma) - L_n(i,j-1,k,\sigma)\right)^2}$$
$$\phi(i,j) = \arctan\left(\left(L_n(i+1,j,k,\sigma) - L_n(i-1,j,k,\sigma)\right)^2, \left(L_n(i,j+1,k,\sigma) - L_n(i,j-1,k,\sigma)\right)^2\right)$$
$$\tag{7.10}$$

An orientation histogram with 36 bins each representing $10°$ is formed from the orientations of points within a region around the keypoint. Each point added to the histogram is weighted by its gradient magnitude and by a Gaussian weight defined by the distance to the keypoint location.

Peaks in this histogram correspond to the principal directions of the gradients around the keypoint and the highest peak is used to define the keypoint orientation. Note that if there are any further peaks which have values within 80% of the highest peak value, then further keypoints are created (which different orientations). Only around 15% of keypoints are typically assigned multiple orientations.

7.4.4   Keypoint Descriptor

The final step in extracting a keypoint is to describe the region around the keypoint so that it can be compared with other keypoints. Again we use the blurred image at the closest scale, sampling points around the keypoint and computing their gradients and orientations. We rotate the image by the keypoint orientation (so that the orientations are normalised with respect to the keypoint orientation). The region around the keypoint is divided into four subregions and a weighted histogram of the orientations (weighted by gradient and location as before) is determined for each of the subregions. The orientations are mapped into the relevant bins and also into all adjoining bins in order to reduce problems relating to quantisation.

7.4.5   Matching Keypoints

To locate a match for a keypoint k we must compare the keypoint descriptor with those in a database. The best matching keypoint can be defined as the being the one with the smallest Euclidean distance to the keypoint k (treating the descriptors as 32 dimensional vectors). In this manner all keypoints will be matched, but we must distinguish matching keypoints from those which have no match in the database. One possibility is to use a global threshold on the Euclidean distance, but this does not prove very useful as some descriptors are more discriminative than others (i.e. some will be very different from all others while some may have several close matches). Instead it was found that it was best to consider the ratio of the smallest Euclidean distance to that of the second smallest Euclidean distance and discard any keypoint matches for which this ratio exceeds 0.8. Experimentally this was found to eliminate 90% of false matches and to exclude only 5% of correct matches.

7.4.6   Recognition

In order to recognise objects (which may be partly or highly occluded) we need to minimise the number of features which we use. Lowe found that as few as three features were sufficient (out of the typical 2000 or more features in each image). In order to find matches where the percentage of correct matches (of the 2000 features) will be low, the Hough transform can be used in pose space (which is four dimensional – two dimensions for location, and the other two dimensions for scale and orientation). This is only an approximation to the full six degree of freedom solution and does not account for any non-rigid deformations. Hence, broad bin sizes of a quarter of the maximum image dimension for location, a factor of 2 for scale, and 30 degrees for orientation are used. To avoid boundary effects in assigning keypoints to bins, each keypoint match puts votes in the two closest bins in each dimension giving 16 entries for each keypoint match.

To locate any match we consider all bins with at least three entries and then define an affine transformation between the model and the image. See Figure 7.15 and Figure 7.16 for examples of matching and recognition.

Figure 7.15 SIFT based matching example. The matches shown between these two parts of two frames from the PETS 2000 video surveillance dataset show (a) some correct matches between the unmoving parts of the background, (b) some correct matches between the features on the moving cars and (c) many incorrect matches. However, it is possible to group the matches together and hence it may still be possible to determine the motion of the car in the scene. The original images are reproduced by permission of Dr. James Ferryman, University of Reading

Figure 7.16 SIFT-based object recognition example, using an image of YIELD sign segmented from its background and comparing it with ten other real road sign images. Many of the matches are between the two YIELD signs and some of these appear to be correct

Figure 7.17 Harris features (centre) and minimum eigenvalue features (right) as derived from the grey-scale image on the left

In OpenCV, to match SIFT features we locate them, extract feature descriptors, match the descriptors and display the matches:

```
SiftFeatureDetector sift_detector;
vector<KeyPoint> keypoints1, keypoints2;
sift_detector.detect( gray_image1, keypoints1 );
sift_detector.detect( gray_image2, keypoints2 );
// Extract feature descriptors
SiftDescriptorExtractor sift_extractor;
Mat descriptors1, descriptors2;
sift_extractor.compute( gray_image1, keypoints1, descriptors1 );
sift_extractor.compute( gray_image2, keypoints2, descriptors2 );
// Match descriptors.
BFMatcher sift_matcher(NORM_L2 );
vector< DMatch> matches;
matcher.match( descriptors1, descriptors2, matches );
// Display SIFT matches
Mat display_image;
drawMatches( gray_image1, keypoints1, gray_image2,
                        keypoints2, matches, display_image );
```

7.5   Other Detectors

There are many other feature/corner detectors (several of which are supported by OpenCV). Two deserve at least a comment in this text:

Figure 7.18   SIFT features (centre) and SURF features (right) as derived from the grey-scale image on the left

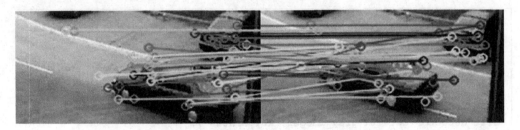

Figure 7.19   SURF-based matching example (similar to the SIFT matching example shown in Figure 7.15). The matches shown between these two parts of two frames from the PETS 2000 video surveillance dataset show (a) some correct matches between the unmoving parts of the background, (b) some correct matches between the features on the moving cars and (c) many incorrect matches. However, it is possible to group the matches together and hence it may still be possible to determine the motion of the car in the scene. The original images are reproduced by permission of Dr. James Ferryman, University of Reading

7.5.1   Minimum Eigenvalues

Similar to the Harris detector, it is possible to just use the minimum eigenvalue at any point as a measure of the feature strength. This is around 25% slower than Harris (as implemented in OpenCV), and returns quite a few extra features (with the same parameter settings). See Figure 7.17.

7.5.2   SURF

A very commonly used feature detector is SURF (Speeded Up Robust Features) (Bay, Ess, Tuytelaars, & Van Gool, 2008) which was inspired by SIFT and was intended to be much faster and more robust. As more efficient versions of these techniques have been developed, SIFT seems to be winning in terms of speed. However, many researchers seem to prefer SURF. SURF is around 35% slower than SIFT (as implemented in OpenCV), and returns quite a few extra features (with the same parameter setting). See Figure 7.18 and Figure 7.19.

8

Recognition

Towards the end of the previous chapter, one of the feature detectors (SIFT) allowed us to recognise objects in images through the comparison of features from a known instance of an object (or objects) and a scene which might (or might not) contain the object(s) in question. This topic of recognition (Cyganek, 2013) is central to most advanced computer vision systems. For example, we may want to

1. distinguish different types of object (e.g. people vs. cars vs. bicycles);
2. recognise specific individuals;
3. automatically read the license plate of a car;
4. locate specific objects to be manipulated by a robot;
5. recognise a page of a book, or a specific painting, or building, and so on, so that we can augment reality in some way;
6. locate eyes so that we can track them to provide advanced user interfaces;
7. classify objects (such as chocolates on a production line) so that a robot can pick them up and place them in the correct location.

This chapter continues this topic and presents a number of different ways of recognising objects. These are appropriate in different situations and are only a small sample of the wide range of techniques which have been presented in the computer vision literature. This chapter concludes with an introduction to the area of performance assessment.

8.1 Template Matching

Template matching (Brunelli, 2009) is very simply a technique where a sub-image is searched for within an image. The sub-image represents some object of interest – which is effectively 2D.

8.1.1 Applications

Template matching may be used for searching for objects such as the windows shown in Figure 8.1. Note that while the two templates are taken from the original image (they were

A Practical Introduction to Computer Vision with OpenCV, First Edition. Kenneth Dawson-Howe.
© 2014 John Wiley & Sons, Ltd. Published 2014 by John Wiley & Sons, Ltd.

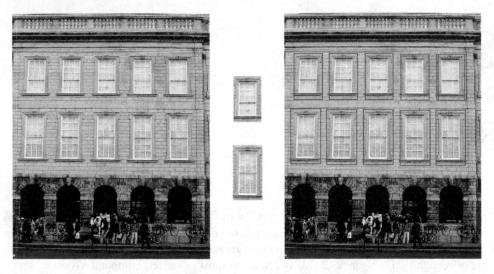

Figure 8.1 An image of a number of windows (left), two window templates (centre), and the located instances of the templates in the image (right). Notice that the upper right window has been located twice

the centre windows), there is quite a bit of variation in the appearance of the windows as the image is narrower at the top due to perspective projection.

Template matching can be used for some recognition applications (e.g. see Figure 8.2) but in this case that recognition is being performed by direct comparison to an image and hence there must not be too much difference between the images. In the license plate recognition example in Figure 8.2 the recognition fails in a few circumstances:

- where the image quality is poor;
- where the font of the characters are different from those in the templates (e.g. the 3 in the third example in Figure 8.2);
- where the characters have not been included as templates – for example only numbers are represented in the template set; letters have been omitted.

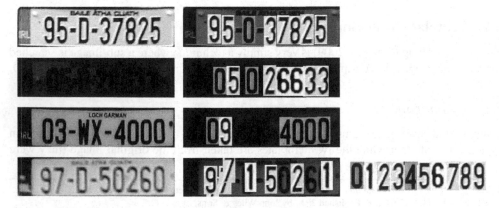

Figure 8.2 Recognition of license plates (original images are on the left, images with recognised characters overlaid are in the middle, and the templates used are on the right)

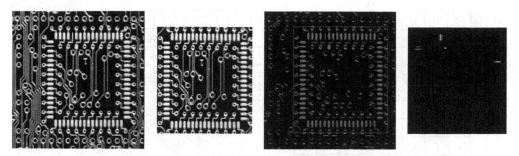

Figure 8.3 Golden template matching. Image of PCB under test (left), golden template image of PCB section (centre left), located template (centre right), and the difference between template and image (right)

There is a common use of template matching in industrial vision referred to as golden template matching. In this usage, a template image of the perfect item (the golden template) is provided, and that template is then compared to all other items presented for inspection. After aligning the golden template with the image, it is usual for a difference image to then be computed and analysed in order to determine if there are any issues. Note that the confidence level of the template match is not sufficient to achieve this as it evaluates global similarity (rather than identifying any local problems). In the example in Figure 8.3 the global confidence was 99% and yet there are clearly some problems with the PCB being inspected.

Template matching has been used quite widely; for example, in stereo vision (where we are trying to determine how far away objects are on the basis of a stereo pair of images) correspondences are sought from one image to the other using very small sub-images; and in tracking of moving objects, where we can typically assume that the appearance of an object being tracked will change slowly from frame to frame and again can use small templates on the moving object.

8.1.2 Template Matching Algorithm

The inputs to template matching are an image (in which we want to search) and an object (generally a smaller 'template' image containing a picture of whatever we are searching for).

Algorithm 8.1

> For every possible position (i, j) of the object in the image
> Evaluate a matching metric and store it in a matching space: $M(i, j)$
> Search for local maxima (or minima) in the matching space above a threshold (T):
>
> $(M(i, j) > T)$ AND $(M(i, j) \geq M(i - 1, j - 1))$ AND $(M(i, j) \geq M(i - 1, j))$ AND
> $(M(i, j) \geq M(i - 1, j + 1))$ AND $(M(i, j) \geq M(i, j - 1))$ AND
> $(M(i, j) \geq M(i, j + 1))$ AND $(M(i, j) \geq M(i + 1, j - 1))$ AND
> $(M(i, j) \geq M(i + 1, j))$ AND $(M(i, j) \geq M(i + 1, j + 1))$

The comparisons (i.e. the values returned by the matching metric) of the template and the image are stored in a matching space which is another array of values (one for every possible

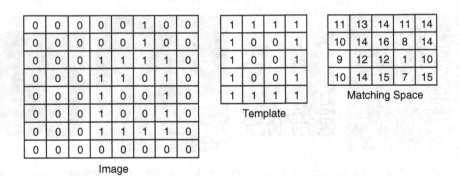

Figure 8.4 A binary image and a binary template compared using the sum of the squared differences. The best match between the template and the image is towards the bottom right of the matching space where a matching score of 1 was obtained. Note that the comparison is only made where the template fits completely within the image and hence the matching space is smaller than the image

position). The matching space will be smaller than the image as the template can only be moved to locations where it is completely within the image. See Figure 8.4. The search for local maxima is done within the matching space. A local maxima within an array is a location in the array where all neighbouring locations have values that are less than or equal to the centre value. Typically, the local maxima must be above some threshold. However, set the threshold too high and you miss some objects, but make it too low and you get false positives.

Also note that 'every possible position' may mean every location (which is a 2D search in image space) AND every possible rotation of the object (which adds another dimension) AND every possible scale of the object (which again adds another dimension). In other words, to apply this operation for an object whose rotation and scale are not known would result in a four dimensional search and matching space. This explosion in degrees of freedom can make the computational complexity get out of hand. Generally we try to restrict these degrees of freedom (e.g. by normalising the size and orientation of characters in character recognition).

The 'matching criterion' (or degree-of-fit) needs to be defined. This criterion may have to deal with problems of noise, partial occlusion, geometric distortion, etc., so an exact match cannot always be expected.

8.1.3 Matching Metrics

To evaluate the difference between the two images (an image in which to search $f(i, j)$ and a template image $t(m, n)$) we can compute the sum of the squared differences between the corresponding pixels, and we can normalise this measure (noting that the closer to 0.0 the better the match):

$$D_{\text{SquareDifferences}}(i,j) = \sum_{(m,n)} (f(i+m, j+n) - t(m,n))^2 \tag{8.1}$$

$$D_{\text{NormalisedSquareDifferences}}(i,j) = \frac{\sum_{(m,n)}(f(i+m, j+n) - t(m,n))^2}{\sqrt{\sum_{(m,n)} f(i+m, j+n)^2 \sum_{(m,n)} t(m,n)^2}} \tag{8.2}$$

We can also extend the idea of Euclidean distance to the notion of distance between the two images, where the number of dimensions is the number of image points being compared. This similarity is measured using the cross correlation or normalised cross correlation:

$$D_{\text{CrossCorrelation}}(i,j) = \sum_{(m,n)} f(i+m, j+n) \cdot t(m,n) \tag{8.3}$$

$$D_{\text{NormalisedCrossCorrelation}}(i,j) = \frac{\sum_{(m,n)} f(i+m, j+n) \cdot t(m,n)}{\sqrt{\sum_{(m,n)} f(i+m, j+n)^2 \sum_{(m,n)} t(m,n)^2}} \tag{8.4}$$

For both of these metrics, the higher the score the better, and in the case of normalised cross-correlation the score ranges from 0.0 to 1.0 (a perfect match). Interestingly, normalised cross-correlation is also invariant to overall lumination (i.e. the same correlation will be returned even if the brightness in the image and template are different), which is quite helpful when matching images.

Note that when using the sum of squared differences or the normalised sum of squared differenced as the degree-of-fit, it is necessary to search for minima, whereas when using cross-correlation or normalised cross-correlation it is necessary to search for local maxima.

To illustrate the matching criteria and the overall technique, a simple illustration is provided in Figure 8.4.

The example in Figure 8.4 raises the question as to what we should do at the boundaries, and in this case (as in many such situations) we have chosen not to compute a degree-of-fit. We could have computed the degree-of-fit based on those points which overlapped between the image and the template, but this calculation would not be consistent with the neighboring calculations and hence might result in strange effects when evaluating the local minima.

In OpenCV, template matching is supported using normalised cross-correlation `CV_TM_CCORR_NORMED` *(although other measures are also supported, such as cross-correlation* `CV_TM_CCORR`, *sum of the squared differences* `CV_TM_SQDIFF` *and the normalised sum of the squared differences* `CV_TM_SQDIFF_NORMED`*):*

```
Mat matching_space;
matching_space.create(
     search_image.cols-template_image.cols+1,
     search_image.rows-template_image.rows+1, CV_32FC1 );
matchTemplate( search_image, template_image,
               matching_space, CV_TM_CCORR_NORMED );
```

8.1.4   Finding Local Maxima or Minima

When processing first derivative gradient images, we had to suppress all gradient points which were not local maxima along some edge (see Section 6.1.1.5). In this recognition technique (and in many others) we need to locate local maxima (or minima) within a matching space (i.e. within a 2D array of the matching scores). The simplest form of non-maxima suppression in this case is to compare each value to the values of the eight neighbouring positions, and to only retain values that are greater than or equal to values of all their neighbours.

It is often necessary to ensure that matches are not too close together (as typically these will represent multiple responses from the same matching object) and in this case we can simply increase the number of neighbours that we compare the current point with.

While we could write a logical test for the identification of maxima as described, it is simpler to perform a grey-scale dilation on the matching space and then simply locate any points whose values have not changed and which are above some threshold as the local maxima of interest. In this case the size of the dilation constrains the minimum distance between maxima. See Figure 8.5.

In OpenCV, to find the local maxima in the correlation image (`correlation`) we perform a grey-scale dilation and look for pixels with unchanged values. We then remove any local maxima whose correlation value is too low (below some threshold):

```
Mat dilated, thresholded_matching_space, local_maxima,
                                    thresholded_8bit;
dilate( matching_space, dilated, Mat());
compare( matching_space, dilated, local_maxima, CMP_EQ );
threshold( matching_space, thresholded_matching_space,
                    threshold, 255, THRESH_BINARY );
thresholded_matching_space.convertTo( thresholded_8bit, CV_8U );
bitwise_and( local_maxima,thresholded_8bit,local_maxima );
```

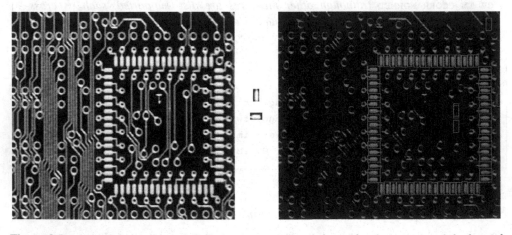

Figure 8.5 A printed circuit board (left), two very small templates of pads (centre) and the located templates (right). The matching was performed using normalised cross-correlation

8.1.5   Control Strategies for Matching

Template matching is a very expensive operation from a computational viewpoint and hence it has made those who have used it consider carefully how it can be implemented efficiently.

We are attempting to localise close copies of a template within an image. The size (scale) and orientation must match and the geometric distortion within the image must be small.

One useful general approach to vision is process images in an image hierarchy (low resolution to high resolution). By processing the low resolution images first we can in effect restrict processing at higher resolutions. In the case of template matching, it is possible to analyse the template to determine the appropriate lowest resolution (this depends on the level of detail in the template) and then after computing the matching criteria at low resolution we can threshold this to identify locations which should be considered at higher resolution in order to locate precise matches.

In fact, we can take this notion further and use the degrees-of-fit from the lower resolution to indicate the likelihood of matching in the higher resolution. Hence we could search the highest probability locations first and stop as soon as we find a strong enough match (assuming we are only searching for one item). Taking this approach means that there is a possibility that valid matches will be missed, as we may find a reasonable match based on a high probability location and then not look any further.

Both of these ideas (looking in high probability locations first, and terminating the search early) are common techniques in the attempt to make operations, such as template matching, more efficient.

8.2   Chamfer Matching

One problem that template matching has is that it is very dependent on the appearance of the object of interest being almost the same (ignoring overall lumination) in the template as in the search image. Any distortion of this appearance can have quite a significant impact on the matching score obtained.

One technique, based on the idea of template matching, which overcomes this problem (to some extent) is chamfer matching (Borgefors, 1988). Before explaining the matching algorithm (Section 8.2.2) we first introduce chamfering (Section 8.2.1).

8.2.1   Chamfering Algorithm

The chamfer value for a pixel is the distance from that pixel to the nearest object (or in this case, edge) point. It would be possible to compute this for every point in the scene by searching from each point for the nearest object point. However, this would be very expensive computationally, so a more efficient two-pass operation has been developed. The first pass (which looks at all points in the image from top to bottom, and left to right) considers points AL (Above and to the Left; See Figure 8.6) of the current point (i,j) while the second pass (which looks at the image from bottom to top, and right to left) considers points BR (Bottom and to the Right; See Figure 8.6). See Figure 8.7 for an example of the two pass algorithm in action.

Figure 8.6   The points relative to the current point (shown by a cross in both masks) in set AL (Above and to the Left of the current point) and in set BR (Bottom and to the Right of the current point)

In OpenCV, to compute a chamfer image from a binary edge image we must invert the edge image so that edges are zero points (for the sake of the `distanceTransform` *routine):*

```
Canny( gray_image, edge_image, 100, 200, 3);
threshold( edge_image, edge_image, 127, 255, THRESH_BINARY_INV );
distanceTransform( edge_image, chamfer_image, CV_DIST_L2, 3);
```

Algorithm 8.2

Algorithm 8.2 to compute chamfered image $c(i,j)$ from a binary edge image $b(i,j)$:

>For every point
>>If ($b(i,j)$ is an edge point)
>>>Set $c(i, j) = 0$
>>Else Set $c(i, j) = \infty$
>For j = min to max
>>For i = min to max
>>>$c(i, j) = \min_{q \in AL} [\text{distance}((i, j), q) + f(q)]$
>For j = max to min
>>For i = max to min
>>>$c(i, j) = \min_{q \in BR} [\text{distance}((i, j), q) + f(q)]$

∞	∞	∞	∞	∞	0	∞	∞	∞	∞	∞	∞	∞	0	1	2	3.8	2.8	2.4	2	1	0	1	2
∞	∞	∞	∞	∞	0	∞	∞	∞	∞	∞	∞	1.4	0	1	1.4	3.4	2.4	1.4	1	1	0	1	1.4
∞	∞	∞	0	0	0	0	∞	∞	∞	∞	0	0	0	0	1	3	2	1	0	0	0	0	1
∞	∞	∞	0	0	∞	0	∞	∞	∞	∞	0	0	1	0	1	3	2	1	0	0	1	0	1
∞	∞	∞	0	∞	∞	0	∞	∞	∞	∞	0	1	1.4	0	1	3	2	1	0	1	1	0	1
∞	∞	∞	0	∞	∞	0	∞	∞	∞	∞	0	1	1.4	0	1	3	2	1	0	1	1	0	1
∞	∞	∞	0	0	0	0	∞	∞	∞	∞	0	0	0	0	1	3	2	1	0	0	0	0	1
∞	∞	∞	∞	∞	∞	∞	∞	∞	∞	∞	1	1	1	1	1.4	3.4	2.4	1.4	1	1	1	1	1.4

     Object pixels (zeros)   After the first stage of processing   Chamfer Image

Figure 8.7   Example of the chamfering algorithm, (left) after initialization, (centre) after the first (AL) pass and (right) after the second (BR) pass

3.8	2.8	2.4	2	1	0	1	2
3.4	2.4	1.4	1	1	0	1	1.4
3	2	1	0	0	0	0	1
3	2	1	0	0	1	0	1
3	2	1	0	1	1	0	1
3	2	1	0	1	1	0	1
3	2	1	0	0	0	0	1
3.4	2.4	1.4	1	1	1	1	1.4

Chamfer Image

1	1	1	1
1			1
1			1
1			1
1	1	1	1

Template

27.4	19.6	12.8	8	27.4
23.2	16.8	10.4	5	9.4
21	14	8	0	6
23.2	16.8	10.4	5	9.4

Matching Space

Figure 8.8 Example of chamfer matching. The template (where the object pixels are marked with a 1) is evaluated, by summing the chamfer values corresponding to the object pixels, in every possible position in the chamfer image (such that it fits within the image). For example, the matching score of 27.4 was computed when the template was compared with the chamfer image in the top left corner. The best match is where the score of 0 was computed

8.2.2 Chamfer Matching Algorithm

Chamfer matching is typically used to compare binary edge images (although any binary image will suffice). The template in chamfer matching is a binary template in which only the object pixels (those set to any value greater than or equal to 1) are considered. This template is compared in every possible location (in the same way that template matching works), but the matching metric in this case is a sum of the chamfer values (derived from the image in which we are searching for the object) corresponding to the object pixels in the template. See Figure 8.8. An example application is shown in Figure 8.9.

In OpenCV, to perform chamfer matching we must write our own routine:

```
void ChamferMatching( Mat& chamfer_image, Mat& model, Mat& matching_image )
{
  // Extract the model points (as they are sparse).
  vector<Point> model_points;
  int image_channels = model.channels();
  for (int model_row=0; (model_row < model.rows); model_row++)
  {
    uchar *curr_point = model.ptr<uchar>(model_row);
    for (int model_column=0; (model_column<model.cols); model_column++)
    {
      if (*curr_point > 0)
      {
        Point& new_point = Point(model_column,model_row);
```

```
          model_points.push_back(new_point);
        }
        curr_point += image_channels;
    }
}
int num_model_points = model_points.size();
image_channels = chamfer_image.channels();
// Try the model in every possible position
matching_image = Mat(chamfer_image.rows-model.rows+1,
                     chamfer_image.cols-model.cols+1, CV_32FC1);
for (int search_row=0; (search_row <=
                     chamfer_image.rows-model.rows); search_row++)
{
    float *output_point = matching_image.ptr<float>(search_row);
    for (int search_column=0; (search_column <=
                     chamfer_image.cols-model.cols); search_column++)
    {
        float matching_score = 0.0;
        for (int point_count=0; (point_count < num_model_points);
                                                        point_count++)
            matching_score += (float) *(chamfer_image.ptr<float>(
                model_points[point_count].y+search_row) + search_column +
                model_points[point_count].x*image_channels );
        *output_point = matching_score;
        output_point++;
    }
}
}
```

8.3 Statistical Pattern Recognition

If it is possible to segment individual objects/shapes from the rest of the scene, then we can attempt to use features derived from these objects/shapes in order to classify them. To do this we first need to learn what feature values are associated with each type of (known) object/shape. Having done this we should be able to classify unknown shapes based on the similarity of their features to those from the known objects/shapes.

This section describes a simple technique for performing this classification, commonly referred to as Statistical Pattern Recognition (Jain, Duin, and Mao, 2000). For example, see Figure 8.10 The section is broken into

- a brief review of the relevant probability theory;
- a description of some sample features which can be used; and
- the statistical pattern recognition technique itself.

Figure 8.9 Location of a bicycle in a video sequence using chamfer matching. The located bicycle is shown (top left) together with a thresholded edge image of the difference between the current image and the background (top right), a chamfered version of that image (bottom left) and the matching space where a local minimum is located which corresponds to the top left corner of located bicycle rectangle (bottom centre). Also shown (bottom right) is the template used for the bicycle

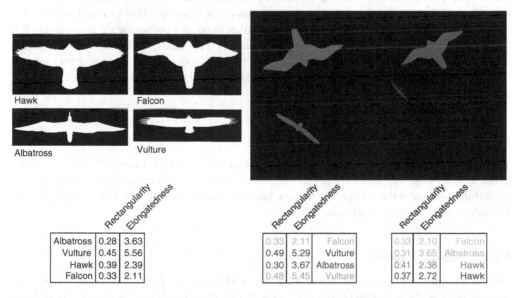

	Rectangularity	Elongatedness
Albatross	0.28	3.63
Vulture	0.45	5.56
Hawk	0.39	2.39
Falcon	0.33	2.11

Rectangularity	Elongatedness	
0.33	2.11	Falcon
0.49	5.29	Vulture
0.30	3.67	Albatross
0.48	5.45	Vulture

Rectangularity	Elongatedness	
0.33	2.10	Falcon
0.31	3.65	Albatross
0.41	2.38	Hawk
0.37	2.72	Hawk

Figure 8.10 Statistical pattern recognition of bird silhouettes (Albatross, Vulture, Hawk and Falcon) based on their rectangularity and elongatedness values. Unknown shapes/regions (the coloured shapes in the picture on the right hand side) are classified using a nearest neighbour classifier in two-dimensional feature space. On the bottom left the feature values computed from the samples on the top left are shown. On the bottom right the feature values computed from the regions in the image (top right) are shown along with their classification using a minimum distance classifier

8.3.1   Probability Review

The probability of an event A can be defined as $P(A) = lim_{n \to \infty} N(A)/n$ where $N(A)$ is the number of times that event A occurs in n trials. For example the probability that the number 5 is face up on a 6-sided dice (in the case of an unbiased dice) will be 1/6 but this figure will only be arrived at after many rolls of the dice.

If there are two events A and B then these events can either be independent (e.g. A = 'today is Thursday' and B = 'it is snowing') in which case the probability of both A and B occurring is:

$$P(AB) = P(A)P(B) \tag{8.5}$$

or can be dependent (e.g. A = 'it is raining' and B = 'there are clouds in the sky') in which case the likelihood of A is dependent on whether or not B has occurred:

$$P(AB) = P(A|B)P(B) \tag{8.6}$$

where $P(A|B)$ is referred to as the conditional probability of A occurring if B has occurred.

8.3.1.1   Probability Density Functions (PDFs)

From a point of view of statistical pattern recognition, we are interested in events such as whether an unknown object belongs to a class W_i in the presence of some evidence (features) x (e.g. the probability that an object/shape is a coin given a measure of its circularity). Through training we can determine the probability that a particular feature's value (x) will occur $p(x \mid W_i)$, by repeatedly computing the features for instances of the class W_i. This probability $p(x \mid W_i)$ is in effect a probability density function of the likelihood of a particular value occurring for that class. We can compute probability density functions for multiple classes. For example, if considering a feature x (e.g. circularity) when viewing objects of class W_1 (e.g. a nut) and W_2 (e.g. a washer) then we will be able to compute separate probability density functions for each class. See Figure 8.11.

8.3.1.2   *A priori* and *a posteriori* Probabilities

The probability $p(x \mid W_i)$ is the *a priori* probability that a feature value/vector x will occur given that an object of class W_i is viewed. We are often more interested in the *a posteriori* probability – what is the probability that we have located an object of class W_i if some feature value/vector x has been observed.

8.3.1.3   Bayes Theorem

We can compute the *a posteriori* probabilities from the *a priori* probabilities and the relative probabilities of the individual classes (i.e. how frequently each class of object occurs $p(W_i)$).

For two classes A and B the *a-posteriori* probability is:

$$P(B|A) = \frac{P(A|B)P(B)}{P(A)} \tag{8.7}$$

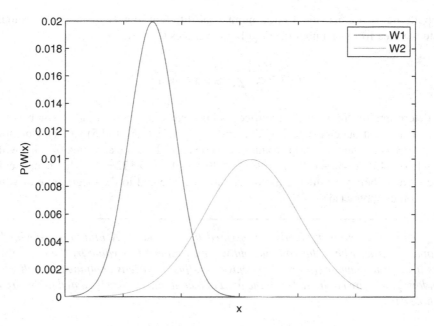

Figure 8.11 The probability density functions P(W|x) for two object classes (W$_1$ and W$_2$) for a single feature x. Note that the two classes are not separable (as their PDFs overlap for the feature) and hence (assuming that only this feature is being used) there will be some misclassification

Where there are multiple classes W_i, we use Bayes theorem:

$$p(W_i|x) = \frac{p(x|W_i)P(W_i)}{\sum_j p(x|W_j)P(W_j)} \quad (8.8)$$

When using this theorem to classify an unknown object, we select the class W_i with the largest value of $p(W_i|x)$. However, we must also ensure that the value of $p(x|W_i)$ is reasonable (above some minimum threshold value) in order to deal with the possibility that the object is unknown.

8.3.2 Sample Features

Statistical pattern recognition is based on the likelihood of occurrence of some features associated with shapes/objects. These features are frequently computed from the object shape characteristics (e.g. aspect ratio), but can equally be based on the colours in the object region, or measures describing the texture of the object, and so on. Here we describe a number of features based on object shape.

8.3.2.1 Area

Computing the area of a shape can be as simple as counting the number of pixels in the shape. Area has proved to be an important metric and vision researchers have developed algorithms to compute the area efficiently from a number of different representations. For example to compute the area from a number (n) of polygon vertices $(i_0, j_0) \dots (i_{n-1}, j_{n-1})$:

$$area = \frac{1}{2} \left| \sum_{k=0}^{n-1} (i_k j_{k+1} - i_{k+1} j_k) \right|$$

The determination from polygon vertices is interesting as it is so simple. The best way to explain it is to try it out on a square with coordinates (1,1), (1,5), (10,5), (10,1). Note that the list of vertices is assumed to wrap around (i.e. vertex n is the same as vertex 0). This will give ½ * | (5-1)+(5-45)+(5-50)+(10-1) | = ½ * | 4-40-45+9 | = ½ *72=36. What is happening is that each pair is being considered as two squares with regard to the origin (one of which is added the other subtracted).

In OpenCV, shapes are typically represented by 'contours'. A routine is provided to compute the area within the contour, but we must reduce this value by the area of any holes inside the contour (although we have to adjust the areas computed as half of the boundary pixels are not included in the area of a contour, and are included in the area of any holes!):

```
vector<vector<Point>> contours;
vector<Vec4i> hierarchy;
findContours( binary_image, contours, hierarchy,
                    CV_RETR_TREE, CV_CHAIN_APPROX_NONE);
for (int contour_number=0; (contour_number>=0);
            contour_number=hierarchy[contour_number][0])
{
   double area = contourArea(contours[contour_number]) +
                   contours[contour_number].size()/2 + 1;
   for (int hole_number=hierarchy[contour_number][2];
                   (hole_number>=0);
                   hole_number=hierarchy[hole_number][0])
     area -= ( contourArea(contours[hole_number]) -
                   contours[hole_number].size()/2 + 1 );
}
```

8.3.2.2   Elongatedness

Elongatedness (i.e. how long a shape is) can be defined as the ratio of the region area divided by the square of its thickness:

$$elongatedness = \frac{area}{(2d)^2}$$

Its thickness can be computed by erosion. In the formula shown d is the number of iterations of erosion before the region disappears completely.

Figure 8.12   The minimum bounding rectangle (centre in black) and the convex hull (right in black) for an arbitrary shape (left)

8.3.2.3   Length to Width Ratio for the Minimum Bounding Rectangle

The minimum bounding rectangle for a shape is the smallest rectangle which will encompass a shape. To determine this rectangle we can consider the minimum rectangle in all possible orientations (which actually means turning it through just one quadrant; i.e. 90°) and locating the smallest one. This search is more efficient than it sounds once the boundary points are determined, although there are other faster (but more complicated) ways of making this determination. See Figure 8.12.

The length to width ratio is just the length divided by the width of the rectangle and provides a useful metric to discriminate some shapes (e.g. it is used in the license plate recognition application to discriminate the number 1 from all other numbers; see Figure 8.19).

In OpenCV, to find the minimum bounding rectangle for a contour/binary region:

```
RotatedRect min_bounding_rectangle =
                minAreaRect(contours[contour_number]);
```

8.3.2.4   Convex Hull Area/Minimum Bounding Rectangle Area Ratio

The convex hull of a shape is the smallest convex shape which encompasses all points. See Figure 8.12. The convex hull can be determined using the following algorithm (see Figure 8.13 for an illustration):

Algorithm 8.3

1. Start with the topmost leftmost point on the boundary (START) and assume that the previous vector direction is horizontal towards the point from the left.
2. Search all other boundary points on the shape and find the point (NEW) with the least angle to previous vector.
3. Switch to the new point (NEW) and the vector from the previous point to NEW.
4. Go to 2 unless NEW == START.

Figure 8.13 Stages in the creation of the convex hull. The START point and the initial 'previous vector' are shown(left). Then, in each of the other drawings, the previous vector from the previous step is extended and the next point on the convex hull is located as that with the minimum angle to the previous vector

---

In OpenCV, to find the convex hull for all contours:

```
vector<vector<Point>> hulls(contours.size());
for (int contour_number=0;
        (contour_number<contours.size()); contour_number++)
{
    convexHull(contours[contour_number], hulls[contour_number]);
}
```

The area of the convex hull can then be calculated using the formula for area based on a list of polygon vertices (see Section 8.3.2.1). The area of the minimum bounding rectangle is simply the length times the width of the rectangle.

The ratio is simply the two areas divided. Again this provides a useful metric to discriminate some shapes (e.g. it is used in the license plate recognition application to discriminate the numbers 1, 4, and 7 from all other numbers; see Figure 8.19).

8.3.2.5   Concavities and Holes

The number and location of large concavities and/or holes in a shape have also proved to be useful for shape recognition (e.g. they are critical in the license plate recognition application to discriminate numbers like 2 and 5, 0 and 8, 6 and 9; see Figure 8.14 and Figure 8.19).

In OpenCV, to find the concavities relative to the convex hull for contours, we must first determine the indices of the points on the convex hull, and then compute the concavities. Each concavity is specified by four integers (the start and end indices of the concavity, the index of the deepest point in the concavity and a measure of the depth of the concavity):

```
vector<vector<int>> hull_indices(contours.size());
vector<vector<Vec4i>> convexity_defects(contours.size());
```

```
for (int contour_number=0;
          (contour_number<contours.size()); contour_number++)
{
   convexHull( contours[contour_number], hull_indices[contour_number]);
   convexityDefects( contours[contour_number],
                           hull_indices[contour_number],
                           convexity_defects[contour_number]);
}
```

8.3.2.6   Rectangularity

The rectangularity of a shape is the ratio of the region area and the area of the minimum bounding rectangle. This ratio has a maximum value of 1 for a perfect rectangle.

8.3.2.7   Circularity

The circularity of a shape is $(4*\pi*area)$ divided by the perimeter length squared. This has a maximum value of 1 for a perfect circle. Calculating the perimeter length is done by tracing around the boundary, but care must be taken when doing this bearing in mind that the calculation is being done in a quantised domain.

> *In OpenCV, the perimeter length can be estimated as the length of the contour as long as the points are all neighbours along the contour (although to be more precise we should consider the distance between the points on the contour):*
>
> `contours[contour_number].size()`

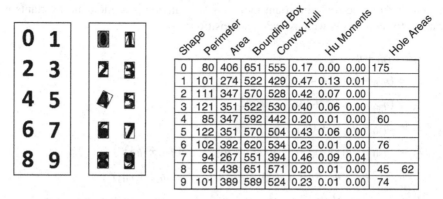

Shape	Perimeter	Area	Bounding Box	Convex Hull	Hu Moments			Hole Areas	
0	80	406	651	555	0.17	0.00	0.00	175	
1	101	274	522	429	0.47	0.13	0.01		
2	111	347	570	528	0.42	0.07	0.00		
3	121	351	522	530	0.40	0.06	0.00		
4	85	347	592	442	0.20	0.01	0.00	60	
5	122	351	570	504	0.43	0.06	0.00		
6	102	392	620	534	0.23	0.01	0.00	76	
7	94	267	551	394	0.46	0.09	0.04		
8	65	438	651	571	0.20	0.01	0.00	45	62
9	101	389	589	524	0.23	0.01	0.00	74	

Figure 8.14   Features computed from digits 0–9 shown on the left. For each, the perimeter length, area (in pixels), minimum bounding box area, the area enclosed by the convex hull and three of the Hu moment invariants are shown. In addition, the areas of any enclosed holes are listed. Any large concavities are also been shown with black lines between the start point, the deepest point and the end point

8.3.2.8 Moments and Moment Invariants

Moments (Flusser, Suk, and Zitová, 2009) measure the distribution of shape and can be used as features in statistical pattern recognition.

$$M_{xy} = \sum_i \sum_j i^x j^y f(i,j) \tag{8.9}$$

From the spatial moments (M_{xy}) we can compute central moments which are invariant to translation (i.e. the position of the shape within the image):

$$\mu_{00} = M_{00} \quad \mu_{01} = 0 \quad \mu_{10} = 0$$

$$\mu_{11} = M_{11} - \frac{M_{10}M_{01}}{M_{00}} \quad \mu_{20} = M_{20} - \frac{M_{10}M_{10}}{M_{00}} \quad \mu_{02} = M_{02} - \frac{M_{01}M_{01}}{M_{00}}$$

$$\mu_{21} = M_{21} - \frac{2M_{10}M_{11}}{M_{00}} - \frac{M_{01}M_{20}}{M_{00}} + \frac{2M_{10}M_{10}M_{01}}{M_{00}M_{00}}$$

$$\mu_{03} = M_{03} - \frac{3M_{01}M_{02}}{M_{00}} + \frac{2M_{01}M_{01}M_{01}}{M_{00}M_{00}} \tag{8.10}$$

$$\mu_{12} = M_{21} - \frac{2M_{01}M_{11}}{M_{00}} - \frac{M_{10}M_{02}}{M_{00}} + \frac{2M_{10}M_{01}M_{01}}{M_{00}M_{00}}$$

$$\mu_{30} = M_{30} - \frac{3M_{10}M_{20}}{M_{00}} + \frac{2M_{10}M_{10}M_{10}}{M_{00}M_{00}}$$

From the central moments we can compute scale invariant moments:

$$\eta_{xy} = \mu_{xy} \Big/ \mu_{00}^{\left(1 + {}^{x+y}\!/_2\right)} \tag{8.11}$$

And finally, from the scale invariant moments we can compute moment invariants which are invariant to rotation (as well as scale and position).

$$I_1 = \eta_{20} + \eta_{02}$$
$$I_2 = (\eta_{20} - \eta_{02})^2 + 4(\eta_{11})^2$$
$$I_3 = (\eta_{30} - 3\eta_{12})^2 + (3\eta_{21} - \eta_{03})^2$$
$$I_4 = (\eta_{30} + \eta_{12})^2 + (\eta_{21} + \eta_{03})^2$$
$$I_5 = (\eta_{30} - 3\eta_{12})(\eta_{30} + \eta_{12})\left((\eta_{30} + \eta_{12})^2 - 3(\eta_{21} + \eta_{03})^2\right)$$
$$\qquad + (3\eta_{21} - \eta_{03})(\eta_{21} + \eta_{03})\left(3(\eta_{30} + \eta_{12})^2 - (\eta_{21} + \eta_{03})^2\right)$$
$$I_6 = (\eta_{20} - \eta_{02})\left((\eta_{30} + \eta_{12})^2 - (\eta_{21} + \eta_{03})^2\right) + 4\eta_{11}(\eta_{30} + \eta_{12})(\eta_{21} + \eta_{03})$$
$$I_7 = (3\eta_{21} - \eta_{03})(\eta_{30} + \eta_{12})\left((\eta_{30} + \eta_{12})^2 - 3(\eta_{21} + \eta_{03})^2\right)$$
$$\qquad + (\eta_{30} - 3\eta_{12})(\eta_{21} + \eta_{03})\left(3(\eta_{30} + \eta_{12})^2 - (\eta_{21} + \eta_{03})^2\right) \tag{8.12}$$

See Figure 8.14 for examples of the first three of the moment invariants.

In OpenCV, the spatial moments, central moments, normalised central moments and moment invariants can be computed as follows (from a contour):

```
Moments contour_moments;
double hu_moments[7];
contour_moments = moments( contours[contour_number] );
HuMoments( contour_moments, hu_moments );
```

8.3.3   Statistical Pattern Recognition Technique

We are addressing a problem of object recognition amongst a number (R) of possible (known) object classes $(W_1, W_2, \ldots W_R)$. We should also be considering the possibility that the object is not one we have seen before (as pointed out in Section 8.3.1.3) but this issue is often ignored.

To recognise the object, we consider information derived from the unknown instances. This information takes the form of a number of features $(x_1, x_2, \ldots x_n)$ which is referred to as the 'input pattern' or feature vector x. We map the features into a n-dimensional feature space and if the features have been chosen appropriately, the different classes will map to clusters of feature vectors in feature space (e.g. see Figure 8.15). Ideally these classes should be separable (again see Figure 8.15) and we should be able to locate hyper-surfaces between them (see Figure 8.15). If the hyper-surfaces are planar then the classes are linearly separable (see Figure 8.15). Unfortunately, for many vision tasks the classes cannot be completely reliably separated (see Figure 8.15) and hence some misclassification results.

To determine which class of object is best represented by a particular feature vector x we define a decision rule $d(x)$ which returns the class W_r. There are many different classifiers which can be used for this purpose and we will consider three of these:

- minimum distance classifier,
- linear classifier,
- probabilistic classifier.

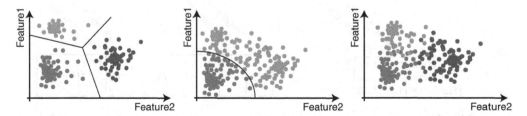

Figure 8.15   Objects of different classes (shown by dots of different colours) mapped into 2D feature space. On the left, the classes are linearly separable, in the centre, the classes are separable and a hyper-surface (a curve in this case) is shown between them, and on the right the classes are inseparable (using these features)

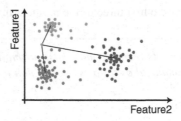

Figure 8.16 The distances considered for the minimum distance classifier from the 2D feature vector (shown in orange) for an unknown object and the centroids of the three object classes (samples shown in green, blue and red). In this case, the vector would be classified as a 'green' object using a minimum distance classifier

8.3.3.1 Minimum Distance Classifier

This classifier decides which class a particular feature vector belongs to based on the distance from the unknown feature vector to a number of exemplars (one or more per known object class). Typically the centroid of a cluster of feature vectors for a particular class is used as an exemplar to represent all feature vectors in that cluster. See Figure 8.16 for an example.

If an object class can appear in more than one fashion (e.g. a CD box which, when viewed from above, typically looks almost square but which may also appear on its side in which case it would appear as a thin rectangle) then it may result in multiple clusters in feature space. Note also that if we want to allow for unknown objects which cannot be recognised then we would need a maximum distance threshold to be set for each or for all class(es).

This approach has significant advantages in computational terms over more complex classifiers, and is often used in order to avoid extensive training. See Figure 8.17 for an example of this type of classifier in action.

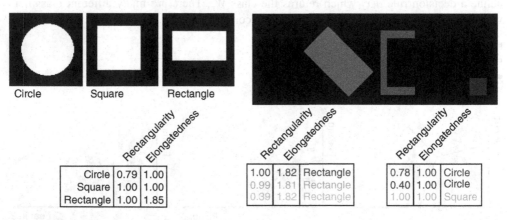

Figure 8.17 Statistical pattern recognition of simple shapes (Circle, Square and Rectangle) based on their rectangularity and elongatedness values. Unknown shapes/regions (the coloured shapes in the picture on the right hand side) are classified using a nearest neighbour classifier in two-dimensional feature space. On the bottom left the feature values computed from the samples on the top left are shown. On the bottom right the feature values computed from the regions in the image (top right) are shown along with their classification using a minimum distance classifier

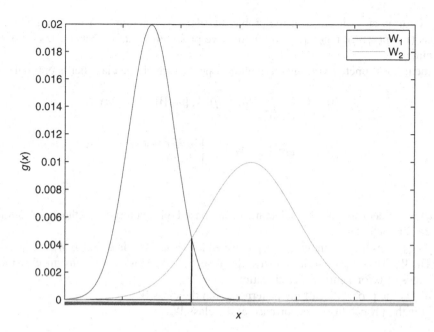

Figure 8.18 The discrimination functions for two object classes (W_1 and W_2) for a single feature x. The coloured line along the bottom indicates which class is returned by the decision rule for each value of x. Note that in this example we have assumed that the two classes are equally likely

8.3.3.2 Linear Classifier

Alternatively, to determine which class of object is best represented by a particular feature vector x we define a decision rule $d(x)$ which returns the class W_r for which the discrimination function $g_r(x) \geq g_s(x)$ for all other classes $s \neq r$. See Figure 8.18 for an example. To allow for the possibility that the object is unknown we should also insist that $g_r(x)$ is greater than some minimum value.

A linear discrimination function is the simplest form of $g_r(x)$:

$$g_r(x) = q_r0 + q_{r1}x_2 + q_{r1}x_2 + q_{r3}x_3 + q_{r4}x_4 + \dots \qquad (8.13)$$

where the q values are constants.

If all the discrimination functions are linear (i.e. for every class) then it is a linear classifier.

8.3.3.3 Optimal Classifier

Errors of misclassification can occur, and to minimise these errors the setting of the optimal classifier should be probabilistic (according to some criteria for loss). The optimal function is the posterior probability and (removing the normalisation factor $\sum_{j} p(x|W_j)P(W_j)$ which is the same for each class) this gives the optimal discrimination functions for each class:

$$g_r(x) = p(x|W_r)P(W_r) \qquad (8.14)$$

This requires an estimation of the probability density function over the feature space for this class (i.e. $p(x|W_r)$) together with the relative probability that objects of this class $P(W_r)$ will occur.

The mean loss function (the function with respect to which the classifier is optimal) is:

$$J(q) = \int_x \sum_{s=1..R} \lambda[d(x, q)|W_s]p(x|W_s)P(W_s)dx$$

$$where\ \lambda[W_r|W_s] = \begin{cases} 0\ if\ r = s \\ 1\ otherwise \end{cases} \tag{8.15}$$

where

- $d(x, q)$ is the decision rule for selecting a class based on a pattern x and the weights for each feature for each class.
- $\lambda[W_r|W_s]$ gives the loss incurred if a pattern which should be classified as W_s is instead classified as W_r. To achieve a minimum loss this is set to a fixed loss of 1 for any misclassification and a loss of 0 for a correct classification.
- $p(x|W_s)$ is the probability of the pattern x given the class W_s.
- $P(W_s)$ is the probability of occurrence of the class W_s.

8.3.3.4   Classifier Training

The quality of decision rule for a probabilistic classifier fundamentally depends on the quality of the probability density functions and relative class probabilities on which it is based. The quality of these probabilities depends largely on upon the quality and size of the training set. This set must be representative of all possible poses of all possible objects (i.e. the set must be inductive), effectively allowing the classifier to correctly recognise presentations of the objects that it has never seen before.

It is not really possible to define the required training set size in advance, so instead the size is gradually increased until the discrimination functions are estimated with sufficient accuracy.

The probabilities have to be learnt and this can be done in a supervised manner (where each sample in the training set is accompanied by a class specification). This allows us to automatically select the features which provide the best discrimination for the samples in the training set.

The probabilities can also be learnt in an unsupervised manner where the samples are unclassified and potential classes are identified by locating clusters in feature space. However, in this case it is hard to automatically select the appropriate features.

8.3.3.5   Example Using Real Data

To finish this section, we illustrate the power of this approach with recognition from real imagery taken in an unconstrained outdoor environment. See Figure 8.19.

8.4   Cascade of Haar Classifiers

This section looks at a specific advanced technique for real time object/pattern recognition as presented in two significant research papers: (Viola, 2001) and (Lienhart, 2002). See

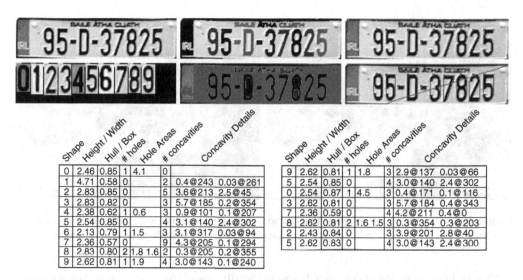

	Shape	Height/Width	Hull/Box	# holes	Hole Areas	# concavities	Concavity Details
0	2.46	0.85		1	4.1	0	
1	4.71	0.58		0		2	0.4@243 0.03@261
2	2.83	0.85		0		5	3.6@213 2.5@45
3	2.83	0.82		0		3	5.7@185 0.2@354
4	2.38	0.62		1	0.6	3	0.9@101 0.1@207
5	2.54	0.85		0		4	3.1@140 2.4@302
6	2.13	0.79		1	1.5	3	3.1@317 0.03@94
7	2.36	0.57		0		9	4.3@205 0.1@294
8	2.83	0.80		2	1.8 1.6	2	0.3@205 0.2@355
9	2.62	0.81		1	1.9	4	3.0@143 0.1@240

	Shape	Height/Width	Hull/Box	# holes	Hole Areas	# concavities	Concavity Details
9	2.62	0.81		1	1.8	3	2.9@137 0.03@66
5	2.54	0.85		0		4	3.0@140 2.4@302
0	2.54	0.87		1	4.5	3	0.4@171 0.1@116
3	2.62	0.81		0		3	5.7@184 0.4@343
7	2.36	0.59		0		4	4.2@211 0.4@0
8	2.62	0.81		2	1.6 1.5	3	0.3@354 0.3@203
2	2.43	0.84		0		3	3.9@201 2.8@40
5	2.62	0.83		0		4	3.0@143 2.4@300

Figure 8.19 Statistical pattern recognition of the numbers in a real license plate (which has been geometrically warped to a standard size). Note that a single sample for each number is provided (shown top left just below the license plate) from which target feature values are computed. The features computed from the sample characters are shown bottom left and those from the license plate image are shown bottom right. The license plate is recognised as 95 0 37825. All of the numbers are correctly recognised but the letter (D) is incorrectly recognised as a 0, partly because of the similarity between the 0 and the D but also because letters have not been included as possible answers in the training data. For the concavities only a normalised area and the angle of the line formed between the centroid of the shape and concavity opening are shown for the two largest concavities. For the hole areas, normalised areas are shown

Figure 8.20. This technique is included in order to demonstrate how different approaches to recognition can be. Bear in mind that this text introduces only basic computer vision and that the range of other techniques which have been developed is quite extensive.

In OpenCV, to recognise (for example) faces using a cascade of Haar classifiers we load the (previously trained) cascade (Note that a number of trained cascades are provided with OpenCV), and pass a histogram equalised grey-scale image to `detectMultiScale`*:*

```
CascadeClassifier cascade;
if( cascade.load(
        "haarcascades/haarcascade_frontalface_alt.xml" )
{
  vector<Rect> faces;
  equalizeHist( gray_image, gray_image );
  cascade.detectMultiScale( gray_image, faces, 1.1, 2,
                CV_HAAR_SCALE_IMAGE, Size(30, 30) );
}
```

Figure 8.20   Face recognition using the cascade of Haar classifiers. Note that this recognition is performed on a grey-scale version of the image and is capable of dealing with faces of different sizes

This technique for object detection learns to identify objects (e.g. faces) based on a number of positive and negative samples. It uses only simple features (which are reminiscent of Haar-like basis functions: in 1D a positive square wave followed by an equal but opposite negative one) to decide if a sub-image contains the object in question. It selects a large number of these features during training and creates classifiers with them which provide an accept/reject response. The classifiers are organised into a cascade (i.e. sequentially) where, if the sub-image is rejected by any classifier in the cascade, it is not processed any further. This has significant computational advantages as most sub-images are not processed past one or two classifiers.

The system is trained using objects at a particular scale in a standard size sub-image, but the classifiers are designed so they are easily resized allowing this object detection technique to be applied at different scales.

8.4.1   Features

The features used are determined by taking the difference of the sums of a number of rectangular regions (usually 2 or 3) of a grey-scale image. See Figure 8.21.

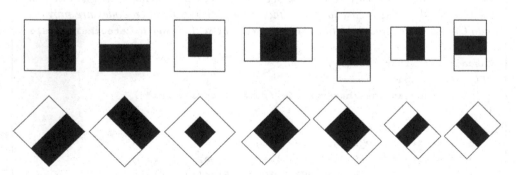

Figure 8.21   The 14 Haar-like feature masks used

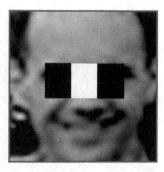

Figure 8.22 A sample face sub-image and the first two features used in the cascade of features for face recognition. These features seem to make logical sense, as the first appears to correspond to the notion that the cheek region will be brighter than the eye region and the second appears to indicate that the space between the eyes will be brighter than the eyes

Given a sub-image, the mask for one of the features is placed at some specific location within the sub-image, and at some particular scale, and the feature value is simply the normalised sum of the pixels in the black area is subtracted from the normalised sum of the pixels in the white area(s). The normalisation adjusts the sums so that the effective areas are the same. See Figure 8.22 to see why these features might be useful.

8.4.1.1 Efficient Calculation – Integral Image

To make the calculation of features more efficient, Viola and Jones (Viola, 2001) put forward the idea of the integral image. The integral image is the same size as the image from which it is derived and contains the sum of all pixels with smaller coordinates. The area of an arbitrary rectangle (defined by its vertices (p, q, s, r)) can be calculated by an addition and two subtractions:

$$ii(i,j) = \sum_{i'=0..i} \sum_{j'=0..j} f(i',j')$$

$$area(p, q, s, r) = ii(i_p, j_p) + ii(i_s, j_s) - ii(i_q, j_q) - ii(i_r, j_r) \tag{8.16}$$

See Figure 8.23. This means that features can be computed at any scale with the same cost. This is very important, as in order to detect objects at different scales we must apply the operator in all pixel positions at all possible scales.

> *In OpenCV, an* `integral` *function is provided which computes the integral image both normally and at 45°.*

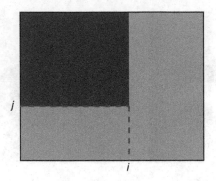 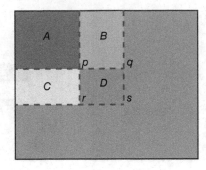

Figure 8.23   (left) The integral image $ii(i,j)$ of some image $f(i,j)$ has every point in the image (i,j) as the sum of all pixels value in $f(i',j')$) where $i' \le i$ and $j' \le j$. (right) To compute the total sum of all pixels in an arbitrary rectangle D: $area(p,q,s,r) = ii(i_p,j_p) + ii(i_s,j_s) - ii(i_q,j_q) - ii(i_r,j_r)$ where p,q,r,s are coordinates in the integral image and $ii(i_p,j_p) = area(A)$, $ii(i_q,j_q) = area(A + B)$, $ii(i_r,j_r) = area(A + C)$, $ii(i_s,j_s) = area(A + B + C + D)$. These diagrams are based on ones (Viola, 2001)

8.4.2   Training

For a typical sub-image, due to the variety of feature types together with the allowed variations in size and position, there are hundreds of thousands of possible features. The training phase for object detection then must identify which features are best to use at each stage in the classifier cascade. To do so the system must be provided with a large number of positive and negative samples.

8.4.3   Classifiers

8.4.3.1   Weak Classifiers

A weak classifier can be created by combining a specific feature with a threshold and through comparison making an accept or reject classification. The weak classifier is defined as $p_j feature_j(x) < p_j \vartheta_j$ where $feature_j(x)$ is the value of feature j at some location x, p_j is a parity value and ϑ_j is a threshold for feature j. The threshold must be tuned to minimise the amount of misclassification (on a set of training data).

8.4.3.2   Strong Classifiers – AdaBoost

To create a strong classifier, a number of weak classifiers are combined using a boosting algorithm called AdaBoost. For example, the two features shown in Figure 8.22 were combined into a two-feature first-stage classifier for frontal face detection by Viola and Jones (Viola, 2001) who reported that it was possible to detect 100% of the faces from a validation training set with a false positive rate of only 40% using these features. Viola and Jones also reported that a single strong classifier constructed using 200 features achieved a detection rate of 95% with a false positive rate of 0.01%.

AdaBoost algorithm 8.3 (based on that described in (Viola, 2001)):

Given n example images $x_1..x_n$ together with classifications $y_1..y_n$ where $y_i = 0, 1$ for negative and positive examples respectively.

Initialise weights

$w_{1,i} = 1 / (2*(m*(1- y_i)+l*y_i))$

where m and l are the number of negative and positive examples respectively.

The weights are changed at each 'round of boosting'. Considering $w_{a,b}$ a is the number of the current round and b is the example image number.

For $t=1,\ldots,T$

T is the number of rounds of boosting.

1. Normalise the weights (i.e. for all i):

   $w_{t,i} = w_{t,i} / (\Sigma_{j=1..n}\ w_{t,j})$

   As a result of this stage the sum of all weights will be 1.0 which means that $w_{t,i}$ can be considered as a probability distribution.

2. For each feature, j, train a weak classifier $h_j(x)$ and evaluate the error taking into account the weights:

   $\varepsilon_j = \Sigma_i\ w_{t,i}\ |\ h_j(x_i) - y_i\ |$

   Training a classifier means taking the single feature and determining the threshold which minimises the misclassifications.

3. Select the classifier, $h_j(x)$, with the lowest ε_j, save as $c_t(x)$, with error E_t

4. Update the weights (i.e. for all i):

   $w_{t+1,i} = w_{t,i}\ \beta_t^{(1- ei)}$

   where $e_i = |\ c_t(x_i) - y_i\ |$ and $\beta_t = E_t / (1-E_t)$

   Update the weights on the images leaving the weights on misclassified images the same and reducing the weights on correctly classified images by β_t.

The final strong classifier is:

$h(x) = 1$ if $\Sigma_{t=1..T}\alpha_t c_t(x) \geq \frac{1}{2}\Sigma_{t=1..T}\alpha_t$
        0 *otherwise*

where $\alpha_t = log\ 1/\beta_t$

The final strong classifier is a weighted combination of the weak classifiers where the weights are related to the training errors from each of the weak classifiers.

8.4.3.3 Classifier Cascade

While object recognition is possible with a single classifier, a cascade of classifiers can be used to improve detection rates AND to reduce computation time.

At each stage within the cascade there is a single strong classifier which either accepts or rejects the sub-image under consideration. If it is rejected by a classifier in the cascade, no further processing is performed on that sub-image. If it is accepted by a classifier, it is passed to the next classifier in the cascade. In this way the sub-images which do not contain the object

Figure 8.24   Face recognition using the technique described in this chapter. Note that recognition has failed on one of the faces. This is most probably due to the angle of the face (i.e. it is not full frontal)

are gradually removed from consideration, leaving just the objects which are sought. Most negative sub-images are rejected by the first couple of stages in the cascade and hence the computation for these sub-images is low (relative to those which have to go through more stages in the cascades). It is this which reduces the computation time.

Note that the classifiers in the cascade are trained using AdaBoost on the remaining set of example images (i.e. if the first-stage classifier rejects a number of images then these images are not included when training the second-stage classifier). Also note that the threshold determined by AdaBoost for the classifier at each stage is tuned so that the false negative rate is close to zero.

8.4.4   Recognition

The complete frontal face detection cascade presented by Viola and Jones (Viola, 2001) had 38 stages with over 6000 features. This was trained on a set of 4916 positive example images and 9544 negative example images. See Figure 8.20 and Figure 8.24 for some sample outputs (of a slightly more advanced version of this system; i.e. which incorporates the ideas from (Lienhart, 2002)). It can be seen from the varying rectangle sizes that the images are being processed at a variety of scales.

8.5   Other Recognition Techniques

There are many other recognition techniques, some of which are supported in OpenCV. A couple are worth mentioning at least.

8.5.1   Support Vector Machines (SVM)

Support vector machines (Cristianini and Shawe-Taylor, 2000) provide a similar mechanism to statistical pattern recognition which attempts to determine an optimal hyper-plane to separate

Figure 8.25 People detected using the histogram of oriented gradients technique. Image from the PETS 2000 dataset. The original image is reproduced by permission of Dr. James Ferryman, University of Reading

classes. This hyper-plane is placed at a maximum distance from the 'support vectors' (which are the instances of the various classes which are closest to the classification boundaries).

In OpenCV, two classes are provided to implement SVMs (`CvSVM` and `CvSVMParams`).

8.5.2   Histogram of Oriented Gradients (HoG)

The histogram of oriented gradients approach was put forward by Dalal and Triggs (Dalal, 2005) to locate people (standing up) in images/video, see Figure 8.25. It uses a linear support vector machine (SVM), which performs classification based on histograms of oriented gradients. The gradient and orientation images are computed as described in Section 6.1.1. All possible positions in the image are considered, and for each position multiple overlapping histograms of orientations are computed, with the gradients being used as the weights to be added to the histograms.

In OpenCV, to detect people using the histogram of oriented gradients:

```
HOGDescriptor hog;
hog.setSVMDetector( HOGDescriptor::getDefaultPeopleDetector() );
vector<Rect> people;
hog.detectMultiScale( search_image, people );
```

8.6   Performance

In Section 8.4.3.2 we talked briefly about the performance of a strong classifier, in terms of the detection rate (95%) and the false positive rate (0.01%). In fact, in all areas of computer vision (not just recognition), both computation time and performance (i.e. success and failure rates) are of great importance. As we frequently process huge streams of (video) data it is important that our algorithms are efficient and fast. At the same time, though, we often need to ensure incredibly high levels of accuracy as many applications of computer vision can be critical (such as medical diagnosis in ultrasound/X-ray/MRI images, automatic guidance of vehicles, obstacle avoidance for robots, biometric analysis of face images and handprints for security systems, etc.).

It is relatively straightforward to measure computation time for vision operations, but to determine how successful a particular vision algorithm is poses significant problems which vary somewhat according to the problem being addressed. In this section we consider some of issues of accessing performance in terms of accuracy.

In OpenCV, to determine how long a piece of code takes to run:

```
double before_tick_count=static_cast<double>(getTickCount());
// Put methods to be timed here...
double after_tick_count=static_cast<double>(getTickCount());
double duration_in_ms=1000.0*(after_tick_count-
                       before_tick_count) / getTickFrequency();
```

We need to assess the success of any vision algorithm using some set of images (or videos). As we want to compare different algorithms it becomes important that researchers share common datasets. These datasets tend to be very specific to individual problems and even then may not be appropriate to assess a particular piece of research if the approach requires that the data take a slightly different form (e.g. trying to recognise faces in stereo imagery rather than in single images). That said, there are a large number of image datasets available and we provide links to some of them in Sections 8.6.1.

Having obtained image data to use in an evaluation we face two further problems. To assess how well any algorithm has performed, we need to know what the perfect answer for each image/video is. This is called ground truth and in general must be provided/annotated by human subjects. As we will see in Section 8.6.2, this ground truth is extremely subjective, and hence different human subjects will annotate the images/videos in different ways.

Assuming we now have satisfactory datasets and ground truth for the algorithm that we want to assess (or more likely the algorithms that we want to compare), we then require metrics with which we can quantify performance. These metrics vary quite a bit depending on what type of problem we are addressing. A number of common metrics are introduced in Section 8.6.3.

8.6.1   Image and Video Datasets

The range and number of computer vision datasets available is quite astounding. A simple search for computer vision datasets will return tens of thousands of hits. There are even many sites providing links to some these datasets, and a few of these are provided here to get the interested reader started:

> http://www.cvpapers.com/datasets.html lists 106 different datasets for computer vision covering detection of cars, pedestrians, logos, classification of objects, recognition of faces, tracking people and vehicles, segmentation of images, foreground/background modelling, saliency detection, visual surveillance, action recognition, human pose determination, medical imaging, and so on.
>
> http://www.computervisiononline.com/datasets lists 79 different datasets for computer vision covering many of the same domains, but including a large number of different datasets and covering some different areas such as joint scene detection, 3D scanning, image quality evaluation, image registration, optical flow, fingerprint recognition, and so on.
>
> http://riemenschneider.hayko.at/vision/dataset/ lists 179 different datasets covering most areas of computer vision.

8.6.2 Ground Truth

One very well known image dataset is the Berkeley Segmentation dataset (Martin, Fawlkes, Tal, and Malik, 2001) (http://www.eecs.berkeley.edu/Research/Projects/CS/vision/grouping/scgbench/) in which 1000 images have been manually segmented by 30 human subjects with an average of 12 segmentations per image (half based on a colour image and the other half based on grey-scale images). Marking by multiple human subjects was intended to allow the identification of features which are considered important by all subjects. However, no two human subjects seem to agree on the segmentation of a particular image, and this illustrates the difficulty of specifying ground truth. See Figure 8.26.

While it is difficult for humans to agree on high level segmentation, perhaps more surprisingly it is also difficult to get agreement on pixel level classification. For example, which pixels are moving shadow pixels in an image (e.g. consider which pixels are moving shadow pixels in Figure 9.3 and compare that to those shadow pixels located in Figure 9.10).

  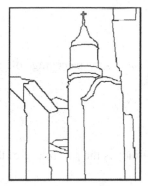

Figure 8.26 An image (left) along with two different human segmentations

8.6.3 Metrics for Assessing Classification Performance

Ultimately, for all the recognition techniques we have considered, we classify each sample as being a member of the positive class (i.e. the class of objects being sought) or a member of the negative class (i.e. not the class of objects being sought). For such tasks we are interested in how successful the classification has been. We want to know how successful we have been at identifying instances of the class being sought while avoiding mis-identifications.

For example, if we are attempting to identify abandoned objects in an airport terminal which represent possible security threats, it is very important that we identify most, if not all, abandoned objects correctly while at the same time not raising too many false alarms. In the first case missing abandoned objects results in potentially serious unidentified security threats. In the second case if the system raises too many false alarms the security guards who have to investigate the threats will lose confidence in the system and most probably start to ignore all warnings generated by it. The measures to assess these two criteria are referred to as **recall** and **precision** respectively and are two of the most commonly encountered performance criteria used in computer vision. They (and some other performance measures) are based on four easily computed numbers:

1. The number of true positives (TP): The number of samples that have been correctly identified as being the class being sought (e.g. that a face exists at a particular location).
2. The number of false positives (FP): The number of samples that have been incorrectly identified as being the class being sought (e.g. that a face exists at a particular location when there is no face present).
3. The number of true negatives (TN): The number of samples that have been correctly identified as not being the class being sought (e.g. that a face does not exist at a particular location).
4. The number of false negatives (FN): The number of samples that have been incorrectly identified as not being the class being sought (e.g. that a face does not exist at a particular location when there is a face present at that location).

Note that the total samples tested is the sum of all four of these number ($TotalSamples = TP + FP + TN + FN$).

Recall is the percentage of the objects being sought which have been successfully located.

$$Recall = \frac{TP}{TP + FN} \qquad (8.17)$$

Precision is the percentage of the positive classifications which are correct (i.e. are not false alarms).

$$Precision = \frac{TP}{TP + FP} \qquad (8.18)$$

Accuracy is the percentage of the total samples which are correct.

$$Accuracy = \frac{TP + TN}{TotalSamples} \qquad (8.19)$$

Specificity, also referred to as the true negative rate, is the percentage of the negative classifications which are correct.

$$Specifcity = \frac{TN}{FP + TN} \tag{8.20}$$

The F_β measure is a weighted measure of precision and recall which can be used to put a different emphasis on precision and recall.

$$F_\beta = (1 + \beta^2) \cdot \frac{Precision \cdot Recall}{(\beta^2 \cdot Precision) + Recall} \tag{8.21}$$

There are three commonly used version of the F_β measure. The F_1 measure puts even weight on precision and recall. The F_2 measure puts a higher weight on recall than precision and the $F_{0.5}$ measure puts a higher weight on precision than recall.

An example of these metrics in use is shown in Figure 8.27.

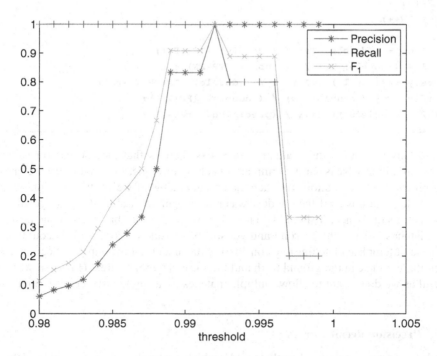

Figure 8.27 Precision, recall and F_1 values for a range of thresholds of the normalised cross-correlation between the template (of the smaller window) and the image from the template matching example in Figure 8.1. The specificity and accuracy values are not shown as they are both approximately 1.0 for all values of the threshold. A threshold value of 0.992 would have given a perfect result

In OpenCV, to determine performance assuming we have binary data for the ground truth and the results:

```
CV_Assert( results.type() == CV_8UC1 );
CV_Assert( ground_truth.type() == CV_8UC1 );
int FP = 0;
int FN = 0;
int TP = 0;
int TN = 0;
for (int row=0; row < ground_truth.rows; row++)
  for (int col=0; col < ground_truth.cols; col++)
  {
  uchar result = results.at<uchar>(row,col);
  uchar gt = ground_truth.at<uchar>(row,col);
  if ( gt > 0 )
    if ( result > 0 )
      TP++;
    else FN++;
  else if ( result > 0 )
    FP++;
  else TN++;
  }
precision = ((double) TP) / ((double) (TP+FP));
recall = ((double) TP) / ((double) (TP+FN));
accuracy = ((double) (TP+TN)) / ((double) (TP+FP+TN+FN));
specificity = ((double) TN) / ((double) (FP+TN));
f1 = 2.0*precision*recall / (precision + recall);
```

One serious issue with the evaluation described here is that the success (or failure) is evaluated on a binary basis. In the template matching example, the ground truth consists of a set of precise correct locations for each matching window. If we get the location wrong by even a single pixel it is as if the window was not recognised at all and we get penalised for an incorrect result. Hence, it should be clear that we need to be able to allow the position of correct matches to be slightly wrong and yet still be considered correct. This could be done (in the case of template matching) by considering the amount of overlap (see Section 9.3.2.2) between the template in the ground truth and the located template area. However, we have to be careful as we don't want to allow multiple matches for a single instance of ground truth.

8.6.3.1 Precision Recall Curves

Where there are parameters (such as thresholds) which can be altered it is possible to determine different sets of values for the metrics. Frequently we determine a precision–recall curve which shows us the trade-off between false positives and missed detections. This allows us to choose the parameter values so that we can select an appropriate precision and recall. See Figure 8.28.

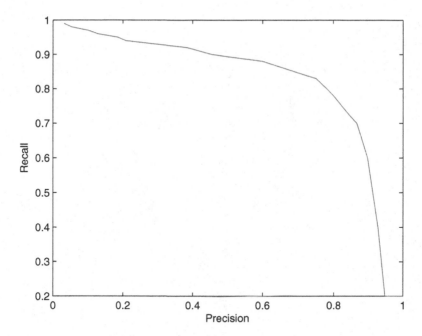

Figure 8.28 Example precision–recall curve where some parameter has been altered giving a range of precision–recall values. Clearly we would want to select the parameter value which results in the best precision and recall values (although what best means depends on the application). In many cases we select the parameter value corresponding to the precision–recall pair which is closest to (1.0,1.0)

8.6.4   *Improving Computation Time*

When developing a computer vision algorithm, the first consideration must always be determining a reliable solution to the problem, as in many cases developing a reliable solution is extremely difficult. After that we can look at making the solution more efficient. Some examples of this have already been introduced earlier in the text and we explicitly amalgamate them here to give an overview of the types of techniques which can be employed.

There are a number of algorithms which have been specifically designed to make solutions to particular problems more efficient. For example, the Perreault algorithm for median filtering (Section 2.5.4), the optimal and Otsu thresholding algorithms (Sections 4.2.2 and 4.2.3), the connected components algorithm (Section 4.5.2) and the chamfering algorithm (Section 8.2.1).

Of the more generic approaches, probably the most significant is the use of multiple resolutions to reduce the amount of processing. Using this approach we can process an image at a low resolution first, and determine locations which warrant further investigation at a higher resolution. This approach has been used in graph searching (Section 6.2.2.3) and template matching (Section 8.1.5) among others.

Other techniques include the use of lookup tables in image processing (Section 4.1), the use of aging when processing video (Section 9.1.4.5), the use of the integral image (Section 8.4.1.1) and the use of a cascade where possibilities are rejected at different levels in the cascade and do not need to be processed further (Section 8.4.3.3).

9

Video

Cameras supply video feeds, but in computer vision they are often used simply to acquire occasional static images from the stream of available video data (for example, in industrial inspection applications). However, as we have progressed from the factory to less constrained environments, we have found that video provides us with much more useful information through the analysis of what is changing in the video scene. Some of the most common such techniques are used for the detection of moving objects (see Section 9.1) within video streams. In this domain, we typically use static cameras (i.e. cameras which are fixed in place and do not pan, tilt or zoom) and hence a background image/model can be derived in a relatively straightforward manner from the video (see Section 9.1.4). Typically, these techniques allow us to identify moving/changing pixels within the scene but have difficulties translating this to moving objects as moving objects frequently overlap, resulting in confusion about which object is which. As a result, another major topic in video analysis is the visual tracking of objects within a scene without use of a background model (see Section 9.2). We finish this chapter by looking in Section 9.3 at performance analysis in video, which can be quite different from the performance analysis for images described in Section 8.6.

9.1 Moving Object Detection

Motion detection is used extensively to analyse video sequences containing moving objects such as cars and people. The relative motion of objects in a scene makes it possible to segment these objects from the rest of the scene (i.e. the background or in some cases the other moving objects).

Motion detection has been applied to

1. Determine if there is any motion in the image (e.g. which could be used to alert a security guard).
2. Detect and localise moving objects. This can range in complexity from just detecting moving objects, to tracking them, recognising them and predicting their likely future positions (i.e. their expected trajectory).

A Practical Introduction to Computer Vision with OpenCV, First Edition. Kenneth Dawson-Howe.
© 2014 John Wiley & Sons, Ltd. Published 2014 by John Wiley & Sons, Ltd.

3. Derive 3D object properties. If multiple views are available of an object (e.g. views from two cameras) these can be used to determine the 3D structure of the object. This is also true if the object is seen in multiple positions or if a single camera moves relative to an object.

9.1.1   Object of Interest

We need to define what the objects of interest are, which is not obvious. If we consider a surveillance video, while we ideally want to understand everything that is happening in the scene it should be clear that we cannot reliably locate or track people or objects in the background of the scene if they occupy very few pixels in each image. Typically, we specify a minimum size (in pixels) for objects of interest.

In addition, we assume that objects have a maximum velocity (e.g. people can only move at a certain maximum speed), that the rate of acceleration of the objects is limited (e.g. an object cannot go from being stationary to moving very quickly in one frame), that all parts of an object exhibit roughly common motion (i.e. they move in more or less the same way; arms and legs obviously move in a periodic fashion with respect to the rest of the body), and that there will be mutual correspondence of object appearance (subject to rotation, occlusion, etc.) from frame to frame.

9.1.2   Common Problems

There are a range of common problems which affect this technique:

- How can we cope with illumination changes, which can be gradual (e.g. as the position of the sun changes in the sky) or sudden (e.g. when the sun goes behind a cloud or a light is switched on)?
- How can we make sure that shadows, which can result in quite strong differences, are not detected as moving object points? There are techniques which can be used to address this by considering the way in which luminance, hue and saturation change. See Section 9.1.5.
- How can we deal with rain? This generally results in a darkening of the scene and also effectively makes the image significantly more noisy.
- What about snow? This radically changes the scene and adds big white blobs of 'noise' in front of the cameras.
- How can we update the background? Objects may enter the scene and become part of the background (e.g. a car when it is parked) or equally a static part of the scene may move away (e.g. a suitcase which is picked up).
- How can we deal with trees or bushes moving in the wind? They are valid moving objects. Should they be ignored? There are techniques that model the background using multiple values for each pixel hence allowing, for example, for a pixel to be green (leaf) some of the time and blue (sky) at other times.
- Is the camera mobile or static? Can it pan, tilt, zoom? Does it have any automatic parameters (e.g. autofocus)? If the camera is completely static (no motion or changing parameters) then the analysis is much simpler.

- What is the time interval between frames? The time interval between frames (together with the object speed and distance from the camera) places limits in terms of the speed at which objects of interest can move within the image.

9.1.3   Difference Images

Simple image subtraction produces a difference image. If the difference is computed between the current frame of a video sequence $f_k(i,j)$ and a background image $b(i,j)$ (an image with no moving objects) then we can identify the moving object points in the scene:

- Binary image output:

$$d(i,j) = \begin{cases} 0 \ if \ |f_k(i,j) - b(i,j)| < T \\ 1 \ otherwise \end{cases} \tag{9.1}$$

- Grey-level output:

$$d(i,j) = |f_k(i,j) - b(i,j)| \tag{9.2}$$

The preceding formulas assume that the input images $f_k(i,j)$ and $b(i,j)$ are both grey-scale images. If we have colour images we must make further choices. Should we process each channel separately and then pick the greatest difference (or the average difference)? Should we just process certain channels (e.g. hue and luminance)? See Figure 9.1.

In OpenCV, the absolute difference between images of any type is computed using:

```
absdiff( frame, background, difference );
```

The resulting binary difference images will hopefully have mainly true positives (where pixels representing moving object points are correctly classified as moving), and true negatives (where stationary pixels are correctly classed as stationary). However, it will normally also have a number of false positives (where stationary points have been incorrectly classified as moving) and false negatives (where moving points have been incorrectly classified as stationary).

We want to minimise these misclassifications but unfortunately, for surveillance applications, we cannot remove them completely as the technique is very dependent on having a high contrast between the moving object and the static background – which we cannot guarantee (because we cannot constrain the scene or the appearance of the moving objects). Some problems are caused by noise, which can be suppressed using a variety of techniques to remove any regions smaller than a certain size (such as binary opening and closing). In addition the threshold (T) may cause too much noise to appear (if T is too low) or too much of the moving object not to be detected (if T is too high). See Figure 9.2. It really is impossible to get it perfect.

Figure 9.1 The current frame of a video sequence (top left), the background image (top right), the colour difference image where the difference for each channel has been computed separately (bottom left) and a thresholded version of the difference image (bottom right) again processed on a per channel basis. The original images are reproduced by permission of Dr. James Ferryman, University of Reading

Figure 9.2 A frame from a video sequence (left) and the moving points detected (centre) where the threshold is too low causing a lot of noise points and the detection of all shadows as moving points; together with the moving points detected where the threshold is too high (right) causing some points (such as the person and parts of the car) not to be detected. The original image (left) is reproduced by permission of Dr. James Ferryman, University of Reading

Figure 9.3 The current frame (left), the static background image (centre), the detected moving pixels image (right). The background image contains some moving objects (the red car and the person at the top of the image), and the corresponding pixels are identified as being moving pixels in the current frame. In addition, the car which has parked since the start of the video has not been included in the background and hence is still identified as moving. The original images are from the PETS 2000 dataset. Reproduced by permission of Dr. James Ferryman, University of Reading

9.1.4   Background Models

A major part of this technique is the acquisition and maintenance of the background model/image (Radke et al., 2005) and there are a wide range of techniques to address this, a few of which are presented here.

9.1.4.1   Static Background image

The simplest approach to the background image is simply to take a static frame of the scene (hopefully without any moving objects present). This is a very common technique, as is evidenced by many sample surveillance videos starting with a completely static scene. This technique cannot deal with objects being added to or removed from the static scene and cannot deal with illumination changes or even minor changes in camera or object position. See Figure 9.3.

In OpenCV, the static background model is very straightforward to implement. Simply save the first frame from a video, and then compute the absolute difference between the current frame and the first frame. We also include some logic to display the moving points from the current frame:

```
absdiff( current_frame, first_frame, difference );
cvtColor( difference, moving_points, CV_BGR2GRAY );
threshold( moving_points, moving_points, 30, 255, THRESH_BINARY );
Mat display_image = Mat::zeros( moving_points.size(), CV_8UC3 );
current_frame.copyTo( display_image, moving_points );
```

9.1.4.2   Frame Difference

One simple technique which overcomes the problems of requiring the background to be updated is the frame difference technique, where a frame is compared with the previous frame.

Figure 9.4 The current frame (left), the previous frame (centre), and the difference image (right). The original images are from the PETS 2000 dataset. Reproduced by permission of Dr. James Ferryman, University of Reading

The difference for moving objects depends on the amount by which objects are moving and on the appearance of the objects (see Figure 9.4). However, the analysis of these difference images is quite difficult.

In OpenCV, the frame difference is computed using:

```
absdiff( current_frame, previous_frame, difference );
```

9.1.4.3   Running Average

In an attempt to incorporate background changes, sometimes the running average is used. The running average should be the average of the last k frames, but this would mean that we would have to store the previous k frames so that we could remove the oldest frame when adding a new frame. For this reason, the running average background is usually approximated using aging:

$$b_{n+1}(i,j) = \propto \cdot f_n(i,j) + (1-\propto) \cdot b_n(i,j) \qquad (9.3)$$

where $\propto$ is the learning rate.

In OpenCV, we can use the `accumulateWeighted` *function to determine the running average background (in this case passing a value of 0.01 as the learning rate, α):*

```
accumulateWeighted( current_frame_gray,
                    running_average_background, 0.01 );
```

The running average as presented will update the background image to account for lighting changes. However, it incorporates moving objects into the running average (e.g. see Figure 9.5).

Figure 9.5 The current frame (left), the running average background image with $\alpha = 0.01$ (center), the detected moving pixels image (right). The processing was started on the same frame as in the static background example (see Figure 9.3), and it is notable that the moving objects from the start frame are no longer visible in the background image. In addition, the parked car has been incorporated into the background. The background image is contaminated by blurred versions of any moving objects. The person to the left of the parked cars is clearly visible in the background image. The white van is not particularly visible in the background image mainly due to the fact that it is just brightening the background somewhat. Note that the background model is a grey-scale image. A colour version of this model is provided in the resources accompanying the text. The original images are from the PETS 2000 dataset. Reproduced by permission of Dr. James Ferryman, University of Reading

To reduce this effect we can set the number of frames (k) to a high value or equivalently the learning rate α to a low value, but, unfortunately, this will mean that the background will be very slow to adapt to lighting or other changes. It is worth noting that we can compute the running average for colour images by simply computing the running average for each channel independently (see Figure 9.5).

Where there are no moving objects there is a very significant reduction in noise, but where objects are moving there are undesirable effects from the moving objects (e.g. see Figure 9.6).

Figure 9.6 Current frame from a video sequence contaminated by significant Gaussian noise (left) together with the running average background (right) with $w = 0.01$. While moving objects are incorporated somewhat (notice the red blurring on the road caused by the moving car) into the background, it is clear that the noise in the video is significantly reduced in the background image. The original images are from the PETS 2000 dataset. Reproduced by permission of Dr. James Ferryman, University of Reading

Figure 9.7   The current frame (left), the running average with selective update background image with $\alpha = 0.01$ (centre), the detected moving pixels image (right). The good news is that the blurred person (from Figure 9.3) has been removed from the background image. However, as the processing was started on the same frame as in the static background example (see Figure 9.3), it suffers from the same problems. The moving objects (the red car and the person) which were present in the first frame have not been removed due to the selective update. In addition, the parked car has not been included in the background but the pixels around the car are updating, resulting in a halo effect around the position of the parked car in the background image. Note that the background model is a grey-scale image. A colour version of this model is provided in the resources accompanying the text. The original images are from the PETS 2000 dataset. Reproduced by permission of Dr. James Ferryman, University of Reading

9.1.4.4   Selectivity

One way to overcome the problem of foreground objects being included into the background model is to only update points which are determined to be background points.

$$b_{n+1}(i,j) = \begin{cases} \alpha \cdot f_n(i,j) + (1-\alpha) \cdot b_n(i,j) \ \dots \textit{if } f_n(i,j) \textit{ is background} \\ b_n(i,j) \qquad\qquad\qquad\qquad \dots \textit{if } f_n(i,j) \textit{ is foreground} \end{cases} \qquad (9.4)$$

This does pose a problem, however, as we must somehow determine if points are foreground or background in order to update the background model. If we simply use a comparison with the existing background model, then objects which enter the scene and stop (such as a car which parks) can never become part of the background (see Figure 9.7).

In OpenCV, to implement selectivity on the running average we need only add a foreground mask to the call to the `accumulateWeighted` *function:*

```
accumulateWeighted( current_frame_gray,
    running_average_background, 0.01, foreground_mask);
```

We can address this by altering the selective update so that the background is updated even for foreground pixels, but arrange that the learning rate is less than that applied to background pixels. For example:

$$b_{n+1}(i,j) = \begin{cases} \alpha \cdot f_n(i,j) + (1-\alpha) \cdot b_n(i,j) \qquad \dots \textit{if } f_n(i,j) \textit{ is background} \\ \alpha/3 \cdot f_n(i,j) + \left(1 - \alpha/3\right) \cdot b_n(i,j) \dots \textit{if } f_n(i,j) \textit{ is foreground} \end{cases} \qquad (9.5)$$

See Figure 9.8.

Figure 9.8 The current frame (left), the running average with selective update background image with $\alpha = 0.01$ for background points and $\alpha = 0.0033$ for background points (centre), the detected moving pixels image (right). Compared to Figure 9.7 we can see that the car on the road on the right of the image has been effectively averaged out of the background, and that the car which parked is slowly being averaged into the background. Note that the background model is a grey-scale image. A colour version of this model is provided in the resources accompanying the text. The original images are from the PETS 2000 dataset. Reproduced by permission of Dr. James Ferryman, University of Reading

9.1.4.5 Median Background Image

The median is the middle value (from an ordered list) of values (e.g. 8 is the median of 1, 1, 2, 2, 3, 3, 5, 8, 11, 12, 15, 15, 15, 18, 19). The median background image is computed by determining the median value for each pixel over the last m frames. Assuming the current frame is n then we can compute a histogram of values for each pixel as follows:

$$h_n(i,j,p) = \sum_{k=(n-m+1)..n} \begin{cases} 1 \ldots if(f_k(i,j) = p) \\ 0 \ldots otherwise \end{cases} \tag{9.6}$$

We must then determine the median value for each pixel from these histograms. Every time a new frame is processed we must remove the oldest value and add the new value for each pixel. This is expensive, from a memory point of view, as it requires us to store the m frames (which are being included in the median) along with a histogram from each pixel.

We must determine an appropriate value for m and typically must limit the quantisation in the histograms so that the amount of data being maintained does not become excessive – particularly where we are considering colour images.

The histograms can be updated very inexpensively using a form of aging:

$$h_n(i,j,p) = \sum_{k=1..n} \begin{cases} w_k \ldots if(f_k(i,j) = p) \\ 0 \ldots otherwise \end{cases} \tag{9.7}$$

where $w_1 = 1$ and $w_k = w_{k-1}{}^*1.005$

This is an approximation to the actual histograms, which works very well in practice (see Figure 9.9).

We can use clever algorithms to update the median for each pixel each time a new frame is processed, as to determine the median directly from the histogram for each pixel for each frame would be extremely expensive computationally. In fact, any change in the median from frame to frame can be determined very inexpensively by simply maintaining a sum of the histogram

Figure 9.9 Current frame from a video sequence (left) together with the median background with a learning rate of 1.005 (centre) and the detected moving object pixels (right). The moving objects from the first frame (see Figure 9.3) have been removed and the parked car has been incorporated into the background. The original images are from the PETS 2000 dataset, reproduced by permission of Dr. James Ferryman, University of Reading.

values which are less than or equal to the current median and doing a little processing after every update of the histogram.

Algorithm 9.1

First frame:
  $total = 1$
  for all pixels (i,j)
    $median(i,j) = f_1(i,j)$
    $less\_than\_median(i,j) = 0$

Current frame (n):
  $total = total + w_n$
  for all pixels (i,j)
    if$(median(i,j) > f_n(i,j))$
      $less\_than\_median(i,j) = less\_than\_median(i,j) + w_n$
    while $\big(less\_than\_median(i,j) + h_n\,(i,j,median(i,j)) < total/2\big)$
                    $\text{AND}(median(i,j) < 255))$
      $less\_than\_median(i,j) = less\_than\_median(i,j) + h_n(i,j,median(i,j))$
      $median(i,j) = median(i,j) + 1$
    while$((less\_than\_median(i,j) > total/2 \text{ AND } (median(i,j) > 0))$
      $median(i,j) = median(i,j) - 1$
      $less\_than\_median(i,j) = less\_than\_median(i,j) - h_n(i,j,median(i,j))$

In OpenCV, the median background model is not directly supported but is relatively straightforward to implement using the aging technique described. A sample implementation is provided in the electronic resources associated with the book.

Note that it is also possible to use the mode (the most common value over some number of frames) in a similar manner:

$$b_n(i,j) = p \text{ where } h_n(i,j,p) \geq h_n(i,j,q) \text{ for all } q \neq p \qquad (9.8)$$

9.1.4.6 Running Gaussian Average

Other than in synthetic images, the values of pixels change somewhat from frame to frame due to a wide variety of factors such as the digitisation process itself, slight changes in the lighting, and so on. For much real world noise, this variation can be measured and modelled using a Gaussian distribution (i.e. a probability density function with average μ, and standard deviation σ). We then define a point as being foreground if it is more than some multiple (k) of the standard deviation away from the average:

$$\left| f_n(i,j) - \mu_n(i,j) \right| > k\sigma_n(i,j) \qquad (9.9)$$

We can update the Gaussian distribution using similar equations to those used by the running average:

$$\mu_{n+1}(i,j) = \alpha f_n(i,j) + (1 - \alpha)\mu_n(i,j)$$
$$\sigma_{n+1}^2(i,j) = \alpha \left(f_n(i,j) - \mu_n(i,j) \right)^2 + (1 - \alpha)\sigma_n^2(i,j) \qquad (9.10)$$

Again, we can apply the selective update mechanism if desired so that the foreground objects don't pollute the Gaussian distribution, with the obvious problematic side-effects (mentioned previously).

9.1.4.7 Gaussian Mixture Model

All of the techniques mentioned so far are unable to deal with background objects which are moving slightly (e.g. ripples on water, trees moving in the wind). To deal with this, Stauffer and Grimson (Stauffer and Grimson, 1999) proposed to model each point of the background using a mixture of Gaussian distributions (typically 3 or 4 distributions per pixel). See Figure 9.10. For example, if a pixel corresponded to a leaf on a tree where the leaf was regularly moved by the wind revealing the sky, then two of the distributions would model the leaf and the sky respectively.

The basic idea is to fit multiple Gaussian distributions to the historical pixel data for each point including both foreground and background values. At any frame (n), each Gaussian distribution (m) has a weighting ($\pi_n(i,j,m)$) depending on how frequently it has occurred in the past frames.

When a new frame is considered, each point $f_n(i,j)$ is compared to the Gaussian distributions currently modelling that point in order to determine a single close Gaussian (if any). A distribution is considered close if it is within 2.5 times the standard deviation from the average value. If there is no Gaussian distribution which is close enough, then a new Gaussian distribution is initialised to model this point. On the other hand, if a close Gaussian distribution is identified, then that distribution is updated. For each point $f_n(i,j)$ the largest Gaussian

Figure 9.10 Current frame from a video sequence (left) together with a weighted image of the GMM background, where the weight of each Gaussian defines how the averages of the Gaussians are combined (centre) and the detected moving object pixels (right). The moving objects from the first frame (see Figure 9.3) have been removed and the parked car has been incorporated into the background. The original images are from the PETS 2000 dataset. Reproduced by permission of Dr. James Ferryman, University of Reading

distributions which sum to at least a set threshold (e.g. 70%) are considered to represent the background. A point is classified as background or foreground if its associated distribution is background or foreground respectively.

To update the distributions

$$\pi_{n+1}(i,j,m) = \alpha^* O_n(i,j,m) + (1-\alpha)^* \pi_n(i,j,m)$$

where $O_n(i,j,m) = 1$ for **the close Gaussian distribution** and

0 otherwise

$$\mu_{n+1}(i,j,m) = \mu_n(i,j,m) + O_n(i,j,m)^*(\alpha/\pi_{n+1}(i,j,m))^*(f_n(i,j) - \mu_n(i,j,m))$$

$$\sigma^2_{n+1}(i,j,m) = \sigma^2_{n+1}(i,j,m) + O_n(i,j,m)^*(\alpha/\pi_{n+1}(i,j,m))^*((f_n(i,j) - \mu_n(i,j,m))^2 - \sigma^2_n(i,j,m))$$

where $\pi_n(i,j,m)$, $\mu_n(i,j,m)$, $\sigma_n(i,j,m)$ are the weighting, average and standard deviation of the mth Gaussian distribution for pixel (i,j) at frame n.

An upper limit is normally placed on the number of distributions to be considered for each pixel, and hence when new distributions have to be created the smallest existing distribution has to be discarded if the limit on the number of distributions has been reached.

Note that this type of learning, as with all of the other background models presented in this chapter, is unsupervised so that the system learns the weights, averages and standard deviations and is able to make classifications for each pixel based on what has been observed at that pixel.

This is the most frequently used method for modelling the background, although more complex (and successful) methods have been developed. It is often used as a benchmark for other background modelling techniques.

In OpenCV, the Gaussian mixture model is supported using the
`BackgroundSubtractorMOG2` *class:*

```
BackgroundSubtractorMOG2 gmm;
gmm( current_frame, foreground_mask );
```

```
threshold( foreground_mask, moving_points, 150, 255, THRESH_BINARY );
```
The shadow points are labelled in the current frame with a lower grey-scale that the moving points:

```
threshold( foreground_mask, changing_points, 50, 255, THRESH_BINARY );
absdiff( moving_points, changing_points, shadow_points );
```

A function is provided to give a visualisation of the GMM background model:

```
Mat mean_background_image;
gmm.getBackgroundImage( mean_background_image );
```

9.1.5   Shadow Detection

Cast shadows are a major problem when analysing surveillance videos as the binary shapes of moving objects are distorted by any shadows that they cast. Hence the removal of these cast shadows is of significant interest. Prati et al. (Prati, 2003) developed a formula for identifying the shadows in HSV space by looking at the changes in hue, saturation and value between the background image and the current frame:

$$SP_k(i,j) =$$
$$\begin{cases} 1 \dots if \left(\alpha < \dfrac{f_k^V(i,j)}{B_k^V(i,j)} < \beta \right) \ and \ \left(\left(f_k^S(i,j) - B_k^S(i,j) \right) < \tau_S \right) and \left(\left| f_k^H(i,j) - B_k^H(i,j) \right| < \tau_H \right) \\ 0 \dots otherwise \end{cases}$$

$$(9.11)$$

The ratio of the values in the current frame and the background frame must be within a defined range, the saturation must fall by some minimum amount τ_S, and the absolute change in hue must be less than a small threshold τ_H. For example, see Figure 9.11.

However, Tattersall (Tattersall, 2003) found that a simplified version of this performed better where only the changes in value and in saturation are considered (as he found that the changes in hue were somewhat unpredictable):

$$SP_k(i,j) = \begin{cases} 1 \dots if \left(\lambda < \dfrac{f_k^V(i,j)}{B_k^V(i,j)} < 1.0 \right) \ and \ \left(\left| f_k^S(i,j) - B_k^S(i,j) \right| < \tau_S \right) \\ 0 \dots otherwise \end{cases} \qquad (9.12)$$

λ was calculated automatically through an analysis of the image data and τ_S was set to 12% of the maximum saturation.

Figure 9.11   The moving pixels detected by the GMM (left) together with the raw moving pixels (white) and detected shadow points (grey). The results are quite good, although it is notable (from the moving object pixels shown on the left) that the very dark shadow under the van has been classified incorrectly and that there is a reasonable amount of noise classified incorrectly as moving object pixels. The original images are from the PETS 2000 dataset. Reproduced by permission of Dr. James Ferryman, University of Reading

9.2   Tracking

Tracking of an object (or multiple objects) in video is an important problem in computer vision (Maggio and Cavallaro, 2010). It is employed in visual surveillance, sports video analysis, vehicle guidance systems, obstacle avoidance, and so on.

Visual tracking is usually not simple, as the object(s) to be tracked:

1. may be undergoing complex motion relative to the camera (e.g. a car in front turning off the road);
2. may change shape (e.g. a person's appearance changes hugely when moving as the arms and legs and head move relative to the trunk);
3. may be fully or partially occluded at times (e.g. a truck passes between a pedestrian and the camera);
4. may change appearance due to lighting or weather (e.g. lights being turned on, or the sun going behind a cloud, or rain starting);
5. may physically change appearance (e.g. a person who takes off a jacket or a hat).

As a result, visual tracking is a very difficult problem and has been approached in a variety of different ways. We consider a number of them in this section:

1. Exhaustive search (see Section 9.2.1), where an image (a template) is tracked from frame to frame searching for the best match in each frame.
2. Mean shift (see Section 9.2.2), where a histogram representation of the object is used for the comparison and a gradient ascent/descent method is used to reduce the amount of comparisons required.
3. Optical flow (see Section 9.2.3) is a technique for determining the direction in which all pixels (or sparse features) are moving from frame to frame. This is often employed to guide trackers. We consider the Farneback method.

4. Feature point tracking (see Section 9.2.4) can be used to track objects if we limit the feature points to those within the object of interest. This can provide a faster and more robust approach.

9.2.1   Exhaustive Search

In its simplest form, tracking by exhaustive search is akin to template matching (as described in Section 8.1). An image of the object to be tracked is extracted from the first frame in which it is seen and this template is compared in every possible position in future frames using a metric such as normalised cross-correlation (see Section 8.1.3). In addition, the object in the real (three-dimensional) world may be moving away from or towards the camera (and hence growing or shrinking in the video), may be turning (and hence rotating in the video) or may be changing its viewpoint with respect to the camera (and hence causing parts of the object to disappear, new parts to appear, and other parts to deform). So at least we need to consider four degrees of freedom (two for image position, one for scale and one for rotation within the image). For each of these degrees of freedom, we can restrict the extent to which we search for a local maximum if we make assumptions about the amount that an object can move from frame to frame.

However, given the range of possible appearance changes for an object, template matching often simply will not work and hence other approaches have been developed.

9.2.2   Mean Shift

Mean shift is an iterative method which uses the probabilities determined by the back-projection of a histogram into an image to locate a target.

To use mean shift, we must be provided with a target image which is histogrammed allowing us to determine the relative probabilities of colours associated with the target. These probabilities can then be back-projected into any image that we wish to search for the target. We must also be provided with an initial estimate of the target location, and mean shift effectively searches for a region of the same size with maximum summed (and weighted) probabilities. Note that the observations in the centre of the target are typically weighted more heavily than those near the boundaries of the target.

Mean shift uses a hill climbing algorithm (one which iteratively moves to a local maximum location) to iteratively locate the best target in the provided probabilities, so it is essential that the initial estimate is quite close to the location in the image being searched. See Figure 9.12.

In OpenCV, given the back-projection probabilities and a starting position (as a rectangle), we can apply mean shift to find the most likely new position as follows:

```
Rect position(starting_position);
TermCriteria criteria( cv::TermCriteria::MAX_ITER, 5, 0.01);
meanShift( back_projection_probabilities, position,
                                         criteria);
```

Figure 9.12 Object location using mean shift. (Top) Frames 100, 140, 180 and 220 from the Bicycles.avi sequence overlaid with the determined object location using mean shift and (bottom) the corresponding back-projections within which mean shift searches. The initial target image (which is histogrammed) is that from frame 100. Reproduced by permission of Dr. James Ferryman, University of Reading

Hill climbing (which is often referred as gradient ascent) locates local maxima by iteratively moving in the direction of the greatest (upwards) gradient beside the current location. In this fashion, the location is gradually changed (one pixel at a time) until the most likely local maxima is found. This technique is generally used in a space where the values represent probabilities (e.g. the likelihood that the current location represents the object being sought). It does not guarantee (or try) to locate the global maximum.

9.2.3 Dense Optical Flow

Rather than (or possibly as an aid to) tracking specific objects, we can compute a motion field for the entire image. See Figure 9.13. The 2D apparent motion field between two images is referred to as optical flow and this shows the apparent motion direction and magnitude for every point in the image. The apparent motion of points within a scene is caused by their motion or the motion of the camera (or both). Optical flow is based on a brightness constancy constraint which states that object points will have the same brightness over a short period of time (Δt). If we consider a point (i, j) in an image $f_t(i, j)$ taken at time t then, assuming the point has moved by $(\Delta i, \Delta j)$:

$$f_t(i,j) = f_{t+\Delta t}(i + \Delta i, j + \Delta j) \tag{9.13}$$

The displacement for point (i, j) at time t is $(\Delta i, \Delta j)$ and $(\frac{\Delta i}{\Delta t}, \frac{\Delta j}{\Delta t})$ is the optical flow. If we compute this flow vector for every point in the image, we will have a dense optical flow field. (A sparse optical flow field is one that is computed for few points in the image; e.g. see

Figure 9.13 Optical flow computed using the Farneback method shown for two frames of the PETS 2000 surveillance video. Note that the optical flow vectors are computed for every point in the scene but are only shown (in green) for every eighth point in both directions (shown in red). The original images are reproduced by permission of Dr. James Ferryman, University of Reading

Section 9.2.4). The displacement for a point $(i_{\text{current}}, j_{\text{current}})$ can be defined as the displacement $(\Delta i, \Delta j)$ which minimises the residual error ε between the images. For example

$$\varepsilon\left(\Delta i, \Delta j\right) = \sum_{i=i_{\text{current}}-w}^{i_{\text{current}}+w} \sum_{j=j_{\text{current}}-w}^{j_{\text{current}}+w} f_t(i,j) - f_{t+\Delta t}\left(i+\Delta i, j+\Delta j\right) \tag{9.14}$$

where a small $((2w+1)$ by $(2w+1))$ rectangular region around the current point is used to assess the similarity of the images. Note that any image similarity measure (such as those described in Section 8.1.3) can be used.

We could exhaustively search the image $f_{t+\Delta t}(i,j)$ to determine the best possible match, but this would be very costly and could potentially give incorrect results (if, for example, the scene contains multiple similar regions; e.g. consider an image of a chessboard). In many situations the motion from image to image is very small and hence we can make use of the spatial intensity gradient to efficiently estimate the displacement and optical flow (e.g. see (Lucas and Kanade, 1981)). From frame to frame, image appearance does not change significantly:

$$f_t(i,j) = f_{t+\Delta t}\left(i+\Delta i, j+\Delta j\right) \tag{9.15}$$

If we assume that the motion from frame to frame is small then we can approximate $f_{t+\Delta t}(i+\Delta i, j+\Delta j)$ as:

$$f_{t+\Delta t}\left(i+\Delta i, j+\Delta j\right) = f_t(i,j) + \frac{\partial f}{\partial i}\Delta i + \frac{\partial f}{\partial j}\Delta j + \frac{\partial f}{\partial t}\Delta t \tag{9.16}$$

In effect, we are approximating the new image by adding estimates of motion in both directions and in time to the image at time t. If we combine the previous two equations we get:

$$\frac{\partial f}{\partial i}\Delta i + \frac{\partial f}{\partial j}\Delta j + \frac{\partial f}{\partial t}\Delta t = 0 \tag{9.17}$$

Now, if we divide by Δt we get

$$\frac{\partial f}{\partial i}\frac{\Delta i}{\Delta t} + \frac{\partial f}{\partial j}\frac{\Delta j}{\Delta t} + \frac{\partial f}{\partial t} = 0 \tag{9.18}$$

which is equivalent to

$$\begin{bmatrix} \dfrac{\partial f}{\partial i} & \dfrac{\partial f}{\partial j} \end{bmatrix} \begin{bmatrix} \dfrac{\Delta i}{\Delta t} \\[2ex] \dfrac{\Delta j}{\Delta t} \end{bmatrix} = -\frac{\partial f}{\partial t} \tag{9.19}$$

The values $\frac{\Delta i}{\Delta t}$ and $\frac{\Delta j}{\Delta t}$ are the rates of change in both spatial directions, which together are commonly referred to as the optical flow (i.e. a flow vector for any point). One widely used approach to solving the optical flow equation is to assume that the optical flow is effectively constant in a small region around any point (Lucas and Kanade, 1981). Hence we have multiple observations of the $\frac{\partial f}{\partial i}, \frac{\partial f}{\partial j}, \frac{\partial f}{\partial t}$ values from the equations and can solve for $\frac{\Delta i}{\Delta t}, \frac{\Delta j}{\Delta t}$ using a pseudo inverse in a similar manner to that shown for determining the transformations in Sections 5.2.2 and 5.3.

There are many other approaches to computing dense optical flow, but the one most commonly employed in OpenCV is tensor-based method by Farneback (Farneback, 2003). This method approximates each neighbourhood of each pixel in each frame using quadratic polynomials, and then estimates the displacements based on knowledge of how exact polynomials change under translation. See Figure 9.13.

In OpenCV, we can calculate (and display) the optical flow between two frames as follows. Note that we are only displaying the optical flow for every eighth pixel in both directions:

```
calcOpticalFlowFarneback (previous_gray_frame, gray_frame,
                optical_flow, 0.5, 3, 15, 3, 5, 1.2, 0);
cvtColor (previous_gray_frame, display, CV_GRAY2BGR);
for (int row = 4; row < display.rows; row+=8)
  for(int column = 4; column < display.cols; column+8)
  {
    Point2f& flow = optical_flow.at<Point2f>(row,column);
    line (display, Point(column,row), Point(
            cvRound(column+flow.x), cvRound(row+flow.y)),
            passed_colour);
  }
```

Figure 9.14 Optical flow computed using the Lucas–Kanade feature tracker is shown for two frames of the PETS 2000 surveillance video. Note that the features used were eigenfeatures, deteremined using Shi's method to compute 'good features' (Shi and Tomasi, 1994). The optical flow vectors are shown (in green) for all selected features (shown in red). The original images are reproduced by permission of Dr. James Ferryman, University of Reading

9.2.4 Feature Based Optical Flow

It can be difficult or even impossible to compute optical flow for all points in a scene. In addition, these calculations can be quite expensive computationally. For these reasons we frequently consider the optical flow only for feature points within the image. As we saw in Chapter 7, features can provide us with distinct patterns that can be used for matching from image to image or equally from frame to frame. Hence, if we have identified an object which we wish to track, we can determine the features which are internal (i.e. not on the boundary) to the object and then match these features from frame to frame. SIFT and SURF features (see Sections 7.4 and 7.5.2) are particularly well suited to this task, and have their own methods for matching features/keypoints. These do not make use of optical flow, and instead exhaustively compare features.

One of the most popular techniques for feature based optical flow is the Lucas–Kanade feature tracker (Lucas and Kanade, 1981) (Bouguet, 2000). The feature points are determined using an eigenvalue technique (see Section 7.5.1) where points with two high eigenvalues are selected, although in theory other feature detectors, such as Harris, would suffice (see Sections 7.2 and 7.5.1). Optical flow is only computed at these feature points. See Figure 9.14.

In OpenCV, we can calculate (and display) the optical flow for features between two frames as follows:

```
vector<Point2f> previous_features, current_features;
const int MAX_CORNERS = 500; int win_size = 10;
goodFeaturesToTrack (previous_gray_frame, previous_features,
        MAX_CORNERS, 0.05, 5, noArray(), 3, false, 0.04);
cornerSubPix (previous_gray_frame, previous_features,
    Size(win_size, win_size), Size(-1,-1),
    TermCriteria (CV_TERMCRIT_ITER |CV_TERMCRIT_EPS ,20,0.03));
```

```
vector<uchar> features_found;
calcOpticalFlowPyrLK (previous_gray_frame, gray_frame,
    previous_features, current_features, features_found,
    noArray(),Size(win_size*4+1,win_size*4+1), 5,
    TermCriteria (CV_TERMCRIT_ITER |CV_TERMCRIT_EPS ,20,0.3));
for( int i = 0; i < (int)previous_features.size(); i++ )
{
  if(features_found[i])
    line (display_image, previous_features[i],
                         current_features[i],passed_colour);
}
```

9.3 Performance

To assess the performance of video processing tasks, such as moving object detection or tracking, we often need a different type of ground truth (see Section 9.3.1) and a different set of performance primitives (see Section 9.3.2) than those presented in Section 8.6.

9.3.1   Video Datasets (and Formats)

Over the last decade there has been a significant research in video processing and a significant number of videos and video datasets have been made available. These cover a range of applications, such as video surveillance, video conferencing, abandoned object detection, event detection and so on. These videos are often supplied with no ground truth, but where ground truth is provided it generally takes one of the following forms:

1. Labelled pixel masks. This form of ground truth consists of labels for each pixel in each image (or at least in a number of frames out of a video sequence). It is very difficult and time consuming to create, but provides the greatest accuracy in terms of evaluating performance. Some examples of this form of ground truth are (i) the PETS 2001 dataset, where ground truth for the moving pixels for some of the videos were provided by Kyushu University; (ii) moving object and shadow ground truth available is provided as part of the LIMU dataset again for one of the PETS 2001 videos; and (iii) CamVid dataset (Brostow, Fauqueura, and Cipolla, 2009) where all pixels in four video sequences (at 1 Hz and partially at 15 Hz) were annotated using 32 different labels (effectively classifying the various types of object in the scene).
2. Bounding boxes. This is significantly easier form of ground truth to create, as each moving object is identified just by a bounding box in each frame. Obviously these bounding boxes include points which belong to other objects and so care must be taken when evaluating performance using them. Well known examples of this form of ground truth are provided in the CAVIAR dataset, which provides 54 annotated videos of people interacting in a lobby and in a shopping center, the ETISEO project which provides 85 sequences corresponding to 40 multi-camera scenes, and the iLIDS project, which was developed by the Home Office in the UK and which contains over 500 hours of video from five different security scenarios.

3. Labelled events. One of the simplest forms of ground truth to create is that of event labels (such as 'luggage abandoned', 'car stopped', etc.). A number of the PETS workshops (2003, 2006, 2007), along with BEHAVE dataset, the CAVIAR dataset, the ETISEO dataset and the iLIDS dataset provide this type of annotation, typically in XML format. The events annotated differ quite significantly; for example, left luggage events, meeting room events, interactions events between people, and so on.

The format of the ground truth limits the manners in which performance can be evaluated. While it is straightforward to determine precision and recall style metrics in the case of pixel based ground truth, it is harder to know what to do for bounding boxes and events.

9.3.2 Metrics for Assessing Video Tracking Performance

Three metrics that are commonly used for assessing tracking performance where ground truth is in the form of bounding boxes are: (i) the dice co-efficient, (ii) overlap and (ii) the number of lost tracks (Doermann and Mihalcik, 2000) (Maggio and Cavallaro, 2005) (Nascimento and Marques, 2006). These metrics are calculated on a frame-by-frame basis, but we can also calculate statistics from the metrics over an entire sequence.

9.3.2.1 Dice Coefficient

The dice coefficient is often used to assess the frame-by-frame accuracy of a tracker (Doermann and Mihalcik, 2000). If we consider an object being tracked in comparison to a ground truth bounding box, then we can determine three areas – one for the bounding box in the ground truth, one for the object being tracked and one which is the area of the overlap between the two rectangles (if any). For two rectangles it is defined as twice their shared area divided by the sum of their areas:

$$Dice\ coefficient = \frac{2.Area_{\text{Overlap}}}{Area_{\text{Object}} + Area_{\text{Ground Truth}}} \quad (9.20)$$

The dice coefficient is calculated on a frame-by-frame basis. To capture the tracker's 'average' performance, we calculate the median (and/or mean) of all of the dice coefficient values returned for a sequence.

9.3.2.2 Overlap

The proportion of the ground truth bounding box that is occupied by the tracker in a given frame is another useful measure of the tracker's accuracy (Doermann and Mihalcik, 2000). This metric is referred to as the overlap:

$$Overlap = \frac{Area_{\text{Overlap}}}{Area_{\text{Ground Truth}}} \quad (9.21)$$

9.3.2.3 Lost Tracks/Proportion of Successful Tracks

Aside from measuring the accuracy of a given tracker on every frame, we also wish to know how it performs overall, that is over the course of an entire tracking scenario. Most importantly, we must determine when we have lost track of an object. The prevalence of such failure cases is a measure of the lack of robustness of a tracker.

We define a track to be lost as soon as its overlap with the bounding box falls below a threshold. Nascimento (Nascimento and Marques, 2006) set this value at 10%, while Kasturi (Kasturi, et al., 2009) sets the threshold at 20%. Both of these are very low, but quite typical, if very 'forgiving' of large tracking inaccuracies.

10

Vision Problems

This final chapter presents a series of computer vision application problems which are possible to solve using the theory (and practice) presented in this text. Images and videos for these problems are provided in the electronic resources accompanying the text.

10.1 Baby Food

On a production line cans of baby food are made by:

1. Fabricating the sides and lid of the can together but omitting the base of the can.
2. Dropping a spoon into the empty upside-down can.
3. Pouring the baby food (powder) into upside-down the can.
4. Sealing the base onto the can.

You are asked to develop an inspection system looking at the can between steps 2 and 3 in order to check that a single spoon has been placed into it (see Figure 10.1).

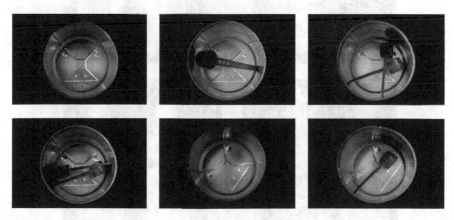

Figure 10.1 Sample baby food can images from the production just after the spoon has been dropped into the can. Examples of no spoon, one spoon and two spoons are shown

A Practical Introduction to Computer Vision with OpenCV, First Edition. Kenneth Dawson-Howe.
© 2014 John Wiley & Sons, Ltd. Published 2014 by John Wiley & Sons, Ltd.

10.2   Labels on Glue

On a production line for bottles of glue it is necessary to perform a number of inspection tests (see Figure 10.2):

1. Check that each bottle has a label.
2. Check that the label on the bottle is straight.
3. Check that the label is not torn or folded.

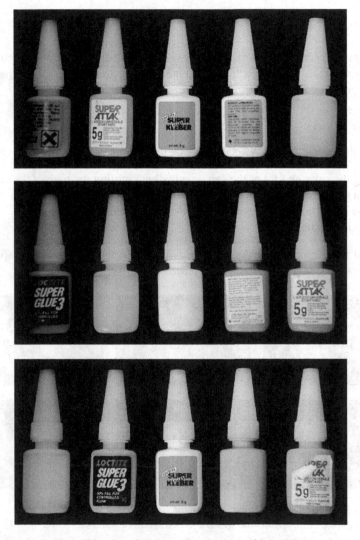

Figure 10.2   Sample images of bottles of glue are shown some without labels and some with crooked (or damaged labels). Note that these are not images from a real production line and in many cases the labels have been manually damaged/removed

10.3   O-rings

You are asked to detect defects (notches and breaks) in rubber O-rings as they pass before an inspection camera (see Figure 10.3).

Good O-rings:

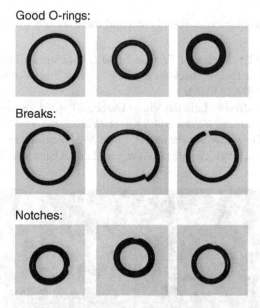

Breaks:

Notches:

Figure 10.3   Sample images of good O-rings (i.e. with no defects; see top row), broken O-rings (middle row) and O-rings with notches out of them (bottom row)

10.4 Staying in Lane

In order to assist drivers, you are asked to develop a system to ensure that they stay in lane, and raise an alarm if they start to drift into another lane (without indicating). Given a video feed from a camera mounted on the dashboard of a car, looking forwards, you are asking to automatically detect the lines on each side of the lane of traffic that the car is in (see Figure 10.4).

This is an area of significant research interest and there are other datasets available online:

1. PETS (Performance Evaluation of Tracking and Surveillance) 2001 dataset 5: 4 videos (2 looking forwards, 2 looking backwards) from a vehicle on a motorway. http://ftp.pets. rdg.ac.uk/PETS2001/DATASET5/
2. CamVid (Cambridge-driving Labeled Video Database): 4 videos looking forwards from a vehicle http://mi.eng.cam.ac.uk/research/projects/VideoRec/CamVid/.
3. Daimler Pedestrian Detection Benchmark Dataset: A small number of long video sequences looking forwards from a vehicle. http://www.gavrila.net/Datasets/datasets.html

Figure 10.4 Sample images from the dashboard mounted camera

10.5   Reading Notices

In order to facilitate auto-translation, you are asked to locate any text within an image and extract the text as a series of characters (see Figure 10.5). You may assume that the text will take up a reasonable portion of the image and will be more-or-less the right way up!

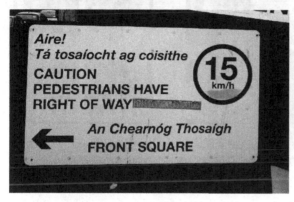

Figure 10.5   Sample images of notices

10.6   Mailboxes

Given a live feed from a camera monitoring mailboxes, you are asked to determine if there is any post in each mailbox (see Figure 10.6). To make the processing a bit easier a pattern of black and white stripes has been put in each box. As people put mail in and take mail from the mailboxes on a regular basis, your solution must be able to cope with occlusion of the camera by moving people (without generating any false mail notifications).

Figure 10.6   Three sample frames from a video of the mailboxes, all empty (left), partly occluded (centre and with mail in three of the boxes (right)

10.7 Abandoned and Removed Object Detection

You are asked to locate any abandoned objects and any removed objects (see Figures 10.7 and 10.8).

This is an area of significant research interest and there are many datasets available online:

1. CAVIAR (Context Aware Vision using Image-based Active Recognition project): 5 videos in a lobby from above of various objects being abandoned and removed. http://homepages. inf.ed.ac.uk/rbf/CAVIAR/.
2. ViSOR (Video Surveillance Online Repository): 19 videos of abandoning and removing objects in an outdoor car-park. http://www.openvisor.org/ and http://imagelab.ing.unimore. it/visor/
3. PETS (Performance Evaluation of Tracking and Surveillance) 2006 dataset: 7 left luggage datasets of videos from 4 different cameras in a train station. http://www.cvg.rdg.ac.uk/ PETS2006/data.html
4. PETS (Performance Evaluation of Tracking and Surveillance) 2007: 7 left luggage datasets of videos from 4 different cameras in a busy airport terminal. http://pets2007.net/

Figure 10.7 Sample object abandonment

Figure 10.8 Sample object removal

10.8   Surveillance

You are asked to find and classify (as people, cars, etc.) all moving objects in a video sequence from a static camera (see Figure 10.9). You must be able to deal with environmental effects (such as changing lighting and the effects of wind, etc.).

This is an area of significant research interest and there are large numbers of datasets available online. For example:

1. CAVIAR (Context Aware Vision using Image-based Active Recognition project): http:// homepages.inf.ed.ac.uk/rbf/CAVIAR/.
2. ViSOR (Video Surveillance Online Repository): http://www.openvisor.org/ and http:// imagelab.ing.unimore.it/visor/
3. PETS (Performance Evaluation of Tracking and Surveillance datasets: http://ftp.pets.rdg. ac.uk/
4. SPEVI (Surveillance Performance EValuation Initiative) datasets http://www.elec.qmul. ac.uk/staffinfo/andrea/spevi.html
5. ETISEO dataset from INRIA. http://www-sop.inria.fr/orion/ETISEO/
6. OTCBVS dataset. http://www.cse.ohio-state.edu/otcbvs-bench/bench.html
7. LIMU dataset from Kyushu University. http://limu.ait.kyushu-u.ac.jp/en/dataset/

Figure 10.9   Four frames from PETS 2001 (Dataset 1, Camera 1). Reproduced by permission of Dr. James Ferryman, University of Reading

10.9   Traffic Lights

You are asked to locate any traffic lights in a camera view and to determine what light is lit (green, amber or red) (see Figure 10.10).

There are videos, available online, taken from moving vehicles which can be used for traffic light detection:

1. CamVid (Cambridge-driving Labeled Video Database): 4 videos looking forwards from a vehicle http://mi.eng.cam.ac.uk/research/projects/VideoRec/CamVid/.
2. Daimler Pedestrian Detection Benchmark Dataset: A small number of long video sequences looking forwards from a vehicle. http://www.gavrila.net/Datasets/datasets.html

Figure 10.10   Three frames from a stationary camera at a traffic light controlled road junction

10.10   Real Time Face Tracking

Assuming that the cascade of Haar classifiers is too slow, propose a way of tracking a face in (close to) real time in a video (see Figure 10.11).

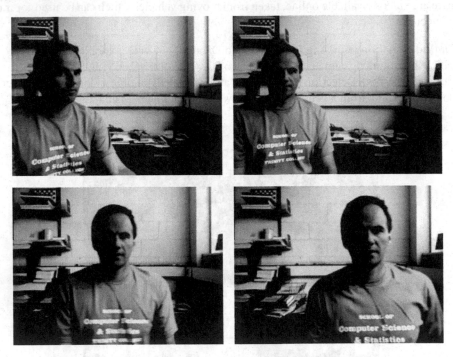

Figure 10.11   Sample frames from a video showing a face to be tracking

10.11   Playing Pool

You are asked to locate the balls on a pool table so that their positions can be analysed for possible shots (see Figure 10.12). Ball positions should be computed only when there is no motion on the table and no one is occluding the table. Also, ball positions should be reported relative to the table (rather than the image).

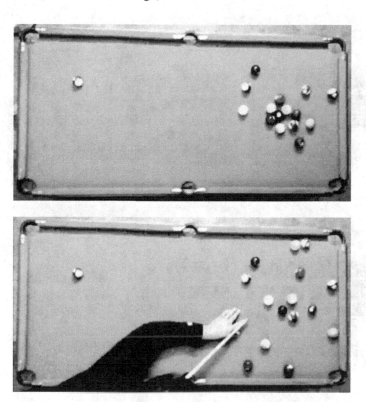

Figure 10.12   Sample images from a video of a game of pool

10.12   Open Windows

You are asked to develop a system to determine what (top-hung) windows are open in images of a building. This is intended to aid in the efficient heating and ventilation of the building (see Figure 10.13).

Figure 10.13   Three images from a camera monitoring a set of windows

10.13 Modelling Doors

Given a video feed from a surveillance camera, you are asked to locate any doors in the view. This can be done during a training phase either from video or still images. This should aid the system when attempting to understand the actions of people within the scene (see Figure 10.14).

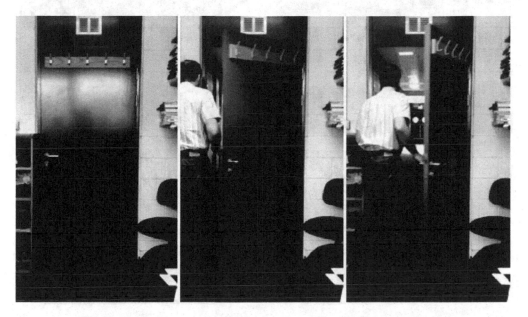

Figure 10.14 Three sample frames from a camera monitoring a doorway

10.14   Determining the Time from Analogue Clocks

You are asked to determine the time from an image of an analogue clock (see Figure 10.15).

Figure 10.15   Sample clock images

10.15   Which Page

You are asked to determine which page (if any) out of a given text a reader is currently viewing so that augmented content can be added to the page through the use of a projector (see Figures 10.16 and 10.17).

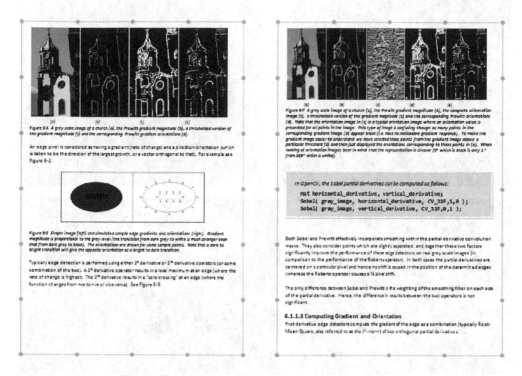

Figure 10.16   Some of the provided sample page images

Figure 10.17   Sample views of the book while it is being read

10.16   Nut/Bolt/Washer Classification

You are asked to classify parts coming down a conveyor line as nuts, bolts or washers (or something unknown) (see Figure 10.18).

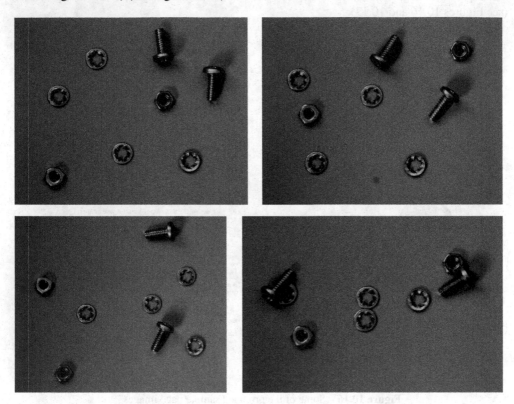

Figure 10.18   Sample views of the parts on the conveyor belt

10.17 Road Sign Recognition

Assuming that you have sample (CAD) images of road signs such as those in Figure 10.19, you are asked to develop a system to automatically recognise these road signs from single images (taken from the dashboard of a car looking forwards). They will appear at different sizes (as the car moves towards them), but should be facing directly towards the vehicle (see Figure 10.20).

Figure 10.19   Sample CAD road signs

Figure 10.20   Sample images (containing road signs) taken looking forwards from a vehicle

10.18 License Plates

You are asked to recognise the number on license plates taken with a handheld camera. You are provided with example images of the digits in two forms (synthetic and real) (see Figures 10.21, 10.22 and 10.23).

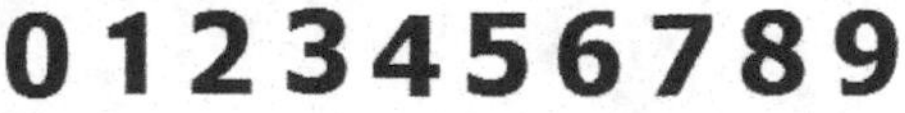

0 1 2 3 4 5 6 7 8 9

Figure 10.21 Sample synthetics digits

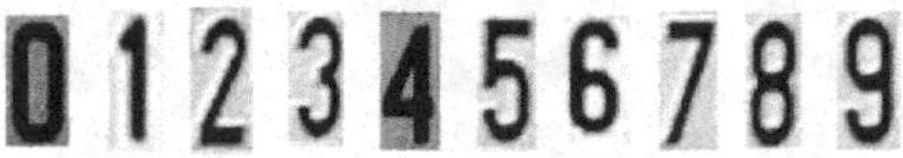

0 1 2 3 4 5 6 7 8 9

Figure 10.22 Sample digits from license plates

06-D-39905
00-C-19986

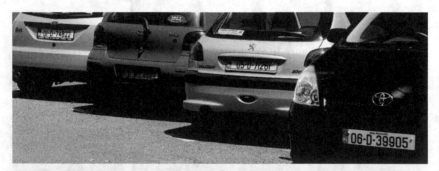

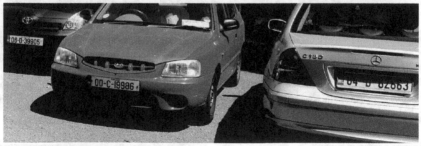

Figure 10.23 Sample images of car license plates

10.19   Counting Bicycles

You are asked to locate any bicycles moving along a path (see Figure 10.24). Note that there can be other bicycles or people walking, and that you must be able to cope with changes in the lighting (as the sun goes in and out) and with the waves on the sea (which are constantly moving).

Figure 10.24   Some frames from the sample bicycle video

10.20   Recognise Paintings

As part of an augmented reality system you are asked to automatically determine the identity of any painting in the view of an observer (camera) (see Figures 10.25 and 10.26).

Figure 10.25   Sample images from an observer in a gallery. Photographs taken by Dr. Kenneth Dawson-Howe at the National Gallery of Ireland

Figure 10.26   Sample known painting images. The painting are: (top left) 'The Marriage Feast an Cana' (late 1660s) by Jan Havicksz. Steen, (top centre) 'A Thunderstorm: The Frightened Wagoner' (1832) by James Arthur O'Connor, (top right) 'Joseph Selling Corn in Egypt' (1612) by Pieter Lastman, (bottom left) 'A Sick Call' (1863) by Matthew James Lawless, (bottom centre) 'A View of the Rye Water near Leixlip' (1850s) by William Davis, and finally (bottom right) 'The Arrival of the 'Kattendijk' at Texel' (1702) by Ludolf Backhuysen I. Photographs taken by Dr. Kenneth Dawson-Howe at the National Gallery of Ireland

References

Ballard, D. 1981. Generalizing the Hough transform to detect arbitrary shapes. *Pattern Recognition*, 13(2), pp. 111–122.

Baggio, D. L. 2012. *Mastering OpenCV with Practical Computer Vision Projects*. PACKT Publishing.

Bay, H., Ess, A., Tuytelaars, T. and Van Gool, L. 2008. Speeded Up Robust Features (SURF). *Computer Vision and Image Understanding*, 110(3), pp. 346–359.

Borgefors, G. 1988. Hierarchical chamfer matching: a parametric edge matching algorithm. *IEEE Transactions on Pattern Analysis and Machine Intelligence*, 10(6), pp. 849–865.

Bouguet, J.-Y. 2000. *Pyramidal Implementation of the Lucas Kanade Feature Tracker - Description of the Algorithm*, Intel Corporation.

Brostow, G. J., Fauqueura, J. and Cipolla, R. 2009. Semantic object classes in video: A high-definition ground truth database. *Pattern Recognition Letters*, 30, pp. 88–97.

Brunelli, R. 2009. *Template Matching Techniques in Computer Vision: Theory and Practice*. Wiley & Sons, Inc.

Canny, J. 1986. A computational approach to edge detection. *IEEE Transactions on Pattern Analysis and Machine Intelligence*, 8(6), pp. 679–698.

Chen, F., Delanney, D., and De Vleeschouwer, C. 2011. An autonomous framework to produce and distribute personalized team-sport video summaries: a basketball case study. *IEEE Transactions on Multimedia*, 13(6), pp. 1381–1394.

Cristianini, N. and Shawe-Taylor, J. 2000. *An Introduction to Support Vector Machines and Other Kernel-based Learning Methods*. Cambridge University Press.

Cyganek, B. 2013. *Object Detection and Recognition in Digital Images: Theory and Practice*. Wiley & Sons, Inc.

Dalal, H. and Triggs B. 2005. Histograms of oriented gradients for human detection. *CVPR*: pp. 886–893.

Doermann, D. and Mihalcik, D. 2000. Tools and techniques for video performance evaluation. *15th International Conference on Pattern Recognition*, 4, pp. 167–170.

Farneback, G. 2003. Two-frame motion estimation based on polynomial expansion. In: *Lecture Notes in Computer Science* 2749, pp. 363–370.

Flusser, J., Suk, T. and Zitová, B. 2009. *Moments and Moment Invariants in Pattern Recognition*. Wiley & Sons, Inc.

Freeman, H. 1961. On the encoding of arbitrary geometric configurations. *IRE Transactions on Electronic Computers*, 10, pp. 260–268.

Gasparini, F. and Schettini, R. 2009. A review of redeye detection and removal in digital images through patents. *Recent Patents on Electrical Engineering* 2(1), pp. 45–53.

Gevers, T., Gijsenij, A., van de Weijer, J. and Geusebroek, J.-M. 2012. *Color in Computer Vision: Fundamentals and Applications*. Wiley & Sons, Inc.

González, R. C. and Woods, R. E. 2007. *Digital Image Processing*. Prentice Hall.

Harris, C. and Stephen, M. 1988. A combined corner and edge detector. *Proceedings of the 4th Alvey Vision Conference*, pp. 147–151.

Illingworth, J. and Kittler, J. 1988. A survey of the hough transform. *Computer Vision, Graphics, and Image Processing*, 44(1), pp. 87–116.

A Practical Introduction to Computer Vision with OpenCV, First Edition. Kenneth Dawson-Howe.
© 2014 John Wiley & Sons, Ltd. Published 2014 by John Wiley & Sons, Ltd.

Jain, A. K., Duin, R. P. and Mao, J. 2000. Statistical pattern recognition: a review. *IEEE Transaction on Pattern Analysis and Machine Intelligence*, 22(1), pp. 4–37.

Kakumanu, P., Makrogiannis, S. and Bourbakis, N. 2007. A survey of skin-color modeling and detection methods. *Pattern Recognition*, 40(3), pp. 1106–1122.

Kanungo, T., Parra, J., Velis, D.N., et al. 2002. An efficient k-means clustering algorithm: analysis and implementation. *IEEE Transactions on Pattern Analysis and Machine Intelligence*, 24(7), pp. 881–892.

Kasturi, R. D., Goldgof, P., Soundararajan, et al. 2009. Framework for performance evaluation of face, text, and vehicle detection and tracking in video: Data, metrics, and protocol. *IEEE Transactions on Pattern Analysis and Machine Intelligence*, 31(2), pp. 319–336.

Kimpe, T. and Tuytschaever, T. 2007. Increasing the number of gray shades in medical display systems – how much is enough?. *Journal of Digital Imaging*, 20(4), pp. 422–432.

Koschan, A. and Abidi, M. A. 2007. *Digital Color Image Processing*. Wiley & Sons, Inc.

Lienhart, R. and Maydt, J., 2002. An extended set of Haar-like features for rapid object detection. *IEEE International Conference on Image Processing*, 1, pp. 900–903.

Lowe, D. G. 2004. Distinctive image features from scale-invariant keypoints. *International Journal of Computer Vision*, 60, 2, pp. 91–110.

Lucas, B. and Kanade, T. 1981. An Iterative image registration technique with an application to stereo vision. *Proceedings of 7th International Joint Conference on Artificial Intelligence (IJCAI)*, pp. 674–679.

Maggio, E. and Cavallaro, A. 2005. Multi-part target representation for color tracking. *IEEE International Conference on Image Processing*, 1, pp. 729–732.

Maggio, E. and Cavallaro, A. 2010. *Video Tracking: Theory and Practice*. Wiley & Sons, Inc.

Marchand-Maillet, S. and Sharaiha, Y. M. 1999. *Binary Digital Image Processing: A Discrete Approach*. Academic Press.

Marques, O. 2011. *Practical Image and Video Processing Using MATLAB*. Wiley & Sons, Inc.

Marr, D. 1982. *Vision: A Computational Investigation into the Human Representation and Processing of Visual Information*. Freeman.

Martin, D., Fowlkes, C., Tal, D. and Malik, J. 2001. A database of human segmented natural images and its application to evaluating segmentation algorithms and measuring ecological statistics. *Proceedings of the 8th International Conference on Computer Vision*, 2, pp. 416–423.

Moravec, H. 1980. *Tech Report CMU-RI-TR-3: Obstacle Avoidance and Navigation in the Real World by a Seeing Robot Rover*, Carnegie-Mellon University, Robotics Institute.

Mundy, J. L. and Zisserman, A. 1992. *Geometric Invariance in Computer Vision*. MIT Press.

Najman, L. and Talbot, H. 2013. *Mathematical Morphology: From Theory to Applications*. John Wiley & Sons, Inc.

Nascimento, J. C. and Marques, J. S. 2006. Performance evaluation of object detection algorithms for video surveillance. *IEEE Transactions on Multimedia*, 8(4), pp. 761–774.

Otsu, N. 1979. A threshold selection method from grey-level histograms. *IEEE Transactions on Systems, Man and Cybernetics* (Vol. SMC-9, (1)), pp. 62–66.

Perreault, S. H. P. 2007. Median filtering in constant time. *IEEE Transactions on Image Processing*, 16(9), pp. 2389–2394.

Plataniotis, K. N. and Venetsanopoulos, A. N. 2000. *Color Image Processing and Applications*. Springer Verlag.

Prati, A., Mikic, I., Trivedi, M.M. and Cucchiara, R. 2003. Detecting moving shadows: algorithms and evaluation. *IEEE Transactions on Pattern Analysis and Machine Intelligence*, 25, 918–923.

Prewitt, J. 1970. Object enhancement and extraction. In: *Picture Processing and Psychopictorics*. Academic Press.

Radke, R., Andra, S., Al-Kofahi, O. and Roysam, B. 2005. Image change detection algorithms: a systematic survey. *IEEE Transactions on Image Processing*, 14(3), pp. 294–307.

Ramer, U. 1972. An iterative procedure for the polygonal approximation of plane curves. *Computer Graphics and Image Processing*, 1(3), pp. 244–256.

Risse, T. 1989. Hough transform for line recognition: Complexity of evidence accumulation and cluster detection. *Computer Vision, Graphics, and Image Processing*, 46(3), pp. 327–345.

Rosten, E. and Drummond, T. 2006. Machine learning for high-speed corner detection. ECCV 2006, pp. 430–443.

Rubner, Y., Tomasi, C. and Guibas, L. J. 1998 A metric for distributions with applications to image databases. IEEE International Conference on Computer Vision, pp. 59–66.

Sezgin, M. and Sankur, B. 2004. Survey over image thresholding techniques and quantitative performance evaluation. *Journal of Electronic Imaging*, 13(1), pp. 146–165.

Shi, J. and Tomasi, C. 1994. Good features to track. *Proceedings of the IEEE Conference on Computer Vision and Pattern Recognition,* pp. 593–600.

Sonka, M., Hlavac, V. and Boyle, R. 2007. *Image Processing, Analysis, and Machine Vision.* Cengage Learning.

Stauffer, C. and Grimson, W. E. L. 1999. Adaptive background mixture models for real-time tracking. *IEEE Computer Society Conference on Computer Vision and Pattern Recognition,* 2, pp. 246–252.

Tattersall, S. and Dawson-HoweK. 2003. Adaptive shadow identification through automatic parameter estimation in video sequences. *Proceedings of Irish Machine Vision and Image Processing Conference,* 57-64.

Viola, P. and Jones,M. 2001. Robust real-time face detection. *International Journal of Computer Vision,* 57(2), pp. 137–154.

von Helmholtz, H. 1868. *The Recent Progress of the Theory of Vision.* Preussiche Jahrbucher.

Wilding, J. 1983. *Perception: From Sense to Object.* Palgrave Macmillian.

Yuen, H. K., Princen, J., Illingworth, J. and Kittler, J. 1990. Comparative study of Hough Transform methods for circle finding. *Image and Vision Computing,* 8(1), pp. 71–77.

Index

Printed in the United States
By Bookmasters